" 'If you write it, Mike,' said Malachi Wald, standing there in the cold Galilee wind, 'every word should be as a knife cutting flesh. For what we learned in 19... everything we ...ved— what we ... deep and brou... We learned a... the world but ...ew. In all the wo... ...no justice for the Jew except that justice which the Jew can take for himself.

" 'That's what we did. We stood at the crossroads then and we turned our backs on Palestine and we started to take our own justice—justice and vengeance!'

"So said Malachi Wald to me.

"There is a Hebrew phrase, a fighting slogan going back to biblical times: *Dahm Y'Israel Nokeam*—'The blood of Israel will take vengeance.' In the first months of 1945, in Germany, Wald and Becker, Judah Klein, Benno the Messenger and Hannah Baum and fifty others left the people they had till then led. They took this fighting slogan for their own and formed the secret organization which came to be known, to those who knew of it at all, by the first letter of each word; the Hebrew letters *daled, yod, nun;* the letters that spell out another Hebrew word: *DIN,* which means 'judgment.'

"And from 1945 until this day they have taken vengeance, and imposed the judgment of the Jew, upon the killers of the Jews."

Forged in Fury

MICHAEL ELKINS

BALLANTINE BOOKS • NEW YORK
An Intext Publisher

BALLANTINE BOOKS, INC.
101 Fifth Avenue, New York, N.Y. 10003

Contents

One / Malachi Wald   1

Two / Illusion and Reality   29

Three / The Jewish Resistance   50

Four / Four from the Furnace

     Ben-Issachar Feld—"The Messenger"   86

     Judah Klein, the Wigmaker   100

     The Little Sister of Rachel Baum   119

     Arnie Berg and the Silver Spoon   147

Five / The Roads   180

Six / DIN—Judgment and Vengeance   194

Seven / The Ways of Poison   224

Eight / The World of Malachi Wald   250

Epilogue   306

References   307

We conjure you: In the name of the shed blood
of our children—*take vengeance!* Avenge our
tortured mothers, avenge our profaned martyrs—
take vengeance for us!

> —MORDECHAI TENNENBAUM TAMAROFF,
> Commander of the Jewish Fighters'
> Organization in Bialystok, killed in
> the revolt of the Jews of Bialystok
> against the Germans, August 1943

Foreword

For more than twenty years there has existed—in Europe, in Israel, and elsewhere—a strange brotherhood, small and secret. Among the men and women who compose it are farmers, merchants, journalists, government officials; one of the women is a well-known poet, one of the men a minister of religion. Whatever their formal work, they share the same voluntary and consuming task—they hunt and kill other men and women.

This is their history, or part of it. In telling it, I have changed some names, some dates and places; I have invented some details. I have done this to protect the people involved and to enable their work, of which I approve, to continue.

And since no man lives outside his time, I have also told something of the history of that time. In telling this, I have changed and invented nothing.

M.E.

One
Malachi Wald

The last time I saw Malachi Wald he was in the orchard of his kibbutz, spreading earthen dikes around the young fruit trees, the bitter Galilee wind whipping his trousers about his long legs, his bony face turning a little blue from the winter cold. I wasn't very happy about the meeting, I'd driven up from Jerusalem to have another talk with him and I didn't want to spend the time squatting on my heels on a windswept hillside.

"I have to finish this," he said, patting the ridge of earth firm with the flat of his spade. "The rains will start soon and if this isn't done the water will just run down the hill, taking the earth with it." His voice, as thin as he, rebuked my impatience; "these trees would die."

Every farmer in Israel sees himself as the right hand of Mother Nature, and there's no arguing; so I put my back against a tree and we talked while he worked.

That was the day before Malachi Wald left for Argentina to kill a man. . . .

Malachi began getting ready to kill this man—among others—on the twenty-third of August, 1943, when he was just over eighteen years old. That was the day he joined the plot to escape from the Ninth Fort.

The Ninth Fort was the last of a chain of concrete blockhouses built half-underground by the Russian czars to protect the town of Kovno near the Prussian border. It wasn't a very successful chain. Early in the First World War, the chain was easily broken by Marshal Pilsudski's

1

Polish legion, then fighting for the independence of Poland with the help of the Imperial German Army. The Russians recaptured the forts with no great difficulty when they counterattacked a year later. Even the ragged Lithuanian nationalists occupied the forts for a time during their own brief and curiously old-fashioned patriotic revolt against Poland.

By the time Malachi Wald was born on July 7, 1925, the nine forts were no more than way stations on a well-traveled path of conquest. And by then, too, the Jews of Kovno had learned that no matter what mission of freedom the temporary possessors of the forts might be engaged upon, a pogrom against the Kovno Jews could always be fitted into the patriotic program. So that when Malachi was six years old and screwed up his courage to ask his widowed father whence came the scar that split the patriarch's bearded face, the answer was: "The Lithuanian *mamzerim* did it, may they lie like onions with their heads in the ground." And when the boy asked why it was done, the old man straightened the skullcap on his son's head and sighed: "The Jewish heart must break a thousand times for the sins of all peoples; it is for that we were chosen by the Holy One, blessed be His Sacred Name."

"Go and study," said Yitzhak Wald, cutting short the question period; and Malachi trotted off to the yeshiva to study the Holy Word under the hooked nose and sharp tongue of Melamed Weintraub, and to wonder—in the brief way of a child—why the God of the Jews allowed things to be so difficult for His people. It was only later that Malachi was to learn that "difficult" was the wrong word and that being a Jew was impossible.

Between the time of "difficult" and the time of "impossible," however, Malachi spent his mornings at the yeshiva, twisting his earlocks and chanting by rote the sometimes meaningless but always compelling liturgy. And in the afternoon he would burst out of the yeshiva and race, earlocks flying and the skullcap pinned to his hair flapping like a sail, to the Ninth Fort to join the other little hellions playing their eternal poignant game:

"Let's say we're not the Jews, those are the Jews down there. We're the Lithuanian *mamzerim* and it's night and we sneak down out of the fort and murder them all."

The years went by like that—yeshiva and synagogue and fort—until Malachi was twelve years old and his father, after consulting with Melamed Weintraub, reluctantly decided that Malachi would never be a rabbi, or even a melamed—a teacher. "Better you should know it now, Yitzhak," said Weintraub, sucking the hot tea through the sugar lump held in his scraggly teeth. "He's a good boy, but what should he do?—the *kopf* for it he hasn't got, a good heart he's got. Nu, it's not so terrible; send him to your brother Shlomo, he should learn him a carpenter."

From Shlomo Wald, Malachi learned more than carpentry. Shlomo was a man nearly seven feet tall and as different from Malachi's father as the oak from the reed. When Shlomo whispered, his voice was rumbling thunder; and when Shlomo roared, which was often, it rattled the walls of the score of houses in the little village eighteen miles from Kovno. Whispering or roaring, Shlomo talked all the time, and all the talk was always the same: the Immortal Return, the Return to Zion, the Jews must go to the Promised Land, to Palestine, to Palestine.

Shlomo was a Zionist. In the four years that Malachi lived with the giant carpenter, the boy became tied to the Jewish dream of that strip of sand and rock along the shores of the Mediterranean Sea as though it were an umbilical cord through which he sucked nourishment. Now when Shlomo's huge hand plucked Malachi from the lathe and his uncle said, "So enough already, go and play," and the boy went out to join the other village kids, it was no longer the game, "Let's say we're not the Jews. . . ." Jews they were, *real* Jews in a Jewish state; farmers they were, on a kibbutz in Palestine, collectively owning the land they sweated over in their minds' eyes. And soon, God willing, the land that was in their dreams would be under their feet.

For four years they worked at their dream. Instead of

the liquid Yiddish, they spoke Hebrew to one another—
the sacred tongue that only Zionists used outside the
synagogue and the yeshiva. They hardened their muscles
on the spade and the hoe, learning to be farmers in the
stubbled fields behind the village. And always there was
Shlomo Wald, keeping the spark alive, telling them of
Ahad Ha'am and Sokolow and the Viennese aristocrat
Theodor Herzl—all the latter-day prophets of Zionism.
Shlomo Wald, seeding them with Zionism as the oak seeds
saplings.

And on June 24, 1941, the oak was chopped down,
casually, stitched across the chest by bullets from a
Schmeisser machine pistol as Malachi, crumpled with terror, lay in the corner of the carpentry shop where his
giant uncle had flung him in the last effort of kindness
and protection. The German army had arrived.

Orphaned, the boy went back to his father in Kovno,
under the shadow of the nine forts.

For the last time—for the last time?—the nine forts
had played their historic pointless role. The panzer brigades of the invading Third German Reich drove right
through them. Only now, behind the panzers, came the
990 men of Einsatzgruppe A, one of the four special task
forces organized by the guardians of German culture and
German purity to help accomplish the mass murder of
east European Jewry.

Within three days, this relative handful of men under
the inspired leadership of SS Brigadier General Franz
Stahlecker managed to organize the murder of nearly five
thousand Jews in Kovno. Of course, they had some considerable help from the local non-Jewish population as
Stahlecker, not one to withhold credit, freely admitted in
his report to SS Lieutenant General Reinhard Heydrich,
his boss at the Reich Main Security Office in Berlin:

> During the first pogrom on the night of June 26th, 1941
> [Stahlecker wrote] the Lithuanian partisans did away
> with more than 1,500 Jews, set fire to several syna-
> gogues and burned down a Jewish district consisting of
> about 60 houses. During the following nights, approxi-
> mately 2,300 Jews were made harmless in a similar way.[1]

But since General Stahlecker was responsible for what the Nazis called "the final solution of the Jewish problem" in all of the Baltic provinces, he couldn't tarry at Kovno. Having provided the first vigorous example, he left the area in charge of Captain Joachim Gratt, a twenty-nine-year-old SS enthusiast who was to become the real genius of the Ninth Fort.

Captain Gratt took over the Kovno area in July 1941, and for a couple of months he had a hard time of it. There were about twelve thousand Jews left in Kovno itself and perhaps another sixty or eighty thousand in the surrounding area. To deal with them, Gratt had only the 193 men of his own SS kommando and another 300 or so Lithuanian partisans under the command of an old-line native fascist named Borisas Klimantis. When they weren't sidetracked by the temptations of rape and robbery, the Lithuanians were ardent Jew-killers, but they went about it in a fashion that was pretty haphazard and was in any case offensive to the German concept of proper procedure. It wasn't long before the Lithuanians' undisciplined activity brought Gratt a reprimand from the Third Reich's Ministry for the Eastern Territories. In the *Daily Situation Bulletin* no. 25 of July 25, 1941, Dr. Alfred Wetzel, the ministry's expert on Jewish affairs, expressed his sharp disapproval of the situation around Kovno:

> There would be nothing to say against the numerous executions of the Jews if it were not that the technical preparation and the method of execution is defective. The Lithuanians leave the executed people where they have fallen without burying them.[2]

When as a result of all this, Captain Gratt told Klimantis that in addition to the privilege of killing the Jews his partisans had the chore of burying them, the Lithuanian patriot replied that his men had joined the crusade as fighters not laborers. And a couple of days later the Lithuanians melted away to do their deeds of valor elsewhere. That left Gratt with a total of just under two hundred men, and the job was clearly impossible.

There were over five thousand rear-echelon troops of the German regular army stationed in the Kovno area, but as far as Gratt was concerned they were useless; worse than useless. The soldiers of the fighting Wehrmacht tended to look down on the black-uniformed SS men who fought, if that is the word, only against an unarmed foe. There were even some beer-heated clashes between the soldiers and the men of Gratt's Death Head kommando. And appeals for cooperation from the Wehrmacht fell on deaf ears. The soldiers would help put down any small Jewish rebellion here and there; or a little casual Jew-baiting might slip, almost unnoticed, over the border of high-spirited clowning and result in a dead Jew. But that was it. For the most part, the soldiers stood around taking pictures of the SS men in action. (It was strictly forbidden, of course, but the photos made fine souvenirs for the folks back home.)

Captain Gratt didn't know about it, but this unsatisfactory state of affairs wasn't limited to his own sector. The higher SS officials in Berlin were already meeting with the Oberkommand Wehrmacht; and the General Staff was persuaded to recognize its Germanic duty and to remind the troops in the field of theirs. The reminder came on October 10, 1941, as an order of the day from Field Marshal Walther von Reichenau:

> The soldier in the Eastern Territories is not merely a fighter according to the rules of the art of war, but also the bearer of a ruthless national ideology. . . . Therefore the soldier must have understanding of the necessity of a severe but just revenge upon subhuman Jewry.[3]

Once the order had been issued, of course, no German soldier could be confused about his duty. Nor, if that had been his inclination, need he concern himself any longer with the abstract issues of morality. So things got better immediately.

Two days after Field Marshal Reichenau's order, Captain Gratt called in the Kovno area commanders of Army Group North and showed them the blueprint by which they were to cooperate in the slaughter of the Jews. It had all been neatly set down by SS Lieutenant General Heydrich in his memo of September 21, 1939, to all Einsatzgruppen commanders:

> The first preliminary measure for attaining the final goal is the concentration of the country Jews into the big towns. . . .[4]

Captain Gratt had already selected the concentration point—Kovno's Viriampole district. It was practically ideal since it was separated from the main part of Kovno by the narrow Memel River, and the river itself was spanned only by a single wooden bridge.

The Wehrmacht began carrying out its part of the business with commendable dispatch. Army patrols fanned out over the countryside to round up the Jews in the neighboring villages. There was little difficulty; most of the Jews were glad enough to get out of the isolated country districts where they were at the mercy of any local band of butchers with guns. There was also a certain sense of security in being together with their coreligionists. In the few instances where Jewish farmers were overreluctant to leave their crops and cattle, it was found that burning down their homes saved a lot of unpleasant argument. In Kovno itself, the few thousand Jews living outside what was to become the Viriampole ghetto were helped across the Memel River by volunteers among their Christian neighbors who relieved them of the burden of transporting their household goods.

At the end of the hectic week, nearly 45,000 people were already jammed into the ghetto. All things considered, the operation was neatly handled. In his October 21 report to his Berlin headquarters, Hans Beibow—the local Gestapo head—pointed out that this mass movement was accomplished at a cost of less than two hundred lives. And of these dead, a score or more were children and old persons who perished, really, of natural causes—such as exposure and fatigue.

While all this was going on, Captain Gratt moved his

SS kommando into the Ninth Fort, which looks down on Kovno from its hilltop not quite two miles away. Around the fort were a number of large pits that had been dug into the surrounding peat bog by the Kovno residents who used the peat for fuel. Gratt borrowed some army bulldozers and set his men to work extending the pits and making such other improvements as they thought useful for the arduous task ahead of them.

Everybody was busy that week, including Malachi Wald. . . .

Malachi spent most of that week of October 12–19 quite literally underground, in the cellar at 7 Mildos Street.

The two-story brick building on Mildos Street contained a cross section of the Viriampole ghetto; a cross section, in fact, of every one of the fifty-five ghettos the Germans had by then established in eastern Europe. On the top floor, in the Hassidic synagogue, the devout swayed and chanted in the ecstasy of the Immanent God. On the ground floor, the black-marketing Rudinetsky family hoarded the well-bitten gold coins they thought would someday buy their freedom. And down in the cellar, as though nurtured by the damp and secret dark, the first seeds of the Kovno resistance movement began to grow.

The seeds were fragile, and sprung from plants themselves hardly mature enough to stand alone. There were forty-six of them, the remnants of the shattered and illegal Zionist pioneer youth movement called Hashomer Hatzair—the Young Guards. Not one of them was yet seventeen, not one of them had ever owned a gun, or fired a shot, or killed man or beast or bird. These children huddled in a cellar and swore in the Hebrew tongue they used to stand against the Third German Reich. Ridiculous even to record it, except for this: they kept their oath and because of it, only Miriam Eideles, Avraham Becker, and Malachi Wald lived to see their twenty-first birthday.

Survival is the first law of resistance. In the ghetto, survival often meant concealment—the ability to hide from the Gestapo agents, from the SS aktions that swept the ghetto without warning, from the wandering patrols and the casual killings. So they built a bunker, dug behind the wall of the cellar, with an entrance through the big peat-burning furnace that heated the building. Avraham Becker and Moshe Ilionski, who worked on the fence the Germans were building with Jewish forced labor around the ghetto, stole the tools and the nails. Shmulik Mordkowski, Leo Ziman, and Michael Gelbtrunk raided the wrecked houses of the ghetto for lumber, oil lamps, anything that was portable and useful. A dozen boys carried the telltale earth away in shopping bags and garbage pails. Malachi, the carpenter, built the timber shoring that kept the walls of the bunker from falling in. They worked day and night, they slept in shifts and snatches. On the eighth day, they finished cementing the bricks that concealed the bunker door cut into the back wall of the furnace. Then, some of them in the bunker and some outside in the cellar, they lit a fire in the furnace. Those outside looked to see whether the fire would burn normally and make the camouflage complete. Those inside waited to know whether they would suffocate from the smoke or broil from the heat. The fire burned; the insulation worked. They had decided never to leave the cellar unguarded, so Avraham Becker and Leo Ziman—who had both been orphaned in the first of the German aktions four months before—stayed behind. The rest of them filtered out of the cellar in twos and threes and went home for the first time in eight days. It was, perhaps, an evidence of the surrealistic nature of the times that, having completed their illegal task at the risk of their lives, most of them shrank from confronting their angry and anxious parents; and they wondered fearfully what lie they might tell in answer to the question: Where have you been?

For Malachi this was not a problem; he answered to no one. His father lived; the Lithuanians and the Germans who had opened the veins of the ghetto four months before had passed by Yitzhak Wald. But the storm of their passing had blown out the light of the old man's mind. The orthodox Jews have a proverb: "The wind of

persecution is the lash of God." One bends like a reed
and breathes the Holy Name, and this, too, shall pass.
The old man bent; the body may bend, but the mind may
break. Yitzhak Wald spent his days cocooned by the
reality of the Holy Word: *Shema Y'Isroel, Adonai Elohaynu, Adonai Echod*—"Hear, O Israel, the Lord our
God, the Lord is One."

Yitzhak Wald's reality was in heaven; his son's was
underground. . . . Not quite so far underground, perhaps, as the reality being prepared by Captain Joachim
Gratt. . . .

October 26, 1941, was a bright sharp day and a man's
breath misted in the frosty air.

Captain Gratt walked briskly on his regular early
morning tour of the Ninth Fort. As he passed, his men
looked up from their labors and smiled as he called out
his cheery good-mornings. He was a good officer, well
liked, skilled in an easy camaraderie that sweetened but
never slackened the necessary discipline.

In the two weeks the SS kommando had been billeted
at the fort, they had worked hard. The fort itself had
been cleared of debris; the interior chambers deep in the
earth had been whitewashed, lined with wooden tiers, the
rusty old steel doors painted. The perimeter of the fort
was circled with a new wire fence rising ten feet high out
of an accordion of barbed wire. Every hundred yards a
high watchtower stood, topped with floodlights. Outside
the fence, hidden by a narrow hump of the hill, there
was an arc of fifteen huge pits dug in the peat bog by the
Wehrmacht's bulldozers. Each of the pits was rimmed on
three sides by mounds of the earth dug out of it. Along
the fourth, open side, at a distance of about twenty-five
yards from each pit, ran a long wooden platform—a little
like a military reviewing stand—raised a foot from the
cold marshy ground. (It was like Captain Gratt, a commander who had the welfare of this men constantly in
mind, to think of a little thing like keeping his men's
feet dry.)

Captain Gratt's tour took about an hour. It was nearly

nine o'clock before he returned to his quarters. By that time, the twenty Wehrmacht trucks had arrived and were already lined up, their motors idling, at the top of the road leading down to Kovno. They were big trucks, six-wheelers. There were four regular army soldiers to each truck: a driver, his assistant, and two men who sat with their submachine guns on a little platform especially built above each truck's cabin.

Captain Gratt climbed into the lead truck, the motors roared, the SS guards at the gate swung away the barbed-wire barrier, and the caravan started down the road to Kovno.

When the trucks turned into the square in front of the big municipal garage at 47 Vitovta Prospekt, there were four thousand Jews waiting for them. Most of the adults sat on their bundles of miscellaneous baggage, but hundreds of children spilled gaily over into the big square where a cordon of Jewish ghetto police auxiliaries kept a benevolent eye on them.

Captain Gratt climbed out of his truck and walked across to where Hans Biebow, the local Gestapo head, stood in conversation with the chairman of the Jewish Council. Biebow was very pleased with himself, he thought his plan was going well. (And so it did go, very well indeed. For this and similar efficiencies, he was made an SS Brigadier General, and six years later for the same reasons a Polish court had him hanged.)

Two weeks before, Hans Biebow had called in the Jewish Council to discuss the ghetto housing shortage caused by the influx of Jews from the areas around Kovno. The problem was acute. Every room in the ghetto was occupied; thousands were sleeping in the streets; synagogues were temporary dormitories for children; there was a serious danger of epidemic.

Biebow had been most sympathetic. He pointed out that the Germans, too, were concerned about the possibility of an epidemic which might spread among their own men. If the council would register everyone who had no housing, he said, he would see what could be done. Eight thousand men, women, and children were listed.

Then Biebow told the council, and the council told the ghetto, that temporary housing had been prepared at the Ninth Fort. Not very nice quarters, perhaps, but better than the streets of the ghetto, and only temporary, until something more adequate could be arranged for them at work camps further west.

On this morning of October 26, the first four thousand people assembled for relocation. And there they were, quiet and cooperative, even eager. The atmosphere was so relaxed that the Chairman of the Jewish Council ventured to raise a question: Most of the men in the group were unemployed and had no industrial skills, they had been farmers before being taken to the ghetto. Did Captain Gratt think there was any possibility that at the Fort they might be given a little ground to work; perhaps they could grow food for the ghetto? The captain considered it. Yes, he thought it could be arranged. It would take time of course, but it might be possible to give each of them a little patch of earth.

It was time to start. Captain Gratt walked over to the loudspeaker truck and called out his instructions: the trucks could take about a thousand at a time; the convoy would make several trips; the baggage would be taken later; families should not separate; parents should carry the younger children. It was all very firm, but pleasant enough. There was a lot of pushing, a few kids cried a little, a few got temporarily lost. Nothing that wasn't to be expected in any large-scale moving operation.

Very soon, the twenty trucks were moving through the bright open suburbs of Kovno, watched curiously by the men and women in the crowded streets outside the ghetto. Then they were past the outskirts and turning onto the road that wound up the hill to the Ninth Fort.

About halfway up the hill, a newly painted sign pointed an arrow up toward the Fort and bore the legend: *Der Weg zur Himmelfahrt*—"The Way to the Heavenly Journey." This bit of special SS whimsy might have been less than riotously funny, but it was at least somewhat more elliptical—and therefore more calming—than the Fort's official designation would have been. In the records of the German Gestapo, the Ninth Fort at Kovno is listed as *Vernichtungsstelle Nr. 2*—"Extermination point no. 2."

Even when the trucks roared into the barbed-wire compound, the Jews were not particularly uneasy. The armed SS men, the machine guns in the guard towers, the fence itself—none of this could be called comforting, but all of it was familiar, part of their war-torn lives. There was all of this in the ghetto, coupled with hunger and the hard bed of the streets. Here at least there would be shelter of some kind; and they had been promised work, and work meant food.

The fifty-year-old fort had been dug like a giant bunker into the crest of the hill so that all three of its levels were underground. Where the hill had been cut away to give access to the fort, the earth rose thirty feet on either side forming a funnel into the fort.[5] It was down this funnel that the Jews poured. The SS men moved them as a dog herds sheep, giving them no time, barking at their heels, but not biting. The Jews were shoved and shouted at; but there were no blows, no bullets, and therefore no terror. Down the earthen funnel, through the steel and concrete outer doors, down the dank corridors, down into the huge cavernous underground vaults. Quickly, quickly, move! until the clanging punctuation of the slamming steel doors brought a full stop and allowed the Jews to look about them. Then fear came, seeping in from the moist walls, panic crouching in the dark corners where the flickering lights in the high ceilings never reached.

Five times the twenty German army trucks went down to Kovno and came up again on The Way to the Heavenly Journey. Until by nightfall four thousand Jews were packed into the Fort and fear lay then like vomit on the concrete floors.

That was the night.

But the morning comes and the Jew puts on optimism with the prayer shawl that he dons to bless the new day. In the morning the doors are flung open and the SS men smile into their faces and call for all men who have done farm work to step forward. No lying now! Only those who can do a good day's work! There isn't a man who cannot. Work means food, obviously, no one can be expected to work long on an empty stomach. Out they file to stand waiting in the corridors while the guards assure the women and children that they, too, will be taken care of very soon.

Out of the fort into the bright day, blinking at the cold sun until they are formed into "work battalions," 120 men to each battalion. The others to wait in the barbed-wire compound while the first battalion is marched out through the gate and around to the other side of the hill where the first of the great pits is revealed and the blow falls on the till-then-unknowing Jews, as sudden and as benumbing as the hammer of God!

How fast it goes! The whips and the clubs are out now. The 120 Jews are beaten and driven to the pit's edge in front of the rifles of the SS men. Captain Gratt gives the order and the bullets that smash into bone and brain shatter the last illusion of the dying Jews. Oh, it goes well! It's efficient! Not forgotten are the two machine gunners who spray the mass in the bottom of the pit, just to be quite sure that nothing squirms there that was once a man.

How fast it goes! But even so, even though the SS men work like dogs—standing there the whole cold day, even after the rain begins—even so, when it is too dark to shoot, there are only 1300 Jews lying on the bottom of the first of the fifteen pits.

And it went less well thereafter, because the camouflage was gone when the "work battalions" didn't return that night. The next day's contingent had to be driven out of the fort; and the day after, the kommando had to shoot some of them in the underground corridors. It took nearly five days to kill the first four thousand. . . .

From October 27 to mid-November 1941, Captain Gratt and his SS kommando butchered ten thousand people at the Ninth Fort. Three of the fifteen pits were filled, and the earth that the bulldozers shoved over the topmost layers of the dead bulged with the swelling rot of the corpses.

To accomplish this considerable bloodletting, Captain Gratt worked his men from dawn to dusk, and it wasn't easy. Several of the men broke under the strain and wandered through the underground halls, scraping at their hands like so many Lady Macbeths, until Captain Gratt was able to arrange for their transfers to somewhat less rigorous duties as concentration camp guards. Among these, somewhat surprisingly, was Gratt's executive officer —Second Lieutenant Hans Groetner. Groetner's extreme youth, he was only nineteen, might be considered a mitigating circumstance; and he recovered sufficiently to play a memorable role, together with Ralf Gerrets, Jan Vijk, Erwin Mere, and Alexander Laak, in the murder of something over a hundred thousand Jews at the Jagala death camp in Estonia. (Groetner was found dead in a ditch in West Germany in 1953; Gerrets and Vijk were hanged by a Russian court in March 1961; Laak hanged himself—with some assistance—in Winnipeg, Canada, in September 1960. The only one left is Erwin Mere, who was boss of the lot and who now lives in England which refused to extradite him to the Soviet Union on the admirable grounds that England does not recognize the Soviet Union's annexation of Estonia. Mr. Mere, who was sentenced to death in absentia by the Russian court that tried his colleagues, says his "conscience is clear." That may be, of course, others of similar ilk went to their deaths with clear consciences and very bloody hands, but Mere is a convicted mass murderer and will some day be called to answer for it.)

The nervous breakdowns among his men were the least of Captain Gratt's problems; for the most part the kommando was made of sterner stuff. But even so, the routine became boring, the winter was severe and the living conditions harsh, and there wasn't much to do to relieve the monotony. One thing and another, Captain Gratt was hard put to keep the morale of his men sufficiently high to enable them to do their work efficiently.

This may have been part of the reason that the drain
of blood from the Kovno ghetto slowed during most of
1942. The aktions against the ghetto were more widely
spaced and on a smaller scale, seldom more than a thousand people at a time. Still, Captain Gratt had no real
reason to reproach himself, the pits were being filled. And
in any case, he wasn't able to devote the entire energies
of his men to killing the Jews of Kovno. For at the same
time, German army interrogation teams combing the
nearby Russian prisoner-of-war camps were sending him
the Jewish soldiers among them for execution at the fort.
And Adolf Eichmann's bureau for Germany's "final solution of the Jewish problem" began shipping Jews to the
fort from deportation depots in Germany, Austria, and
Czechoslovakia. There were even clients from western
Europe on whose behalf Eichmann's harried transport
officers somehow managed to divert freight cars badly
needed by the German army. It is hard to understand
why these people had to travel clear across Europe to be
buried in the pits at the Ninth Fort when it was clearly
more efficient to add them to the thousands who were
being killed and shoved into the earth at any one of a
score of places the Germans maintained for the purpose
closer at hand. But every now and then such examples of
bureaucratic frailty did occur, and scratched on the walls
of the Fort can be found—for example—the names of
Wolf Zelikstein of Brussels, Isaac Hayat of Marseilles,
Phillip Klein of Paris, Jules Herskowitz of Antwerp. . . .

In any case, by the winter of 1942 about ninety thousand people—give or take a couple of thousand—had
ended their "Heavenly Journey" at the Ninth Fort. Nearly
half of these were from the Kovno ghetto.

It was Ika Grinberg, an inspector in the Jewish ghetto
police, who first brought the news of the October 27
massacre at the Fort to the Jewish Council. Grinberg had
it from a Gestapo man who strained the story out through
the bottom of his schnapps glass. Most of the council
members dismissed it as a horror tale told by an idiot,

and a drunken one at that. The reasons for this disbelief were many: isolated in the ghetto by the fence and the guards and the hundreds of miles of German-held territory beyond, the Kovno Jews knew nothing then of what was happening elsewhere; pogroms they knew about and had suffered themselves, but to the eastern Jew the pogrom was an age-old eruption of primitive Jew-hate that flared up like a fire and destroyed and was gone. Their minds boggled at the concept of mass murder organized as government policy and carried out by the most highly civilized people on earth. Then, too, the Germans had already organized factories in which the Jews made coats and boots for the German army; would the Germans kill off the labor force they needed for their own war effort? All weighty reasons, but finally it came down to this: a man must believe that his life has some meaning, that his work has some value. The council members were buried in the tragic and overwhelming task of keeping their people alive—finding food, shelter, medicine, safeguarding the newborn, burying the dead. They could not, in sanity, believe this was all a monstrously useless charade.

So most of them swallowed the illusion that what had happened at the Fort had not happened; that the Fort was—as the Germans said—a way station on the road to resettlement. "Resettlement"—the same carrot of illusion that the Germans dangled before the Jews everywhere and that helped to lead them, for the most part all-unknowing, to the edge of the abyss.

But there were some in the Kovno Jewish Council who were able to look upon horror and know it for truth. Among these were Dr. Simon Elkes, the new chairman, and his deputy—Leib Gorfunkel. They didn't scream the news from the housetops for they knew this would spread panic through the ghetto to no useful end. Mass resistance in the conditions of the ghetto was not possible and could lead only to certain massacre in place of the grim but, at that time, still uncertain future. So Elkes and Gorfunkel and the policeman, Ika Grinberg, took their news instead to the cellars where the Zionists were organizing their underground groups. And Malachi Wald was sent as a messenger to 8 Broilu Street where the small group of Communists remaining in the ghetto were building a partisan group under the leadership of the remarkable Chaim Yellin.

No one speaks of the Kovno ghetto today without mention of Chaim Yellin. Thin, shy, with a manner so retiring as to render him almost a shadow, he drifted through the ghetto like a phantom; but the phantom had the substance of the hero. At the time the Germans came to Kovno he was twenty-two years old. Five years before he had put aside the religion to which he'd been born and embraced instead the secret orthodoxy of communism. One of the very few Jewish students at the Lithuanian University of Kovno, Yellin was already famous as a Yiddish poet and author and it was widely predicted that he had important achievements ahead of him. And so he did—in sabotage, forgery, arms smuggling, and fighting.

It was Chaim Yellin who brought together the small and scattered groups that were beginning to think of some kind of resistance. The first meeting was on the night of November 18 in the cellar at 8 Broilu Street. There were Yellin, Dmitri Gelperin, and Pesach Gordon from the Communists; Dr. Elkes and Abraham Golub of the Jewish Council were there as representatives of the Zionist Center parties that dominated the council. The Hashomer Hatzair—Malachi Wald's Zionist Young Guards—sent him and Abba Diskont, who led the group, and Avraham Becker. Moshe Levin, the chief of the ghetto Jewish police auxiliary, was there, and two of his men.

They had little in common, one with the other, when they went into the meeting and not much more when they came out. But between the going in and the coming out, they had formed a loose confederation of the Jewish resistance in Kovno. Within this confederation, the groups were autonomous, but there would be a coordinating committee called *der schwarzer shtab*—"the black staff" —headed by Chaim Yellin.

None of the groups—small, unarmed, inexperienced,

MALACHI WALD   19

totáling at that time less than two hundred people—
thought then in terms of organizing any really effective
resistance. Their aims were more limited than that: to
organize *some* resistance, some token of their dignity as
human beings; and to break the isolation that walled in
the ghetto, without knowledge of what was happening beyond the fence and the guards and the patrolling dogs.

Even within this common ground, the groups saw their
work differently. The Communists focused their gaze beyond the ghetto. It was their aim to find and somehow
to join the ranks of the Soviet partisans they were sure
must be hidden in the Augustava forest a hundred miles
to the west and in the Rudniki woods eighty miles or so
southeast of Kovno. The activity of the Communists,
from first to last, was to organize an escape route, to get
men and women capable of fighting out of the ghetto and
into partisan formations. Chaim Yellin put it bluntly:
"We shall not forsake the ghetto, but our principal aim
is to fight openly in the ranks of the Soviet partisans. Any
member of our organization is a partisan." Everything—
money, forged papers, stolen weapons, homemade bombs,
the fake German army uniforms sewed from materials
stolen from the clothing factory in which the Germans
forced the Jews to work; everything—the bunkers dug in
the cellars for the men and women to hide in when the
Germans roamed the ghetto in an aktion to feed the pits
at the Ninth Fort; everything—the quick knife in the
night-dark alley; everything, all of it was for the Communists preliminary to and part of the organization of an
escape route out of the ghetto to the partisans in the
forests, a route for people willing to fight and trained to
do it.

This was the Communist way. One cannot say that it
was easy. It was hard and frightful and heroic beyond
imagining: to creep through the fence, to be shot in the
fields or torn apart by the patrolling dogs, to freeze and
starve in the maze of forest and sucking swamp, to be
betrayed in the streets of Kovno by the Lithuanian inhabitants whose Christian fervor was so great that it was
never necessary for the Gestapo even to offer rewards for

the capture of escaped Jews. . . . They did it all, the Communists in the ghetto suffered it all. This was their way and nothing turned them from it. Nothing—not the eight dead for every one who succeeded in escaping; not the ferocious reprisals in which the Germans killed fifty Jews for every weapon found in the ghetto; not the danger outside or the misery within; nothing stopped them. And finally Chaim Yellin went out of the ghetto alone to the Rudniki forest and made contact with the commander of the Soviet partisans there—a woman known only as "Albina"—and she came back into the ghetto with him to see whether the Jews could be serious fighters, worth helping. Albina spent three days in the ghetto and went out again. From then on there was a thin trickle of arms that came in to the Communists; and a training base in the forest to which the ghetto escapees came. Until, at last, there were enough of them to form a regular partisan battalion and they called it "Death to the Occupiers." That took a year—a year and a half. . . .

That was the way of the Communists in the Kovno ghetto, hard and bitter and infinitely dangerous. The Zionists, Malachi Wald among them, went the same way and other ways also, and with more anguish. For the Zionists saw themselves not as part of the Soviet struggle against the invader, with natural allies among the Soviet resistance forces. They saw themselves as Jewish fighters, avenging Jewish blood. Their war was a war as Jews against an enemy bent upon exterminating them because they were Jews. And to fight, even to fight, was not enough. This alone even—impossible thought!—even were it successful, would not suffice unless it carried with it the protection and the survival of the Jewish people. Not only that the Jews should live, but that they should live as Jews!

No one fights a hopeless empty-handed fight without a philosophy. This was the Zionists' and it made their dangerous way even more difficult, ambushed at every turning by doubt and uncertainty and pain. They would not turn their backs upon the ghetto; and they could not forsake the opportunity to form effective bands in the secret woods. So they did both. Some went out to the woods; some stayed in the ghetto. Some went out for a time and returned again. They risked their lives at sabotage and flash raids; and risked them again in the desperate endeavor to preserve what still remained of the social and public forces in the ghetto and to prevent them from being swept totally away in the tide of deportations and massacres. They organized forbidden schools, they taught the forbidden Jewish history, the forbidden Hebrew language. They anticipated the German raids and hid the young in the secret bunkers and smuggled them out of the ghetto by bribery and deception to keep them alive in the forests—to guarantee the survival of a Jewish people.

Simon Elkes and Moshe Levin searched out the guards who could be bribed; Abba Diskont and his men stole the trucks and the gasoline; Malachi Wald and twenty men in fake German uniforms escorted the trucks and bluffed their way past the wandering Wehrmacht patrols, or ambushed them.

For weeks at a time the work would stop while the infuriated Germans ran wild in the ghetto and reinforced the guards and threw two armored battalions across the countryside to block the ways between the ghetto and the sheltering forests. But at Stalingrad and elsewhere the Soviet armies were bleeding the Germans white and they couldn't spare the men to keep the blockade tight for very long. So the patrols would be diminished and the resistance fighters would start again and Malachi was out in the nights again in his German uniform. Four times he was wounded and twice captured and twice away. Until, on July 26, 1943, with a twisted leg and a lung ruptured by tuberculosis, he was brought to the Ninth Fort and flung like a hurt dog at the feet of Captain Joachim Gratt.

Captain Gratt and the Gestapo specialists who worked with him on such matters had high hopes for the eighteen-year-old kid they had their hands on. Malachi was the first of the resistance leaders to be captured alive. (Well, not actually the first; Leo Ziman and Moshe Ilionski had been caught earlier. But Ziman had ripped his veins open with a rusty nail he'd found in his cell the night they caught him and by morning he was dead and useless to them. And Ilionski had gone insane when they'd put out his eyes; and though they kept him around in the hope that he'd recover, he was still just a babbling lunatic crawling about in the five-foot-square box they kept him in.) So there was only Malachi Wald who could tell them enough to break the resistance in the Kovno ghetto; and even with him it wasn't so simple. The problem with Malachi was not that he was so tough, it was that he was so sick that they couldn't really explore how tough he might be. If they tortured him enough he'd start coughing up blood from his tubercular lung, and if he coughed up enough blood, he'd die and that would be the end of it. They knew who he was all right, and that he was important, one of the women they'd taken from the ghetto to wait her turn at the pits told them as much after some persuasion; but that was all they knew.

It isn't certain that it was Captain Gratt's idea, but either he or one of his colleagues thought to look for Malachi's family and one day they brought his father in to see him. The old man was barely coherent at all and he knew nothing of his son's activities; but it seemed a reasonable guess that the boy might talk to spare his father pain. Yitzhak Wald didn't last long enough to make it a fair test. But in any case, Malachi watched it as long as it went on and all he did was spit at them until Captain Gratt—exasperated beyond endurance—knocked out his front teeth and had him dragged away unconscious, and they were no further along except that the doctor warned them the boy's hold on life was very tenuous.

So they left him alone for a while, and that while saved his life. Early in August 1943, the Gestapo at Kovno received orders to destroy the evidences of mass murder at the Ninth Fort, to exhume the corpses and burn them. The orders were that it had to be done by the end of the

year in view of the possibility that the German armies
might have to evacuate the Baltic provinces. There were
something over a hundred thousand bodies in the fifteen
pits at the fort; so Captain Gratt had a lot to do and not
a lot of time in which to do it.

Right or wrong, Captain Gratt didn't feel he could
order his own men to do the work. After all, they'd killed
the Jews once and oughtn't to be asked—as it were—to
do it again. Gratt thought about it for a time and after
a bit he hit upon a solution that was both ingenious and
ironic.

A hundred men were selected from among the prisoners at the Fort and put to work. They were divided into
four squads, each of which did a particular part of the
job. The first squad of "miners" shifted the top cover of
earth from the pits and with their shovels removed the
first layer of corpses. After that they used ladders to go
deeper into the pits, pitchforking the bodies out layer by
layer.

When the corpses had been brought up by the miners,
the "porters" piled the bodies on boards and logs—a
layer of bodies, a layer of logs, a layer of bodies, and so
on. Then the "burners" went to work. Kerosene was
poured over the piles of dead and the whole thing set on
fire. When the flames burned down, the fourth—"re-
moval"—squad shoveled the ashes and odd bits and
pieces onto trucks which dumped them over a wide range
of the countryside.

The men of the SS kommando guarded the Jews and
supervised the work. They didn't like it very much for it
was widely believed that the smoke of the burning bodies
was unhealthy. Nonetheless, the work went pretty well
and over a period of time they managed to achieve a
productivity norm of about four hundred bodies reduced
to ashes daily.

During this time, except for an occasional bit of dis-
ciplinary bloodletting, the killing at the Fort ground to a
halt. Of course, there was still a pretty high death rate
from starvation and similar natural causes, but the slaugh-

ter was over. Clearly, it would not have made much sense to shove more bodies into the pits while at the same time expending every energy to get them out.

It wasn't only the dead who were being moved in those autumn months of 1943. From August, the Ninth Fort was being used as an assembly point for thousands of Jews who were being transported from concentration camps in the path of the advancing Soviet armies to Sachsenhausen, Dachau, and Belsen further to the west. Finally, by the end of November, the permanent population of the Fort was down to about a thousand prisoners, among these the men of the special burning squads.

By then, the original hundred men had been reduced to sixty-four, the rest having died or been helped to die when they became unfit for the work. Among the sixty-four remaining was Malachi Wald, who had been added to the group by some quirk of humorous dispensation on the part of Captain Gratt.

As things went at the Fort, the men of the burning squads were an elite group. They slept together in one of the underground halls; each man had a blanket; they had two rations of bread and watery soup each day instead of the customary one. While it cannot be said that, even in such luxury, the men actually thrived, they were able to maintain a minimal level of health and even some certain resemblance—unusual among the prisoners—to normal human beings. They were also, of course, able to work better and it seems reasonable to assume that Captain Gratt was motivated by this consideration rather than some sudden influx of warm regard for the welfare of the people in his care. But in thus subverting the National Socialist principle of keeping the untermenschen submissive by starvation, and in unconsciously adopting instead the Socialist principle of "To each according to his labor," Captain Gratt overlooked still another principle known to slavers of ages past. It might be put this way: "If a slave is strong enough to work, he is strong enough to scheme."

And that's what happened. The sixty-four men of the burning squads schemed to escape from the Ninth Fort.

No one now remembers who first talked about the plot, but it was hatched into action by Abba Diskont, Malachi Wald, and Avraham Becker of the Kovno ghetto; and by Captain J. L. Vasilienko of the Red Army. Diskont was the leader of the Zionist resistance movement in the ghetto, but he'd been swept up in one of the casual SS aktions and Captain Gratt seems to have been unaware of the importance of the fish he'd netted. And Vasilienko had been sent from a Russian prisoner-of-war camp at Kalvaria to the Fort for execution on the good grounds that he was Jewish *and* a Communist. Since in addition to all that he was also tremendously strong, Captain Gratt put him to better use tossing bodies up from the pits.

Abba Diskont, who was occasionally used by the Germans as a translator, had managed to steal a plan of the Fort from Captain Gratt's office. The diagram showed that a locked steel door in the underground hall where the burning squads slept led to an unused storeroom. Avraham Becker, a man of many skills, took an impression of the lock in the door with a scrap of soap. Malachi, who at that time worked in the Fort's machine shop sawing logs for the fires that burned the corpses, fashioned a key under the nose of the SS supervisor.

From then on, when the lights went out at seven o'clock, the men scraped with their food pans and stolen bits of metal at the wall of the storeroom. Every morning they smuggled out the scrapings of stone and earth in the slop buckets or in their clothes and then scattered them surreptitiously in the pits. They worked in shifts all night after each day's bitter hard work. Terrified that their work would fall off and that they would be replaced and killed, the men increased their quota of bodies destroyed to 450 and then to nearly 500 a day. They worked all the long days and dug all the long nights. Four times the tunnel collapsed, breaking through the makeshift cement fashioned of earth and excrement and urine. The first time it buried Moshe Kowalski and he strangled to death before they reached him. That seemed the end of it. If they left him where he was, the morning count would be short and the resultant search would bring them death. If he were taken to his bed, to be found dead with his face swollen and his eyes popping, asphyxiated with no apparent cause, there would be an investigation and they were done. It was the Russian captain, Vasilienko, who thought of hanging the dead man with a strip of his own blanket. And in the morning when the guards came, they found Kowalski—just another one of the not-infrequent suicides.

The fourth time the tunnel collapsed Yossi Siekow was pulled out with a smashed hip. But he was alive and though they discussed it all night under his wide stricken eyes, there were none of them able to try the "suicide" trick again with a living friend. So, finally, they told him to lie in his bunk and they would report him sick and then see. But when the guards came, Siekow called out and told them he'd fallen from his bunk during the night. The guards took him out and shot him, and his friends burned him that morning.

After eleven weeks of it, they were bludgeoned with fatigue, fevered with anxiety. But the tunnel stretched 150 feet under the wall, under the courtyard, under the fence, and within a few feet of where the earth fell away into the first of the fifteen pits around the fort.

It was December now; cold to kill a man out in the open and not clothed for it, snow on the ground to betray a running man by the line of footprints, blizzards to blind him. It was the worst time, but every day birthed the risk of discovery and they could not wait. They set the date for Christmas Eve. Abba Diskont slipped a note for Chaim Yellin in the ghetto to the ancient Jew who came wheezing up the hill with a wagonful of ersatz bread from the ghetto bakery every second day. And they waited. . . .

Christmas Eve, 1943, at the Ninth Fort. In the barracks, the SS men crowd around the glowing iron stoves, stuffed with the Christmas feast, drugged with heat, doped with drink, hoarse from bellowing the hearty German songs thick with love of the German home, the German mother, wife, child. In the Fort itself, a thousand skeletons—non-German and therefore beyond love—twist and freeze on their bare board beds. In the storeroom and the tunnel beneath the Fort, sixty-two men wait, pressed close together, close to freedom, close to death. And outside, the ice-bladed winter wind whips and tears at the thinned-out guards, huddled in their furs, warmed with schnapps, waiting for their hour tour of duty to end and their relief to come, cursing the cold whimpering dogs that press against their legs and trip them as they walk.

It was the dogs that the escapees feared most. Because of the dogs, the tunnel was dug into the side of one of the pits. So the men, stinking of the dead they handled every day, would crawl out of the tunnel, out among the remaining swollen corpses in the bottom of the pit; the whole thing presenting only the clutching reek of death to the quivering noses of the killer dogs.

Two o'clock in the morning, or about that, and Vasilienko is first, tearing the screen of earth from the tunnel mouth and out among the corpses at the bottom of the pit. One at a time they come, until all of them are crouched among the staring skulls and the rotting entrails. Vasilienko then, and Diskont and Malachi Wald, out of the pit, drifting like ghosts down upon the huddled sentry and the dog curled at his feet, both of them hugging the shelter of one of the gun towers, empty now because it is the Lord's day and a good time to be inside and drunk. And at the last moment, the stench of death comes close and the dog lifts its head and growls and the guard moves to question but it is too late and the three are on them; dog and man dead in the snow with Malachi tearing the throat out of the man until Abba Diskont lifts him away and thrusts the submachine gun into his hands and motions him to wait and watch while the other two go back to the pit and get the others.

That's how they go, all of them, drifting past while Malachi crouches against the tower, the German machine gun in his hands, the taste of German blood fine in his mouth. Past they go and no one sees them, Malachi coming last, running for the thin scrub of trees where Chaim Yellin waits with ten armed men and three stolen trucks.

Only a moment to cry and kiss each other and cry. Then into the trucks. Malachi and his group going west to the Augustava forest, Diskont and his men southeast to the partisans in the Rudniki woods. The big Russian captain to strike straight east through the German lines toward the Soviet armies; and Avraham Becker with five men going with him, hoping to get arms and men and Soviet planes and parachute into the ghetto ahead of the advancing Soviet troops. Last of all, Chaim Yellin, left behind to smuggle those too sick to live in the woods back into the nearby ghetto to hide them there.

A moment, only, for Malachi to ask, "Where will we meet again? When?"

"After," Diskont tells him, "when it's over; we'll bring the group together again." And the Hebrew watchword of the Zionist fighters called softly from truck to truck: *Chazack v'amotz!*—"Be strong and courageous!"

Malachi Wald, eighteen years old, out of the Ninth Fort and on his long way to kill—among others—a pig of a man in Argentina. . . .

Two

Illusion and Reality

From early 1941 to April 1945, between five and six million Jews were butchered—mostly in eastern Europe—by citizens of the Third German Reich and those who cooperated with them. The majority of these Jewish millions did not resist their murderers, and the question arises: Why did they not? Often it is put more bluntly, with a harshness akin to contempt, and the formulation is: "Why did they go like sheep to the slaughter?"

One might for many reasons wish the question gently phrased. It is, after all, asked from the safety of distance and the clarity of elapsed time by those who are alive and, usually, themselves without personal experience of horror. And those of whom it is asked and who might authoritatively answer out of the weight of their own terrible knowledge are, for the most part, dead. It would seem some humility is called for.

But however it is framed, the question deserves discussion in the hope that out of this some answers will emerge, each of them partial only and even the sum total of them partial, like a jigsaw puzzle in which the last piece is missing, was indeed never carved, and must be supplied by each player out of his own inner search.

Of the five to six million victims, nearly two million are outside the frame of our discussion. Something over a million of these were children or aged; more than a quarter million were the blind, the crippled, the mentally ill, the diseased. And, although the Jewish ethic as

generally interpreted does not teach nonviolence, there
were about three hundred thousand adult Jews in eastern
Europe whose failure to resist was, as they saw it, the
very essence of religious duty. These last were members
of the Hassidic sect of orthodox Jewry which believes that
only in His fullness of time can God's design come clear
to man, and that evil is the concealing cover for the
ultimately-to-be-revealed good. These Hassidim—the father of Malachi Wald was one of them—accepted the
Nazi persecutions as a manifestation of the unfathomable
will of God.

In this time of holocaust, they put their lives—as they
had always put them—in the hands of the zaddikim, "the
righteous men," the devout, unworldly leaders whom the
Hassidic creed holds to be intermediaries between God
and man. And these leaders had before *their* eyes the
obscure but meaningful and holy vision set down in the
Book of Job. To the early persecutions the Nazis visited
upon the Jews of eastern Europe—the hatreds, the harry-
ings, the starvation, even the eruptive and apparently patternless first pogroms—to all these the zaddikim had Job's
answer and silenced the distressed and the doubters
among their people as Job did his wife: "What? Shall
we receive good at the hand of God, and shall we not
receive evil?"

And when the bloody road was walked to its end and
the pits were open before them, the Hassidim stood unresistant, constrained by the dazzling nimbus of revealed
truth. For was it not God's will? As seven centuries earlier
the iron knights of the Crusades thundered into battle
with that same cry—*Deus le veult!*—so these iron-willed
zaddikim led their people, not to kill but to be killed.
God wills it!

If the slaughter was terrible for them beyond true understanding, the evil too shattering for them to detect
the good their faith taught them must lie within all God's
works, why so was it also for Job. And that awful riddle
stood as example before their believing eyes. They were
answered with the same bludgeoning nonanswer given to
Job when he asked why he suffered *his* incomprehensible

agony: "Then the Lord answered Job out of the whirl-wind and said . . . Knowest *thou* the ordinances of Heaven? Canst *thou* set the dominions thereof in the earth? . . . Moreover the Lord answered Job and said, Shall he that contendeth with the Almighty instruct Him?"

They bowed their heads and accepted the unknowable will of God. Embraced their loved ones. Told their terrified children—"Don't cry. Sh-h, what's to cry? Soon we shall all live with God in His house." And believed it so. They went down into the pits and stood on the corpses of those who had gone before; lifted their eyes above the rifles and the machine guns to the heavens and called the ancient—and joyous!—Hebrew affirmation of the reality of God!—*Shema Y'Isroel, Adonai Elohaynu, Adonai Echod.*

If it is all strange to us, well, then, it is strange to us. How much do we really understand of man's relationship to God? It is not strange to history, nor is it unique to the Hassidic Jew. The early Christians went similarly bemused and joyous to their martyrdom in the amphitheaters of Rome. And one might usefully inquire why the Christians are remembered as exemplars, sanctifying the Holy Name, while for the God-oriented immolation of eastern Europe's equally devout Hassidic Jews the descriptive terms are less ennobled and they are considered to have gone, somehow shamefully and less than brave, "like sheep to the slaughter."

Children or aged or ill or offerings to the glory of the living God, the Nazis killed them all. But we may not join their murderers in seeing no difference between them and the rest of the victims of the holocaust when we frame the harsh question: Why didn't they fight? These nearly two million, being what they were, could not have fought; they could only die. . . .

The question hangs in the air, now, only over the memory of those others of the dead who might have fought; but we may not ask it yet, for there are other things to understand before we begin to peel this bitter onion of truth. . . .

It is self-evident that the Jews could not have fought
a war; what we speak of here is underground resistance.
There are differences between such a resistance and warfare. Warfare is conducted by nations against nations,
armies—weaponed and equipped—against other armies
similarly endowed, mass against mass. Underground resistance is, in these terms, a lonely art.

The people of a nation can be ordered into war by
leaders good or bad, for reasons good or bad. All the
techniques available to a sovereign nation, all its media
of information and propaganda can be used and are always used to persuade the people of the exalted purpose
or the tragic inevitability of each particular war. Those
segments of a society that remain unpersuaded can be
dragooned by social pressure or by governmental force.
And there are always the jails to ensure a final quarantine
for those hard-core carriers of the disease of division and
doubt who remain unpersuaded.

An underground resistance has none of these means.
No one can order or force such a resistance into effective
being; nor, if it exists, can it be held together by order
or force. It is created voluntarily and individually. It is
composed always of persons each of whom has made a
free, deliberate, and dangerous choice. And this decision,
once made, must be reaffirmed over and over, each time
with all its original difficulty and doubt, by each participant during the entire life of the resistance.

One thing more: the Germans decreed death by
shooting or hanging as the legal punishment for an act
of resistance.

All this constituted part of the canon law governing
all resistance movements. If one thinks carefully and
personally about the fortitude required to accept this
law and to live by it, the result is likely to be humbling.
And thus humbled, we are ready to begin an examina-
tion of the Jewish resistance, which had all the problems
of all other resistance movements—and more. Because for
the Jew under the Nazis there were also other laws and
other risks.

The resisting non-Jew braved swift death. Sometimes

the death was slowed and rendered more painful by a
local German commander with a taste for brutality, but
the German military and SS regulations with regard to
the non-Jewish resistance specified the noose or the bullet
as the usual maximum punishment. For the Jew, this punishment was minimal and merciful, and rare. The regulations specified that a resistant *Jew* might be killed "in
any manner considered most conducive to discipline and
deterrence of further resistance."[6] In the province of Lublin, where SS Lieutenant General Odilo Globocnik was
the Lord God, the Jew caught with a gun or in an act of
sabotage was hung by his scrotum on a hook. The same
fate, as exactly as anatomical differences allowed, awaited
the Jewess similarly caught. Nor was Globocnik unique,
except in the genital drift of his imagination. His coun-
terpart in Minsk, SS Lieutenant General Maximilian von
Herff, had a different whimsy, perhaps attributable to his
scholarly researches at the University of Mainz into
the history of the Germanic peoples. Herff's fifth-
century forebearers—the Vandals—moving south from
the valley of the Oder River, blinded their captives with
hot irons and sent them back to their people as a deter-
rent to resistance. Fifteen centuries later Herff used the
same punishment for the same purpose. History records
that the Vandal King Gunderic died in bed; Herff, happily, was hanged in Minsk on February 6, 1948. Artur
Greiser, gauleiter of Warthegau, burned Jewish resistance
fighters at the stake, and was hanged for it in Posen on
July 20, 1946, despite the personal intervention of Pope
Pius XII.[7] Baron Gustav von Waechter favored the
thumbscrew and the iron boot during his six months'
rule at Krakow; and died peacefully on September 10,
1949, as a good Catholic monk in the Capuchin mon-
astery on the Via Siciliani in Rome, where out of the
same curious concept of Christian charity, Father Benedetto had earlier hidden Adolf Eichmann before supplying him with a Vatican laissez-passer to enable that
hunted hound to run again.[8] And SS Major General
Fritz Katzmann, who fed captured Jewish resistants spas-
modic poison so they could die in agony for the edifica-

tion of his dinner guests in east Galicia, is free now in
Cairo as are Bernard Bender—who put his captives into
pits with starving wolfhounds—and Leopold Gleim—
who reconstructed the rack of the Spanish Inquisition
and used that to tear them apart. . . .

One could go on endlessly. The rack, the thumbscrew,
the stake, the hot irons—these were the medieval deaths
the Jew of the ghetto faced when he rose in revolt. In
this, as in all other things, the Jew had a special fate
under the German New Order. It was only the Jew who,
caught in an act of violent resistance, was made to tarry
on his way to the torture chambers to witness the deaths
of all the members of his family—father, mother, brother,
sister, wife and child, grandparents and grandchildren.

Under the German doctrine of collective responsibility
as it was applied to the Jews, retribution eddied out from
a single act of resistance until it bathed the entire ghetto.
An act of sabotage in a factory could bring death to all
the workers. Everyone might die in a building where a
gun was found. As everyone in a building might die for
the resistance slogan scrawled on a wall; everyone—innocent or not, young or old, whether he had read the forbidden words or written them, whether indeed he could
at all read or write or was, perhaps, a nursing infant and
therefore unlikely to have done either. And killing a German was, of course, the ultimate crime, to be washed
away only by the river of blood let out of the bodies of a
thousand Jews.

The purpose of this policy was always clear—to drown
a Jewish resistance in blood, to paralyze it with indecision. For facing this terrible retribution, the Jew who
thought to take a gun—if he could find a gun—had other
thoughts to give him pause. A brave man may decide to
risk his death and the many cruel ways of his own dying.
Decided. Done. And then? What of the others who do
not so decide, but die nonetheless out of his decision?
His, not theirs. How many innocent unconsulted lives does
a man earn the right to endanger because he is willing to
risk his own?

Thus dreadfully bedeviled, even the most resolute heart is host to the worm. . . .

The singular savagery of German reprisals, and the moral dilemma they created, were themselves sufficient to render the birth of a Jewish resistance more agonizing than that of any other resistance movement. But there were also other problems which faced the Jews and faced no other people in Nazi Europe; an understanding of these is essential if we are ever to approach the reality of the eastern ghettos.

It is axiomatic that no resistance movement can successfully exist among a people who are hostile to it. The active membership of a resistance is normally limited, but the movement itself must be popular, otherwise the people will refuse it help and will ultimately fight or betray it.

In the Second World War, the strength of the resistance movement in each country was directly proportionate to the anti-Nazi sentiment in that country. And the corollary was also true—where nazism was massively and overwhelmingly popular, there was no resistance.

There was, for example, no anti-Nazi resistance to speak of in Germany, unless one demeans the term by attaching it to the dithering plot to kill Hitler hatched by a cabal of Wehrmacht officers. As part of the enthusiastic effort to rewrite German history, it has become fashionable to speak of this hesitant conspiracy as "a German resistance" and the West German government has published a book about it somewhat wistfully titled *Germans Against Hitler*.[9] The facts contained within the book have a smaller impact than the title might indicate. Of the seventy million Germans, there were 154 people known to be involved in this "resistance movement." Some of these were unquestionably honorable, heroic, and anti-Nazi. By far the greater part, however, were high-ranking officers who had gone along with Hitler merrily enough when he was winning, but whose revulsion against nazism grew as the inevitability of Germany's total defeat became increasingly clear. The fiddle-footed attempt on Hitler's life, for which the conspiracy was formed, took place on July 20, 1944—eighteen months after the German debacle at Stalingrad, a year after the Germans had been thrown out of Africa and Italy had surrendered, and a month after the Allies had broken out of the Normandy beachheads. By that time, the handwriting on the wall was written large enough for even such Nazi careerists as SS Major General Artur Nebe to read, so there he was, among the freedom fighters. No one, apparently, boggled at the fact that just before joining the group, Nebe had been commander in Russia of Einsatzgruppe B which had butchered 45,476 Jews in a single five-month period.[10] It was a bit hard on the Jews, of course, but it made fine cover; with such a record, who would suspect Nebe of being an anti-Nazi? Who, indeed?

There were certainly Germans during the war who were truly anti-Nazi and acted as such, among these: the seventy-five Germans who formed the Rote Kapelle and were hanged for supplying military information to the Russians; the students Hans and Sophie Scholl, who were hanged for distributing anti-Nazi leaflets at Munich University; the twenty-six men and women—mostly Jews— led by Herbert Baum, who carried on sabotage in Berlin munitions factories for eighteen months until they were caught and tortured to death on July 11, 1942.[11] There were others, but not even West German sources today number these in more than the hundreds; and these honorable exceptions scarcely constitute a German resistance movement. There was none. No organized sabotage; no program of anti-Nazi propaganda; no partisan fighters. None.

The Germans created no resistance movement because the German people were not anti-Nazi.

So it was also in Austria, Hungary, Rumania, Bulgaria. There were anti-Nazis in all these countries, and isolated acts of resistance; but no resistance movement because the people would not support it.

This rule—that a resistance must grow in fertile soil

—pressed most harshly upon the Jews. For, *wherever* the Jews were in eastern Europe, they were among their enemies, among peoples who were violently and historically anti-Semitic, in countries where Jew-killing was endemic. Even before Germany's "final solution of the Jewish problem" got underway, thousands of Rumanians went howling through the streets of Jassy on June 25, 1940, and slaughtered seven thousand Jews.[12] At Czernowitz, a year later, there was a friendly competition between the Rumanian "Iron Guard" fascist organization and Kommando 10b of SS Major General Otto Ohlendorff's Einsatzgruppe D. At the end of it, 58,000 Jews were dead and Ohlendorff was compelled to record in reluctant admiration that the Rumanian volunteers had outstripped his own professionals by four victims to one.[13] It went on like that. The Lithuanians helped to kill the Jews at Kovno; the Latvians at Riga and Dvinsk; the Estonians at Tallin and Jagala; the Ukrainians killed them by the thousands at Lvov, Zhitomir, Kiev, Dnepropetrovsk, Vinnitsa.[14]

All this, it is true, happened in areas where the people were overwhelmingly pro-German, at least while the Wehrmacht was winning. But these were the areas in which the ghettos were; and if there was to be a Jewish resistance movement it had to germinate, contrary to all the rules, in this barren ground and among these hostile people.

But the Jews learned, to their cost, that even where the people were anti-German they could also be ferociously anti-Semitic; and that even within the resistance movements, the Jews could not safely assume that the fight against the common enemy necessarily softened an ingrained hatred of the Jew. In Poland, for example, the underground Armia Krajowa—which took its orders from the Polish government-in-exile in London—had no unified policy toward the Jews. In Volhynia and Ternapol, Jews were welcomed into the Polish partisan units; in the Narocz forests, the Armia Krajowa formation under General Kapusta sheltered the Jews escaping from the ghetto and the brigade under General Markov slaughtered them. Armia Krajowa units murdered Jewish partisans in the forests outside Lublin; other AK groupings patched together a temporary truce with SS Einsatzgruppe B in order to help the Germans liquidate the Vilna ghetto; and in the forests outside Bialystok and surrounding Krakow, the Armia Krajowa disarmed the Jewish partisans and left them naked to their enemies.[15] On April 23, 1943, when the Warsaw ghetto revolt was at its height and the Jews appealed to the Armia Krajowa for help, or at least guns, the answer the local commander, Colonel Konar, sent was, "For us the time is not convenient." Unfortunately, the Jews couldn't pick a more convenient time. One might, nevertheless, insist in sorrow that there were overriding military considerations that compelled the Armia Krajowa to refuse such help at that time; but it is hard to produce military reasons why the Poles refused—as they did refuse—to help hide the few battered survivors of the Warsaw ghetto revolt who crawled through the sewers into the "Aryan" sector of Warsaw.[16]

So it comes to this: unlike any resistance movement in history, no Jewish resistance movement in the Jewish heartland of eastern Europe could safely seek allies among the general populations; not even, for the most part, among those who were themselves fighting the Germans.

The Jew who thought of fighting the Germans and thought his way past—or ignored—the questions "At what risk?" and "Who with?" came finally to the question "*What* with?"

A fighting resistance must have weapons with which to fight. The concept of fighting an enemy "tooth and nail" makes for inspiring poetry but suicidal practice.

The non-Jewish resistance movements in World War II got their arms in one or more of the following ways: in the beginning, soldiers out of the defeated armies joined the resistance and brought their equipment with them; in certain areas, the munitions depots were opened to the resistance fighters before the German armies reached them; later on, most of the equipment—especially plastic explosives, gelignite pencils, antipersonnel mines, hand grenades, machine guns, even mortars—was parachuted to the various resistance movements by planes operating from the territory of the Allied powers. Once a resistance movement was armed enough to fight effectively, they could also take weapons from the enemies they fought.

No Jewish resistance could obtain arms in any of these ways. The Jews of Germany, Hungary, Austria, Rumania, Bulgaria, never had weapons to begin with because they had not been in the armies of those nations. Jewish soldiers coming out of the western European armies joined the general resistance there. The Jews in the Soviet armies retreated with those armies or were captured, disarmed, and for the most part killed by the enemy. The German advance through Poland and western Russia was so rapid that it overran the arms depots before any partisan resistance could be organized. In Poland, the Armia Krajowa disarmed the Jews coming out of the Polish army. And at no single time anywhere on the eastern front did any Allied power parachute, or otherwise supply, any arms whatever into the ghettos or the forests for the use of a Jewish resistance.

One thing more must be recorded in the list of burdens that crushed down on a Jewish resistance—the terrible isolation of the six million Jews crammed into the eighty-five ghettos scattered across eastern Europe from the Baltic Sea to the Black Sea. They were a universe apart.

Around each ghetto was a wall, with the towers and the searchlights and the machine guns and the SS guards; then came the prowling dogs—the *Hundestaffel,* trained to kill; then the volksdeutsche auxiliaries recruited from among the Latvians, Rumanians, Lithuanians, the Polish fascist bands, and all the other anti-Semites; then the security patrols of the German army rear-echelon troops; then the hundreds of miles of field and forest, with friendly shelter uncertain, very rare, and come upon only by chance, like a lone piece of driftwood—blind fortune's gift—in a hostile sea; and only then, after all this, the next ghetto and the Jews therein.

Each ghetto was a world to itself, and what was happening in the next ghetto was happening in another, unknown world; and death lay between them. It took a long time, and many dead, before the Jews organized a precarious system of messengers, with forged papers, traveling—for the most part—on foot, at night, and in dreadful danger, to bring information from one ghetto to another. There were no secret radio senders and receivers to bridge the terrible gap; no informative and encouraging messages beamed from the BBC in London or from Radio Moscow to the Jews in the ghettos. Only in the midst of the Warsaw ghetto revolt did the fighters hear from the BBC how brave they were. By that time they knew how brave they were, and what they were listening for was for news of what brave attempts might be made to help them. This they didn't hear.

The Jews were alone in their ghettos.

The physical isolation of the Jews began on the 21st of September, 1939. That was three weeks after Adolf Hitler pledged to a cheering Reichstag ". . . the annihilation of Jewry";[17] it was three weeks after the Wehrmacht's invasion of Poland had opened up the eastern heartland of European Jewry and began to make the führer's promise realistically possible.

On September 21, 1939, SS General Reinhard Heydrich, chief of the Security Police and overlord of the Gestapo, sent a memorandum to the heads of the newly formed Einsatzgruppen, to all bureau heads of the Gestapo and the Security Police, and to the Army High Command. The memorandum was marked "Reich Secret" and was titled "The Jewish Question in the Occupied Territories." It said, in part:

I would like to point out once more that the total measures planned (i.e. the final aim) are to be kept strictly secret. A distinction is to be made between:

1. The final aims (which will take some time) and
2. Sections of the aim (which can be carried out within a short space of time). . . .

I. The first preliminary measure for attaining the final
goal is the concentration of the country Jews in the
big towns. This is to be carried out immediately. . . .
Care must be taken that only such towns be chosen
as concentration points as are either railroad junctions themselves or at least lie on a railway. . . .[18]

The significance of Heydrich's order that the future
ghettos should be "either railroad junctions themselves or
at least lie on a railway" was to become clear to the Jews
only years later when the trains ran from the ghettos to
the pleasant countryside stations marked Auschwitz,
Treblinka, Buchenwald.

On September 21, 1939, Reinhard Heydrich, called
"the Hangman," took over what was to become the Nazis'
"final solution of the Jewish problem." He wasted no
time. Six days later he called a conference at Gestapo
headquarters in Berlin. There were fifteen of them, all SS
officers, ranging in rank from a then obscure captain,
Adolf Eichmann, to three major generals, Best, Beutel,
and Streckenbach.

These were the top technicians of "the final solution."
It was their job to translate Heydrich's orders of the
week before into practical action, to concentrate the millions of Jews (they spoke of 11 million), to strip them
of their possessions, to transport them to locations in
which it would be convenient to guard them, starve
them, use them as slave labor, and finally—though this,
as Heydrich ordered, was for the secret future—murder
them all.

The conference's first decision was: *Juden so schnell
wie möglich in der Studte*—"Jews as quickly as possible
into the ghetto." The second decision was to establish the
ghettos primarily in Poland. The third decision was to
sweep up thirty thousand gypsies together with the Jews
and send them to ultimate death in Poland also. They
planned the expansion of the concentration camps, and
their discussion was even projected years ahead to the
problems that might arise when the Wehrmacht would be
sent smashing into the Soviet Ukraine.[19]

They did a first-class job of technical planning, these fifteen men, and for some of them the rewards were immediate. Adolf Eichmann became Heydrich's right-hand man, head of the Gestapo Bureau 4 B IV, in charge of Jewish affairs; Artur Nebe, Professor Franz Six, and Otto Ohlendorff were all made brigadier generals and respectively headed Einsatzgruppen B, C, and D. Major General Streckenbach went on to become head of the Security Police for all Poland, Dr. Konrad Meier and Oswald Schaeffer became top officials of the concentration camp administration.

But of the fifteen planners—sixteen, including Reinhard Heydrich—only some can as yet be considered to have received recognition really proportionate to their contribution to "the final solution." Two Czech resistance fighters, Jan Kublis and Josef Gabeik, tossed a bomb at Heydrich outside the Czech village of Lidice on May 29, 1942. Kublis and Gabeik were caught and killed, as were 1331 men, women, and children of Lidice; Heydrich died in slobbering agony of a shattered spine.

Otto Ohlendorff and Erich Naumann were hanged in Landsberg prison on June 8, 1951, by the judgment of the International War Crimes Tribunal, and the Polish courts had Bruno Fischer hanged. Beutel and Meier were caught by some of Malachi Wald's men in Bavaria in October 1945 and were beaten to death.

Eichmann, hiding in Argentina, was found by Wald's men, brought to Israel, tried, convicted, and hanged.

The rest of them are alive. In its book *Germans Against Hitler,* the West German government lists Nebe as having been executed for participating in the July 20, 1944, plot to assassinate Hitler, but that's not true. In September 1956, Nebe was traced to Turin, Italy, but got away and was reported to be with SS kommando leader Otto Skorzeny in Ireland in the winter of 1960. He was gone again when the men arrived to take him. Bruno Streckenbach was caught by the Russians and sentenced to death, but the sentence was never carried out; between 1956 and 1958 he was loose in East Berlin; and by the end of 1958 he was free again in West Germany.

Best was sentenced to death by Denmark in 1946, the sentence was commuted to life imprisonment in 1948, and he was released from the Copenhagen prison on August 29, 1951, and disappeared. Georg Filbert was taken into "protective custody" by the West Germans in 1949, and the custody must have been very protective indeed, because he has never been brought to trial and his present whereabouts are unknown. Mueller has never been traced.

The resourceful Major General Professor Franz Alfred Six was sentenced in April 1948 by the International War Crimes Tribunal to life imprisonment. Life imprisonment in this case turned out to be a little less than four years. Professor Six and eight hundred other major war criminals benefited from the amnesty decreed in 1951 by John J. McCloy, who was then American High Commissioner for Germany and subsequently became President John Kennedy's advisor for disarmament problems. All things considered, Six did pretty well for himself in postwar West Germany. He became a member of the top management of the billion-dollar Mannesmanne Werke.

The rest of them—Gustav Rauff, Oswald Schaeffer, and Ludwig Damzag—are also in West Germany, though they have come down in the world since the good old days. Still none of them have any cause for complaint. They are free and they have lived many more years than most of the people who were set in motion toward the ghettos and the firing squads and the gas chambers by the decisions these men and their colleagues took in the Berlin Gestapo headquarters on the twenty-seventh of September, 1939.

Juden so schnell wie möglich in der Studte, the SS planners decided, "Jews as quickly as possible into the ghettos," and within two weeks the decision was beginning to be implemented all over the central and east European areas then controlled by the Third Reich. By October 5, eighty thousand Jews from Bohemia and Austria were shoved into Adolf Eichmann's freight cars and hauled off to Nisko, the first of the new ghettos to be established in the half of Poland the Germans then occupied. Hundreds of thousands were being crammed into the ghettos in cities like Warsaw, Krakow, Kielce, Radom, where Jews had lived for centuries.

Further east, in the areas the Germans were not to reach until they struck into the Soviet Union two years later, the Jews—sensing disaster—were also on the move. Out of the towns and villages they came, seeking the safety of numbers in the crowded Jewish neighborhoods in Minsk, Vilna, Riga, Kiev, Odessa. So that when the SS troops and their auxiliaries arrived in the wake of the triumphant Wehrmacht, there were the Jews already—in effect—ghettoized.

Whether shoved by the Germans or impelled by fear, the Jews in those early months of the war went into the ghettos pursuing the same wraith of safety. All during 1940, "the final solution of the Jewish problem" roiled in the minds of the SS leadership and the Oberkommand Wehrmacht. It was—as it were—ready in the wings, but the tragic drama was not yet onstage; the players were being gathered, bludgeoned into the theater of operations, tricked into it by deception and illusion.

Thousands of Jews were already dying of brutality, disease, and starvation in the concentration camps at Dachau, Auschwitz, Bergen-Belsen. But this was casual butchery, not yet extermination. The gas chambers were not yet invented; that was to come with the first experimental gassing of two hundred Jews in Auschwitz on September 23, 1941. Treblinka, Mauthausen, Sobibor, Birkenwald—all the camps designed solely for extermination were not yet built and the Jews could not know that they were planned.

This is the key. The Jews did not know what was planned for them. With this comprehended and added to what has gone before, we can enter the terrible reality of the eastern ghettos. Without it, we stand outside the walls and are blind. Without it, we are deaf to understanding and the voices of the dead are mute.

The Jews did not know what was planned for them!

They went into the ghettos believing there was safety to
be found. Not "safety" as we understand it—security,
peace; but safety in its most basic, pitiful, primitive meaning—the absence of violent death. Not for all of them,
there was too much killing all around for them to hope
so greatly; but for most of them, anyway, for many of
them. And if there is even that much hope, if some may
live, each man may think—*must* think—that he may
live; and if not he, then his!

The Germans wrapped them in illusion and moved
them by the millions; even the brutality with which it
was done made the deception easier: "Where are you
taking us?"—"To join all the other *dreckischer Juden*
in Warsaw, or Radom, or—later—in Vilna or Kiev. . . ."
(So? It can be believed. Didn't they always say they
wanted us out of *their* Europe. . . .) "How will we live?"
—"For once you'll have to work! All of you, you'll sweat
blood, believe me! You'll be working for the Third Reich!"
. . . (Nu, it makes sense. With all of them in the army,
they need workers. . . .) "Move along, pig! You fall
behind, you're dead! . . ." (So, think! It stands to reason,
if you can keep up, if you can move along, if you can
work—you'll keep alive, they'll let you live. Would they
take us all the way to Warsaw to kill us? Foolishness!
They could kill us here, no?) . . .

Out of such sane logic is illusion crafted—when the
world is mad.

It did make sense; surely it made sense in the beginning.
The Germans shoved them into the ghettos, and murdered those who fell behind on the way or got sick on
the way, but the others lived. They starved them in the
ghettos, but not quite to death, some food the Germans
did supply; and those who could survive on it were allowed to live. The Germans killed them if they bumped into them on the sidewalks, but if they stepped down into
the gutter and took off their hats . . . The Germans killed
them in casual fits of bad temper, but if one kept out
of their way . . . if one worked in the German factories
outside the ghetto . . . if one was skilled in something
they needed . . . could make uniforms, turn a lathe for

the manufacture of shells . . . had a trade . . . if one was tough, and lucky . . . if only one was lucky . . .

It was the most evil deception ever created and the Germans molded it with loving care.

They set up the Judenrats—the Jewish Councils to "govern" the ghettos—and the Jewish leaders joined them. Some joined to stand between their people and the terror; some to save their own lives; and both concepts were illusion, availing nothing, though this they learned later. In the beginning, the mere existence of the Judenrat deceived the Jews into thinking they had some control over their destinies. They had none. Sooner or later, in every ghetto, the Judenrat became a conveyor belt to the pits and the gas chambers. When the Germans demanded a thousand Jews, or five thousand, or ten, it was the Judenrat who made up the lists. They drew up the lists, thinking—if these thousands die, others will live. Or they drew up the lists, thinking—if we do not, we will die and others will come and the lists will be made anyway; so to what end do we refuse? Or they refused, and they died, and others did draw up the lists. So it went, and in the end, all the members of the Judenrat—good or bad and however motivated—died, too. They all died. But that was later. . . .

The Germans passed out work cards and sent the word throughout the ghetto that the man who worked would live, and his family would live. So the Jews fought to get those cards, begged for them, bribed for them, stole them, forged them. And in the end, they all died. But that was later. . . .

Doctors, nurses, sanitationists—those who slaved to keep down the ravaging plagues in the ghettos—got special gray cards with their photographs on them, called the *Lebenscheine,* the "life cards." Surely they would live, for a plague could also ooze out of the ghetto and knew no difference between Jew and German. Surely *they* would live! In the time to come, they died; but that was later. . . .

Even in the beginning, of course, the Germans were murdering the Jews. But it was not by the hundreds of thousands; and it was camouflaged, often by devices won-drously inventive.

In Krakow, for example, SS Major Fritz Kutschera enlivened a dull week by asking the Judenrat for three hundred Jews, "female, intelligent, unmarried, possessing at least three languages including German." They were to be put to work indexing and preparing for shipment to Germany some thousands of books in the Krakow library. Nearly a thousand women showed up and Major Kutschera and his men selected carefully; sometimes angrily reject-ing those who tried to pretend linguistic ability in order to get the precious work cards. About five hundred were approved, and told to report to the library the next day prepared to sleep in until the job was done.

The Jews worked hard for a week and ate and slept in the library. Major Kutschera provided extra rations and he would wander among them at night asking amiably if all was well. Then the job was done, the books on the trucks, and Kutschera asked for volunteers to accompany the trucks and to drop off in Warsaw for a similar job at the library there. They would be back in a week or ten days, he said, with extra food rations for their families. Three hundred went. A week later the Judenrat in Krakow was informed that the women had decided to remain in Warsaw and had been given more work.

Four years later, on January 23, 1944, Polish partisans caught Kutschera masquerading as an SS sergeant, and hanged him. Three years after that, the Krakow books and three hundred female corpses were found in the woods forty miles from Krakow by the Polish War Crimes Commission.

There were other incidents, similarly ingenious, aimed also at accomplishing the death of a number of Jews without revealing any program of general mass murder. There was, for instance, the unknown SS humorist in Lodz—a lieutenant, apparently—who on May 24, 1940, had his men stop the passersby in front of the Women's Hospital. The SS men looked them over, and those who seemed particularly feeble were sent into the hospital "for treatment." When a thousand such were in the hospital, together with the regular patients, the doors were locked, and the hospital was burned down with the SS guards outside to shoot anyone who tried to escape. The Germans then posted signs in the area to say there had been typhus in the hospital and the action, draconian and regrettable but necessary, had been taken to spare the ghetto a deadly epidemic. . . . This device proved such a happy success that it was repeated in Zhitomir and half a dozen other ghettos. In Czestochowa it was the Austrian *Ordnungpolizei* who demonstrated their own brand of gemütlichkeit. Late in May 1940, according to a report by Gauleiter Artur Greiser, an Austrian unit took two thousand Jews out of town to dig antitank ditches, shot them there, and buried them in the ditches they had dug. Then the Austrians told the Judenrat that the men had rioted; and so they took another thousand out and killed *them,* as a lesson to the Jews of Czestochowa not to riot. . . .

It went on like that in all the ghettos—a few hundred here, a thousand there. The Jews were killed, but it was apparently patternless, and it was not—annihilation.

So, at the beginning, locked in the separate walled world of each ghetto, the Jews saw their lives as dangerous, filled with hardship and endless labor; but they saw no further than that. They knew they were being brutalized, enslaved to the German Reich, to the German army, to the profit of I. G. Farben and Krupp and Volkswagen. The Jews knew disease, hunger, fear, and death. But in those days, death was still individual—however many the individual dead. They could not foresee the days that would come when violent death would be their collective fate. They could not think the Germans planned to murder them all.

There is a woman named Zivia Lubetkin, who lives today in an Israeli kibbutz called Lochemei HaGetaoht, the Ghetto Fighters. She fought in the Warsaw ghetto revolt and came out afterward through the sewers through the forests through the DP camps through the British blockade to Palestine. She remembers it this way: "During the first few years we could not believe that a nation in the twentieth century could pronounce a death sentence upon a whole people. We knew that they meant to degrade us, to make us lose the face of God, to turn us into a nation of slaves, ignorant. This we knew, but this was not total extermination."[20]

This was the German masterpiece, the weaving of such a veil of illusion that the Jews—isolated, confused, their sight obscured, lost in the long night of terror—could not perceive that in the heart of the darkness was the ultimate, limitless, inconceivable horror. It is true that the Germans found an ally in the eternal tenacity of man's capacity for hope and in the human refusal to believe—until the Germans taught us how—that an entire nation can be capable of absolute evil. Nonetheless, the German plan was brilliantly conceived and wonderfully successful. It accomplished the murder of millions of people and deprived them of the dignity of choosing the manner of their dying. It choked the wellsprings of heroism, and when the flood could be contained no longer, illusion and hope were still combined to divide the Jewish people.

So the wonder that emerges is this: not that the majority of the Jewish millions went unresistant to their death, but that—despite the isolation and the terror of their reality, despite the paralyzing seductiveness of their illusion and hope and their belief in God and man—the time of the heroes did come, and the Jews in their hundreds of thousands in the eastern ghettos did resist. . . .

Three

The Jewish Resistance

In 1939 and '40 and '41, the Prophets of Israel were long ages dead and the Jews in the ghettos, though sprung from their loins, had not their gift. The future was unknowable, but the known present was desperate enough to demand total concentration on the immediate problems of survival. So when the Jewish resistance arose at last in each of the isolated ghettos, its purpose was to resist the dangers that they then knew and against which some measures of partial defense might de devised. It was not a fighting resistance. This was beyond their powers, it could not have answered their needs *as they then understood their needs,* and it would have been crushed by mass reprisals against the entire ghetto.

The resistance movements that rose in the early years risked only the lives of those who participated in them, and this they were prepared to risk. This underground was not intended to take German lives, but to save Jewish lives; to frustrate the German intention as the Jews then understood that intention: "to degrade us, to make us lose the face of God, to turn us into a nation of slaves, ignorant." It was an unarmed underground movement and it came to be called "the white resistance."

The white resistance called upon every element in the ghetto: the community leaders, the Zionists, the anti-Zionists, rabbis, doctors, teachers, and the youth, especially the youth—most especially the halutzim, the Zionist "pioneer" youth movements. This significant role of the halutzim was partly an accident of organization. The leadership of an underground movement must be tightly knit, each member knowing and trusting the capabilities of the others, receptive to a voluntary group discipline. Discipline is the key to survival, a breach in the wall may let in death; so discipline must be not only rigorous but habitual, automatic. The halutzim had this habit. In training as they were for life on the collective farm settlements of Palestine, they were close groups, accustomed—even before the war—to living together, working together, sharing everything. For them, more easily than for any other Jewish groups, the practice of sharing could be extended to the sharing of terrible danger. And they were young, most of them not yet twenty, with the resilience of youth.

Youth or adult, politically left or politically right, the organizations of the Zionist movement held in common the mystique of Jewish nationalism, the immutable faith that the Jewish people were a nation and would survive to be recognized as such among the nations of the world. In this sense, the Zionists, however irreligious, were spiritual brothers of the religious Jews. Having come on different paths to similar shrines, each of these groupings —as we shall see—made its special, central contributions to the white resistance.

There was another group that held neither the mystique of the Jewish nation nor of the Jewish faith, whose shrine lay neither in the synagogue nor in Palestine, but within the high minarets of the Kremlin. The Jewish Communists had been a group apart, but when the ultimate night descended upon the Jewish people in the eastern ghettos, they—too—stretched out their hands to their brothers in the dark.

And, finally, there were the worldly men and women who warmed at no shrine whatever, who belonged to nothing except the Jewish birth and thus—bound, as it were, by the rites of circumcision—found their own individual ways to the common risk and the common sacrifice embraced by all who joined the movement.

The white resistance was a *reactive* movement, reacting to the German persecutions and to the German aims as the Jews then knew them. It was intended, first of all, to ensure the physical survival of the Jews and to safeguard that absolute minimum of human dignity without which man becomes animal.

The first fight was against starvation. An adult who does no work needs a minimum of 2100 calories a day; a working adult male needs from 2800 to 6000, depending on the kind of work. A baby needs 1200 calories daily; a thirteen-year-old boy needs 3200. Failing this, the penalties are malnutrition, tuberculosis, rickets, pellagra, scurvy, anemia, death. And all this presupposes the other necessities—adequate shelter, clothing, heat, sanitation. The Jews in the ghettos had none of these. They were clothed in rags, they had no heat, they defecated in holes dug in the courtyards of houses in which they were crammed ten and twenty to a room. And the nutritive values of the food the Germans supplied to the ghettos—for which the Jewish Councils had to pay by taxing the Jews themselves—approximated 200 calories a day. On this ration, the Jews in the ghettos would have been exterminated within six months had the Germans never even laid a hand on them! The difference between that and the survival of the Jewish people until the Germans were themselves compelled to murder them was the measure of the white resistance.

It was death to be caught smuggling food into the ghetto. The people of the undergrond smuggled it in. Before the walls went up, children scavenged in the garbage pails of the Aryan quarters in every city in which the Jews were concentrated. When the ghettos were walled in, men and women and youths broke out to steal food and carry it back, sneaking into the lines of returning workers with the scraps of food tied between their legs; and they died for it.

The Jews who died in the ghettos were brought in crude coffins to the cemeteries outside. By orthodox religious law, a Jew is buried in a winding sheet, without a coffin, so the coffins were brought back. The white resis-

tance decreed that every Jew—religious or not—would be
buried so, and they smuggled back food in false bottoms
of the coffins. As time went on and the coffins fell apart
and the winding sheets could not be spared, the sheets
alone were used over and over for the dead. And when
the bodies were laid naked in their graves, the bundled
sheets carried food back to the ghetto. Even the sheets
that had covered those dead of contagion were used;
they were preferred, the Germans would not risk the
plague to search them.

The food came in a hundred secret ways, until in most
ghettos enough was brought in to supply nearly a thousand calories per person, to be distributed evenly by the
Judenrat. A thousand calories a day, month in and
month out; not enough to grow on, not enough to keep
disease away; not enough even for all to survive. But
enough so that—despite the highest death rate the world
has ever known—enough of the Jewish people survived
so that when the Germans wanted them dead, *they* had to
kill them.

Under German law anyone in the ghetto who was sick
with a contagious disease had to be reported to the Judenrat, and the Judenrat had to report him to the German
ghetto administration. A health measure, to prevent epidemic. Only it went a little bit further; the patient so reported was taken to the registered hospitals and there
the Germans watched him killed by injection. So the sick
were not reported. The white resistance built hospitals underground—quite literally, under ground; the doctors and
nurses came there and the people of the resistance stole
and smuggled in medicines. They did it all at the risk
of their lives.

A people dies and disappears if no one is born to it.
The Germans decreed death to the mother of an unre-
ported newborn baby. If the birth was reported, why,
only the baby died—the mother was allowed to live,
if she could then live. So the women concealed their
pregnancies and went down into the underground hospitals, to a kind of "natural childbirth" undreamed of anywhere, where the mother may not scream and the first

cry of the baby is smothered in a cloth, lest that first sound of its entrance into life should usher it also into death.

It was death to perform or participate in a Jewish wedding ceremony. The rabbis and the lovers went underground and the weddings went on. . . . It was death to teach Yiddish or Hebrew or what it is to be a Jew. The teachers and the pupils went underground and the teaching continued. . . .

Every act—however small or ordinary—that ensured survival, or helped it, physical, spiritual, ethical, was an act of resistance. The Germans decreed death, and the Jews struggled to live. This was resistance.

The hundreds of thousands who risked their lives through the months and the years in every ghetto of eastern Europe were heroes. This was resistance, brave and dangerous, or the words have no meaning at all.

Until the time when the ultimate German aim began to come clear; when it was no longer a matter of casual sporadic butchery; when the stink of total death was carried on the long winds; and the definition of "resistance" began to change. . . .

On June 22, 1941, the Wehrmacht crashed eastward into Russia with 185 divisions and within three months the Germans held a belt of Russian territory five hundred miles deep and stretching more than a thousand miles from the Baltic to the Black Sea. Behind this belt lay all of Poland, Estonia, Latvia, Lithuania, Byelorussia, much of the Ukraine. And in this area nearly six million Jews were caught, netted by the rear-echelon troops of the German armies and held by them for the SS whose task was, as the Wehrmacht's Field Marshal Walther von Reichenau plainly informed his staff officers, "to exterminate the Jewish enemy. . . ."[21]

The SS had had nearly two years to prepare for the job since they were first entrusted with it in September 1939. In that time, the Death's Head divisions had grown from 26,000 to 348,000 men. Working with the SS on the eastern front were 15,000 Ukrainian fascists and perhaps another 50,000 anti-Semitic auxiliaries recruited from every country along the Russian border. And one ought, in accuracy, to add to the list the 35,000 *Helferinnen,* the German women who served in the SS field auxiliaries, the members of the gentler sex who carried the little whips of leather plaited over flexible steel —so that even a woman could flick a man's eyes from his head, or open the flesh to lay the bone white and bare in the welter of blood.

From the first day of the invasion, the SS killing formations—the Einsatzgruppen—moved in behind the advancing German armies, protected by them, supplied and given transport by them; and within a month the hard-working men in the black uniforms had shoved a hundred thousand Jews into the mass graves. The curtain had risen on Germany's long-planned "final solution of the Jewish problem"—but the Jews didn't know it.

The German camouflage was fine and illusion died hard in the walled and isolated ghettos. It was only in the winter of 1941 that here and there, by accident and happenstance, some few of the Jews began to see the dim and distant outline of what was to come upon them, had indeed already come. Even then they saw it imperfectly, partially, uncertainly, like bits of a landscape bewilderingly revealed by the fitful flashes of lightning that slash the night open and the blackness closes down again before the mind can register what the eye, perhaps, has seen. So it was that even for these few who saw it, the questioning understanding of what was happening even within the areas of the ghetto in which they lived was a blind leap into the incredible. Most of the Jews could never make this leap, and none of them knew the full pattern of the holocaust until it was far too late.

At Vilna, for example, the partial understanding came to a handful of young men in the white resistance in November 1941. From June to November, the Germans had taken 47,000 Jews out of the Vilna ghetto. Those remaining were told that the others had been taken to a labor camp at Ponar, and that they too would go when the camp and the factories were able to absorb them.

It was all, the Germans told them, part of the plan to transfer the Jews out of the cities and get them into isolated centers where their labor could be exploited for the Third Reich, and where they wouldn't contaminate the Christians. This seemed harsh enough to be the truth, so the Jews gave it credence. But in November a woman named Sara Menkes—a girl, really, nineteen years old—shoved away the dead bodies that lay upon her and came crawling up out of the pits of Ponar to go twenty miles in a single night through the frozen forest back to Vilna where she staggered into a band of food smugglers come from the ghetto to raid the farms at the edge of the "Aryan sector." They didn't believe what she said had happened at Ponar. Who could believe a raving lunatic babbling of forty thousand people dead in a ditch? But anyway they took her to Abba Kovner, the young poet who had organized the food smuggling for the white resistance, and *he* believed her, he and Itzik Wittenberg and Abram Hornick and a few of the other members of the Zionist youth who were called Hashomer Hatzair—the Young Guards—in Vilna.

They believed her and they took her story to the older leaders of the resistance and to the heads of the Judenrat—the Jewish Council—and there the believing ended. . . . What! Were they crazy! The girl was crazy—poor girl!—was the madness catching? Who could do such things, and why would the Germans do it, didn't they need the Jewish workers? Weren't they even, right there in the ghetto, being forced to work like dogs sewing winter uniforms for the German pigs? Would the Germans be working them in Vilna and killing them in Ponar?

And so it went for a month. Kovner and Wittenberg and Hornick argued, but what they did they have to go on really? So they sent Shmuel Glassmann out through the woods to Ponar, and six others after him when he didn't come back; and that made seven gone and nothing more than Sara Menkes's story.

The argument raged in the leadership of the white resistance; Kovner, Wittenberg, Hornick, and Yosef Glasman and Nissan Resnick—who had joined them—demanded that the people in the ghetto be told what Sara Menkes had said; the older community leaders forbade them to spread panic in the ghetto. The young men argued that the unarmed effort of the Jews to ensure their survival was nonsense in the face of a German policy of extermination; if the Jews were all marked for death, better to die fighting. And the others faced them with a wall of unanswerable questions: "You call for a fighting resistance knowing it cannot win and the reprisals will be death to the entire ghetto. You ask us to throw our lives away, and not our lives only, because you say we will all die anyway—so you *say,* but do you *know?* And if you are wrong, and we are all uselessly dead? . . . Even if those in Ponar were killed, do you *know* that they intend to kill us all? Must we all die because you think you know, and you wish to die as heroes? . . ." And finally this last from the heads of the white resistance—all of them brave enough and risking enough so they could not thus be challenged—"If you act, you yourselves, endangering us all and all our work, by what right do you do it? Who put *you* as leaders over us?"

The question held them paralyzed with indecision for a month—"Who put you as leaders over us?"—and it was not ever answered. But on December 28, the Germans took another two thousand Jews out of the Vilna ghetto to Ponar; and on January 1, 1942, this leaflet went out from Abba Kovner and Itzik Wittenberg hand-to-hand among the young men and women in the white resistance:

> Jewish youth, do not believe those who are trying to deceive you. . . . All the Gestapo's roads lead to Ponar and Ponar means death. Those who are taken out through the gates of the ghetto will never return. Ponar is not a labor camp; all of them are shot. . . . Brethren, it is better to die fighting like free men than live at the mercy of the murderers![22]

With that leaflet, they broke the discipline of the white

resistance and opened a split in the movement that was
to cost Itzik Wittenberg his life; but it was also the beginning of a fighting resistance in the Vilna ghetto. On
that New Year's Day a small group of young men and
women—not one of them older than twenty-three—set
their feet on a bitter path that was to bind them together
tighter than the love of family or the love of man and
woman and that was, in the years to come, to lead them—
some of them—to a searing and unending mission of
vengeance at the side of Malachi Wald. . . .

It happened differently elsewhere: In August 1941, a
plump little man named Viktor Brack—an ordinary mid-
dle-level civil servant in the German Chancellor's Office—
was sent from Berlin to Poland on the sort of mission
ordinary German civil servants undertook in those days.
He was to supervise the construction of the first death
camp at Chelmno, complete with gas chambers. Brack
had little stomach for the job, or so he was to argue—
albeit in a fashion somewhat peculiar—at his trial for
war crimes at Nuremberg five years later. Brack was,
according to his later testimony, against the extermination of the Jews; the thought of the gas chambers made
him ill, although, apparently not quite for the reasons
one might expect. He felt that the Jews could better
serve the Reich alive as laborers and he coupled this
concept with a plan for sterilizing three million male
Jews by exposing their genitals to a concentrated X-ray
bombardment.[23] Brack had had some experience with
this as far back as 1940 when he was administering the
German government's program of sterilizing patients in
the state insane asylums. Brack's experience showed that
most of the men so treated died within a few years;
and so, as he told the war crimes tribunal, he suggested
to Heydrich that his plan would bring the "Jewish problem" to its desired "final solution" just as surely as the
gas chambers with the added dividend that while the
Jews lived they could at least make themselves useful.
It is clear Brack's plan could not be expected to
endear him to the court, which had him hanged in 1946;

but the reasons why so efficient a system failed to appeal to Heydrich are somewhat more obscure and were, as Brack petulantly told the court, never made known to him. All he knew was that the plan was rejected and, like it or not, there was Viktor Brack building gas chambers in Chelmno in August 1941.

By December 5, the gas chambers were working and despite occasional breakdowns attendant upon a running-in process, the bodies were piling up satisfactorily—like cordwood for the burning. In those primitive days, the crematoria had not yet been designed and they simply burned the bodies in the open fields just beyond the inner barbed-wire fences. On windy days, the smoke of the burnings blew into the eyes of the SS guards and what with this and the stench it sometimes happened that the guards grew a bit careless and didn't always see what was going on. So it was that, on the eighteenth of December, they didn't see a man named Moshe Podhlebnik when he crawled out of the fire. Podhlebnik had not been gassed, he'd been shot in the head for a minor infraction of the rules, and though he was nearly dead from his wound and a good part of him had been burned black in the flames, he managed to crawl a hundred yards or so through the charred and stubbled field until he fell into the open culvert that carried the sewage from the camp. There he lay, smothering his keening pain in the filth and garbage of the culvert until night came.

No one at all knows now how Podhlebnik dragged himself for a mile and a half that night and through the outside perimeter fence and past the SS patrols that kept the curious far away from the surroundings of the Chelmno camp. But he did it, and a Jew delivering slaughtered cattle to a German army unit bivouacked nearby found him and piled the tortured dying thing into his cart and took him to Rabbi Yehoshua Aaronsohn in the village of Sanik. Podhlebnik told what he knew, through blood and pain, and the news was out about the Chelmno gas chambers. Podhlebnik somehow survived, and—because of what he told—so did others.

Rabbi Aaronsohn sent the word to Mordechai Anielewicz in the Warsaw ghetto and it went from there to Mordechai Tennenbaum-Tamaroff in Bialystok and to Abba Diskont in Kovno, and these people spread it further. It took a time to get around, through the winter snows and traveling for the most part at night; and by then news of the massacres in Lithuania and Latvia and in Kiev were also filtering into the ghettos. In those days the news was too fantastic for most people to believe—especially for those leaders of the Judenrats and of the white resistance organizations who had to believe that their life-preserving work had meaning. But in every ghetto there was someone to believe the unbelievable truth; and in every ghetto that someone began to look for a gun. . . .

The first thing was the gun. How would a Jew in a ghetto find a gun? One way, clearly, would have been to slip a knife into some German soldier strolling down a ghetto street and take it from him; and the killing of the German was a good thing, too. But a German gun and a German death so gotten could cost a thousand Jewish lives in the reprisal that would follow and the price was too great, and the time was wrong. It wasn't at the beginning that they were going to kill Germans, not one at a time and a thousand for one. It wasn't to kill one German at a time that they were organizing a fighting resistance, and to do more than that, they needed time and training and guns. . . .

There were two ways left, then, to get the guns—buy them, or steal them. They did both.

They stole the gold and the jewels their parents had hoarded hoping to buy their lives with it, or their children's lives. But the "children" knew what the parents refused to know—that the hope was illusion; and they had a need for the gold. So they stole it from their parents, or from their friends' parents, or from any Jew who had anything that could be used to buy a gun. They stole. They had all stolen before for the needs of the white resistance; but this was the first time they stole from Jews.

This was the first of many hard lessons in the teaching that an underground fighting resistance is born ruthless, or it is born dead.

They gave the gold and the jewels and the items for barter to the most Aryan-looking youths among them and smuggled them outside the ghettos to the areas that mushroom in every city in wartime, where you can buy anything for the kind of money that doesn't lose its value no matter who wins the war. They bought guns from the thieves who had them as part of their trade, and from the volunteer Jew-killers among the native Christian population who had them as part of their hobby. They went into the saloons and the whorehouses to buy guns from any German soldier whose ears could hear the clink of coin above the call of duty. The gun buyers were the lads with the blond hair and the blue eyes and the straight noses, un-Jewish-looking, so that nothing should lead the Gestapo back to the ghettos and because the story they had to tell was always the same plausible story and it went with the Aryan look: they said they wanted the guns to do a little pogrom-making of their own.

For such purposes—and for gold, of course—there were always guns to be had. When the gold and the jewels in the ghettos ran out, or couldn't be found, they stole from the German factories in which they labored as slaves—running the greater dangers of exposing the resistance. They stole army shoes, leather, cloth, tools, anything they could somehow get out of the factories and into the black markets to sell for guns.

Then the guns gotten outside the ghettos had to be brought in, to the secret bunkers being prepared by the organizations. There were German guards at the ghetto gates to search the people going in and out, Germans at the machine guns in the watchtowers that lined the walls, the German patrols and the killing dogs who paced the floodlit walls at night. Getting the guns in was the most difficult and dangerous task, not only for the death the gunrunners faced, but because discovery could expose the fighting resistance and the organizations were too young, too small, too new to withstand exposure.

At first they brought in the guns as they had earlier learned in the white resistance to bring in food and medicine—in false bottoms of the coffins in which the dead were carried out to the cemeteries and which were brought back into the ghettos to be used again. But in many places the leaders of the unarmed white resistance refused to allow it. The coffins were needed for smuggling food and medicine. A German guard might be bribed to close again the coffin lid he had opened, if what he saw was only food, but not if it was ammunition or guns. A man smuggling food might die for it, but a man caught smuggling guns killed thereby his entire family—at least. And besides, the white resistance was opposed to the black and often looked upon the fighting groups as suicidal, and worse than that, as endangering the entire ghetto.

So the incipient fighting organizations were thrown back on their own resources. Then, for a time, girls brought in guns, slung between their legs as they returned from the factories outside. They went in groups, the pretty girls carrying nothing and the leering guards searching them diligently; the homely ones pushed aside and into the ghetto with the guns under their skirts. This worked well enough, but it was slow and it was risky. They looked around for another way.

The way was found. Not in every ghetto; but in Vilna and Warsaw and Bialystok, in many other ghettos. They used the sewers.

They sent people down to explore the sewers; slim youths, girls, the smallest among them. Gradually they mapped the sewer systems, finding the ones which led to the rivers, to the larger conduits, which led out to secluded streets in the Aryan quarters and which came up in the midst of German installations. The sewers were to become the most important single route whereby arms came into the ghetto and people got out. But before this, there were those who died in the preliminary explorations —lost and gone mad in the noxious dark, or caught and smothered and drowned in filth where a pipe narrowed in a turning and one could go neither forward nor back. And when this happened, the others had to go down to pull out the dead, lest the blocked sewage back up into the streets of the ghetto and some sharp-eyed Gestapo man should see it and be curious. It took a special kind of courage to slither through the reeking horror of the sewers on such a mission, and to come back hauling the body of a loved comrade—often little more than a child —with his face eaten away by the ravening rats. . . .

But they went down into the sewers, and charted them; and then the gunrunners used them, holding the guns and the munitions up above the running stinking filth. . . . In time to come, the Germans would block the exits of the larger conduits, and occasionally they tossed gas grenades into the sewers; but this was mostly thoroughgoing precaution. Not until the last days of the Warsaw ghetto revolt did the Germans realize that the sewers were the ghetto fighters' highways. . . .

Sometimes the guns came in easier ways. For the most part the Polish partisans and the Russian guerrillas gave nothing to the Jews, neither weapons, nor food, nor shelter, nor help. In the cases where the partisan bands were willing to accept Jewish fighters within their formations, they demanded that the Jews come to them already armed. But there were exceptions, and there were partisans in the Lublin region, near Krakow, around Kovno, who helped. This help, when it came at all, came late; in the first year when the Jewish fighting units were organizing, there were no Polish or Russian partisans on anything like an organized basis.

Even at the beginning, though, there were Christians who stood as human beings above the animal hate that engulfed the Jew. There must have been many such, but there were only a few who were able to join decency with great courage and stand forth where the Jews could see them as friends, and brave.

In Krakow, for example, a German named Oscar Shindler ran a factory making uniforms for the German army. For a year Shindler wandered in and out of the

Krakow ghetto bringing medicines under his coat. When the fighting unit was formed in the ghetto, the medicines changed to grenades and ammunition. Shindler was never caught—who searched a German official, Aryan for ten generations, with two sons dead on the western front? Who peered at such a man to see if the light of an un-Germanic humanity shone in his eyes?—and he lived to snatch a thousand Jews from the SS when the black-uniformed killers moved in on his plant in 1944. . . . No one even knows the names of the three Ukrainians who came on May 23, 1942, to the black resistance in the Dnepropetrovsk ghetto with 150 kilos of industrial dynamite hidden in the pestilential carcass of a rotting horse they told the guards they were selling to the Judenrat. . . . In Vilna, after the massacres in December 1941, the mother superior of the Bendictine Convent of St. Catherine came into the ghetto on what she described as "an errand of mercy"—and so it was, the mercy armed. She found her way to Abba Kovner, and asked the slight young poet of the resistance to turn his back. When the cloth of her nun's habit ceased its rustling and he turned around again, she was holding two hand grenades out to him as though they were—as indeed they were!—a votive offering. For nearly a year thereafter, until the Gestapo caught them sheltering Jewish fugitives and hanged them for it in the Lukishki prison, the Sisters of St. Catherine brought grenades and guns into the ghetto and hid the gunrunners in the convent on St. Ignatius Street. . . .

There were other such cases—in Minsk and Riga and Kovno, in Tulczin, Warsaw, Kiev—but there were not many. For most of the Christians in eastern Europe, the brotherhood of man—when they felt it at all—was only a pious hope for a shining future, too dangerous a concept to be given practical expression in the bloody-needful present. . . .

The months went by and one way or another the ghetto fighters got some weapons; not enough, surely, never enough and never the right kind; no heavy machine guns, no mortars, no mines, no antitank weapons, no gelignite pencils or plastic explosives; nothing that an army gets to fight an army with. But every unit had some weapons of some kind. Statistics are hard to establish, but the evidence of those still alive among the fighters themselves indicates that it averaged out at one or two light machine guns in each ghetto, something around fifty hand grenades, one pistol and a couple of handfuls of cartridges to every three men, one rifle to every five or six men in the fighting resistance movement.

They had some weapons, now, but they knew nothing of how to use them: The bullets in the clip and the clip goes here and the bolt works this way, and then what? . . . what's this on top marked a hundred meters, two hundred, three hundred? . . . how long do you cut a fuse if you want it to burn for five seconds? . . . how do you "lead" a running man so you won't keep shooting just behind him? . . . what do you do if the gun jams? . . . how do you throw a hand grenade from behind a barricade without exposing yourself? . . . how do you cover an advance? a retreat? establish enfilading fire? . . . how do you do anything?

It was hilarious, they knew nothing, it was very funny. You could die laughing. Only with great rare luck was there ever an experienced soldier in a fighting unit; most of the men and women were much too young ever to have had such experience. They had to learn from the beginning, from before the beginning. Alexander Guttman remembers how he sneaked into the libraries of Sosnowiec and Bedzin and tore out of the encyclopedias the pages that carried descriptions of a revolver and a rifle. They made copies of these and distributed them to the fighting units.

It's clear, now, that they did learn; some of them learned very well—Guttman, for example, learned well enough to command a brigade later in the 1948 Israeli-Arab War and then to become staff officer in the Israeli army. They sat in cellars and learned to take their guns apart blindfolded. They looked in their chemistry books and read up on explosives and began to build homemade bombs in the workshops they installed in their secret bunkers.

Some were blinded and some were maimed and some were killed in workshop explosions or when they tested their handcrafted bombs in the sewers. But in time, in each ghetto, the most common weapons were those they had learned to make themselves. The "Molotov cocktail" was the simplest of these—a bottle of kerosene with a rag tied around it. Set the rag on fire and throw the bottle; when it smashed, the target was enveloped in liquid flame. . . . They made a crude kind of mine—two metal plates hinged together at one end, filled with dynamite, with a percussion cap at the unhinged end between the plates. The "mine" was covered with loose rubble in the road and when a car or a man went over it, the two plates banged together on the percussion cap and the dynamite blew up—if it hadn't blown up before and taken the hands off the man who was setting it. . . . There was the "ghetto grenade"—a tin can filled with nuts and bolts packed tightly around a paper twist of explosive with a sputter fuse to set it off; or a length of pipe, like a bangalore torpedo, stuffed with explosive.

It was with this sort of junk that the ghetto Jews proposed to fight—and, indeed, did fight—the German army. . . .

Everywhere, in that bitter winter of 1941–42, the newly formed Jewish fighting groups tried to break the isolation of the ghettos, to make contact one with the other. And after a time, at the cost of many lives, the emissaries made their hazardous ways from ghetto to ghetto, bringing news and encouragement. The news was bleak and the encouragement harsh, but at least then each group knew that it was not entirely alone. And out of these contacts they formed the loose confederation that came to be called the Jewish Fighters' Organization. It was never to become an underground army in any full meaning of the term; the isolation of the ghettos, the difficulties of communication, the distances between the groups prevented this. It was only in the last weeks of the war that Jewish partisan units were to come together for larger operations. But from the beginning, by its very name, the Jewish Fighters' Organization affirmed the belief of the fighting Jews in a Jewish national existence.

The Jews could give each other love and pride, but guns and help had to be sought elsewhere. So the emissaries went out again, into the forests, seeking the partisan bands they thought must surely be forming behind the German armies in Poland and in the western border areas of Russia. These reconnaisance missions were terribly dangerous. The SS and their uniformed auxiliaries, the Wehrmacht patrols, the regular police, these could be recognized and, seen in time, could be avoided. But the agents of the Gestapo could not be identified; and one never could know whether a band in the woods were the partisans one sought or the informers one feared. No one knows any longer how many hundreds went out on this dangerous fruitless quest, but few came back—and none came back in those days with help.

Seven times, Israel Lapidus—the leader of the ghetto fighters in Minsk—sent units out to filter through the German lines, seeking the partisans. None got through, save only a fifteen-year-old boy named Fimka Pressman who went 180 miles toward Smolensk, only to learn from a group of escaped Russian soldiers—starving in the woods—that the city had fallen and the Red Army had been rolled back to the gates of Moscow. Back came Pressman, all the way back, sending the hard word by runners before him, until the exhausted boy himself reached Minsk—to hang, after all this time, on the barbed wire of the ghetto fence, chopped into a bloody rag by machine-gun fire from one of the guard towers encircling the ghetto.[24]

Soon after the boy—Pressman—died, the messengers went out again; eleven times more, and only Fedia Shedletki lived to make contact with a small band of partisans, led by a Russian army captain named Vyacheslav Bystrov, who had escaped from a German prison train. Captain Bystrov sent the messenger back to the ghetto with greetings and advice; and the advice was—wait;

train, and wait.[25] When Chaim Yellin, from the Kovno ghetto, found the "Albina" partisans in the Rudniki forest, he came back with the gift of one pistol and the same advice—wait, the time for action has not yet come. . . .

We know, now, that it wasn't until after the Germans were beaten at Stalingrad in 1943 that the Red Army dropped its agents behind the German lines and began organizing the partisans in the forests. We know, now, that the Jews were ahead of their time; but they had no other time. They could not wait. The maquis in France could wait, the Polish underground Armia Krajowa could wait. They could wait in Greece, in Italy, in the lowlands of Holland and Belgium. They could bide their time while the arms were dropped to them and the agents to organize and teach them parachuted down and the secret radio communications were established. They could wait until the Allied landings in Sicily or Italy or Normandy, until the Russians were hammering the German armies back through Poland. They were brave men and it is no slight upon them that they waited; they were right to wait until the time was ripe to fight. But the Jews could not wait. By mid-1942, 229,052 Jews had been slaughtered by the Einsatzgruppen in the Baltic states alone, 14,000 were killed in three days in Kharkov, 27,000 were dead in Riga, 32,000 in Vilna, the ghettos were wiped out at Simferopol and Zhitomir, the Jews of Dvinsk were dead, 112,000 corpses filled the Babi Yar ravine outside Kiev; the gas chambers were operating at Auschwitz and Chelmno and Belzec.[26]

Time was running out for the Jews, borne on the tide of blood that gushed from the ghettos. Of all the fighters in the European undergrounds, only the Jews could not wait for the best time to fight; so they fought as they could, where they could, with no help, and before they were ready. . . .

Late in 1942, the flames of resistance flared for the first time and flicked at the Germans along a thousand miles north and south from the Baltic to the Black Sea.

Chaim Yellin and twelve others went eastward out of Kovno in a stolen army truck until they stood in sight of the ruined ghetto of Dvinsk—with the smoke of its burned buildings still drifting over the rest home the Germans had established in a pleasant glade nearby for the war-worn officers of Army Group North. The Jews had come at dusk, they lay in the fringe of trees till dark and left again before the late rise of the moon. They stopped the truck with its motor idling at the bend of the road climbing up to Zolataya Gorka and waited, looking back. When the flare of the dynamite lit the sky behind them, they went on, and there were thirty dead German officers to follow the ten thousand Jews who had died in the ghetto of Dvinsk.

Malachi Wald took his group in fake German uniforms from Kovno northwest toward the German Naval Ordinance Depot at Lepaya. They were gone four days and when they were back in their bunker at 7 Mildos Street, there were fourteen dead in the explosion at the depot that deprived the German submarines in the Baltic Sea of torpedoes for nearly a week.

The Sisters at the Convent of St. Catherine in Vilna's Aryan quarter were saying good-bye to a colleague. She had been with them for just over a year and they had come to love her and the parting was hard. She was the youngest of them, and—though she wore the somber costume of the Benedictine order—she was not a nun, nor was she Catholic. Her name was Vitka Kempner, and she was a nineteen-year-old Jewess from the Vilna ghetto.

For a year the nuns had sheltered her, provided her with the "cover" of their order and the false Aryan papers under which she had functioned as a liaison between the white resistance in the ghetto and those Christians of Vilna who were Christian. But that was done. Vitka Kempner—at her own insistence—was going back to live in the ghetto and to do a different work. And now, in the hidden pockets under her dress, instead of medicines for the underground hospital in the ghetto, she carried dynamite for the fighting resistance.

She went into the ghetto that afternoon, joining a file of returning workers, showing her own *Arbeitskarte* which listed her as a seamstress in the factory making uniforms for the Wehrmacht. A week later, Vitka went out again. This time at night, through the sewers, with three other girls, carrying the dynamite again—fitted with percussion caps.

They went half a kilometer through the sewers, and then another thirty kilometers along the tracks of the railroad running east from Vilna to Moscow. For half an hour they worked, scrabbling in the darkness, setting the dynamite under the crossties. Then they waited, listening tensely for the sound of an approaching train.

After all the waiting, the train was upon them almost before they realized it and the explosion that tore the night apart came as though unexpected and held them, for a moment, motionless and shocked. Then they ran, stumbling in the loose gravel of the embankment, tossing hand grenades into the windows of the coaches, while the German soldiers cursed and died and then the submachine guns started spitting from the coaches and the girls turned and floundered and fell and stumbled on in their race for the planned shelter of the nearby swamps with the Germans afraid to follow, fearing ambush.

The next morning the train was on its way again, and the girls lay in the swamp, watching the line of soldiers combing the ground between them and the smoking twisted skeletons of five jettisoned coaches. The girls lay still, and the one who was dying died without a sound, biting back the need to give voice to pain. . . . The soldiers left after a time, the tangle of swamp and underbrush defeating them; the girls buried their comrade then in the only way they could, pushing her down into the mush of earth and swamp.

So there were three of them left, all wounded, with the holes in Vitka's legs bleeding her life into her shoes, until finally the blood clotted against the plugs of cloth they bound about their wounds. All day they lay in the swamp and when night came they started back to the ghetto, leaving behind them the wrecked coaches of the first military train to be blown up in all Lithuania; leaving behind them one girl dead, even her name lost now to history, her name lost—but not she. . . .

Raiders went out from the Vilna ghetto almost every night during the following weeks. It was training for them. They tested the ghetto escape routes—the bribed guards, the guards who drank themselves into carelessness, the weak spots in the ghetto walls, the sewers. They learned to move quickly and quietly at night, to take advantage of natural cover. They learned other things too—where to slide the knife so the dying man cannot scream, how to set an ambush, where to stand to cut down the men who pour out of the whole length of a dynamited train. They were hard lessons, learned hard, and the price they paid in learning was high—10 percent of the ghetto fighters were killed in the raids of those first few weeks.

Twenty miles from Vilna, on the railroad line to Moscow, stood the farm village of Oshmiana, with its tiny ghetto jammed up against the railroad tracks. Tiny; three hundred families, too small even to bother walling in, guarded only by the armed volunteers from the thousand or so volksdeutsche whom the Germans had brought in to take over the farms and the houses of the village when the Jews were moved into the ghetto. The whole place was only a dot on the largest of maps, hardly worth noticing, never noticed until the Engineering Corps of Army Group Central decided to requisition the area because Oshmiana was just the place for a secondary munitions dump to be held in reserve for the coming push on Moscow. So the Engineering Corps asked Einsatzgruppe B to assign a few competent machine gunners to liquidate the ghetto—ten good men could do it in a day and be back for dinner.

The orders came to Gestapo headquarters–Vilna, which served as a letterbox for the busy Einsatzgruppe, and the word came from there through one of the Jewish ghetto police to Itzik Wittenberg, the head of the Vilna ghetto fighters. Wittenberg sent Lisa Marum to warn the

Jews in Oshmiana and to guide them into the forests to wait for the help he would be sending later.

The girl got to Oshmiana and those who believed her, perhaps a hundred people, went out with her into the forest. But the rest didn't believe her, or were afraid to go, and Lisa Marum went back to them, to try again. And was caught there when the men with the Death's Head uniforms came and some poor terrified Jew betrayed her. So they hung her by her hands nailed to a cross—to watch while they butchered the Jews of Oshmiana.

It was, as they had thought, only a single day's work, especially since they hadn't the added chore of shoving the carcasses into the ground. The bulldozers of the army engineers did that, rolling over the girl on the cross and the dead and the houses of the dead; leveling them all together, blending them into the receiving earth. Four days later, the munitions trains began rolling along the Oshmiana siding and within a week there were tons of munitions and explosives tucked neatly under camouflage netting, standing on a patch of land where only Jews had stood before.

Wittenberg led them then, in the name of Lisa Marum, sixty of them out of Vilna—a fifth of all the ghetto fighters—in the largest action they had ever planned. They knifed the sentries, set off a chain of explosions in the munitions stores, machine-gunned the volksdeutsche from the two stolen trucks in which they rocketed through the village streets, and were back in the ghetto—except for the four dead—before daylight.

As in Vilna and Kovno, so it was elsewhere; not everywhere, but in more than half the eastern ghettos there were men and women banded together to fight without hope of victory or of personal salvation.

In Krakow, Shimshon Draenger and his wife, Justina, led the Jewish fighting units in ambushes so successful that the SS moved in a special battalion under Major General Oskar Dirlewanger to make the roads safe from the raids of a few score starving Jews. Dirlewanger is a thief and a murderer. And he had been convicted in the

early days of the Nazi Reich for sexual offenses against
minor children.[27] But he redeemed himself in Nazi eyes
when he fought with the other convicts in the German
Condor Legion for the cause of Generalissimo Franco in
Spain; and ever since then he had been doing particularly
dirty jobs for Himmler.

The Draengers were taken finally, both of them, and
escaped—killing their way out of Gestapo headquarters
—and were caught a second time and hanged quickly
lest they do it all again. The leadership of the resistance
fell then to Dolleck Liebskind and Judah Tennenbaum,
until the night the men they led bombed thirty German
officers to death in a café and were hunted down and
killed in a bunker, with Liebskind and Tennenbaum com-
mitting suicide at the end to avoid capture.

After that, General Dirlewanger broke the Krakow resistance, but it took him time and it wasn't easy. To help
him bear the strain of the struggle, Dirlewanger borrowed
the amusements developed by his friend and colleague,
SS Major General Fritz Katzman in East Galicia, and
brought Jewish girls captured among the fighters to his
officers' mess where they were given strychnine injections
so their death struggles could add to the general con-
viviality.[28]

Like Katzman, Dirlewanger is now in Cairo; and
though he has exchanged his SS uniform for that of a
colonel in the Egyptian army's training command, the
German Knight's Cross of Gold still gleams on his chest.
Both Dirlewanger and Katzman hold valid West German
passports and the Bonn government has never asked
Egypt for their extradition as war criminals, so they can
presumably return to Germany at any time. But whether
they remain in Egypt or not, there must be some comfort in the knowledge that their memory is kept green in
the homeland they served with such distinction: both
have their photographs and biographies prominently included among the "Heroes and Martyrs" in the perennial
best-selling book, *Die Ritterkreuzträger der Waffen SS*—
"The Bearers of the Knights' Cross of the Waffen SS."

While Dirlewanger's battalion was busy in Krakow, the

Germans were being harried by the Jewish fighters all along a thousand miles of territory. Perhaps "harried" is too big a word to describe what the Jews could do with their pitiful resources. But what they could do, they did. Even in the tiny ghettos of Lachwa and Miesweiz, where the Jews had no weapons—none at all—the raiders went out against the Germans with knives and hammers. . . . In Minsk alone there were twelve fighting units. One of these was a group of girls led by Lena Meiselis and Nadia Shuser, who blew up part of the Wehrmacht's clothing factory. There was a group led by David Lerner that sabotaged the workshop making communications equipment for the German army. Another unit went deep into the Aryan quarter of Minsk to poison the liquor stocks kept in a warehouse for shipment to the German officers needing comfort during the cold siege of Moscow. . . . From Warsaw came Mordechai Tennenbaum Tamaroff, to organize the black resistance in Bialystok, and—in time—to die there with the men he'd banded together. . . .

The whole future of the Jewish fighting resistance hung in the balance during those first few months. Everything had to be done at once. They had to organize, acquire some weapons, train the men and women who had never held a gun—the boys and girls who had never even seen one except in the hand of the Germans. They had to forge some kind of a loose chain of communications to link the widely separated ghettos; they had to build the hidden bunkers, try to persuade the uncertain and frightened Jewish masses that the fighting resistance was not merely a provocation to mass reprisals, but the only possible instrument of national dignity. There were so few people in the black resistance then that everyone had to do everything, and they all had to learn the dangerous jobs by doing them.

Under these circumstances, it was impossible to organize the movement into units with special functions and with the tight minimal contact between units which is vital to the security of any illegal organization. The leaders were everywhere, the roots of the movement were too near the surface for the safety of the organization.

So it was that a day came when from Kovno south through Vilna and Bialystok the raiding stopped, the leaders hid, the fighters went into the secret bunkers and awaited the coming of the German tanks and the flame-throwers. Anton Schmidt had been taken near Vilna, and he could betray them all.

Schmidt was a key member of the fighting resistance, though he was not Jewish, and he did not fight. He was a lieutenant in the German army, commanding a special services company assigned to rounding up German soldiers who had strayed into the rear-echelon areas and returning them to their front-line units.

Schmidt's contact with the resistance began on a day in January 1942 when he walked into the Vilna ghetto on a "sight-seeing tour." There was nothing unusual about this. German soldiers often wandered through the ghetto in their leisure moments, staring at the curious sights for all the world like so many tourists, snapping photos of the starving children—exotica for the folks back home. Schmidt had no camera; what he had instead was a note from the Mother Superior of the Convent of St. Catherine to Abba Kovner. It took some time before he found a terrified boy willing to admit that he even knew the name of the poet-leader of the black resistance and that he might try to find him. The boy took the note, and Schmidt waited in the courtyard of a building. He waited quite a while, pretending not to notice the men who filtered into the court and lounged about with their hands in their pockets, or those who were leaning casually on the parapets of the surrounding roofs. Then Kovner came, risking the trap.

They talked a long time; it takes a long time to approach a point by careful narrowing circles, until they decided to trust each other. Then Schmidt gave Kovner the results of his work during many dangerous weeks—a documented list of the names and crimes of the SS men who were executing in the field the "final solution of the Jewish problem." He also turned over the secret orders of the Einsatzgruppen. He wanted Kovner to pass the material on, he said, for some day there must come a judgment, and the guilty should not escape.

It was Anton Schmidt, in January 1942, who first stripped the anonymity from Adolf Eichmann. "There is a man," he said to Kovner and to Itzik Wittenberg, "a dog named Adolf Eichmann, and he is organizing all this." Nearly twenty years later, Schmidt's words were to help convict the "dog named Adolf Eichmann" when Abba Kovner repeated them to the Israeli judges trying the ex-Gestapo colonel for mass murder.[29]

In the months that followed that first meeting, Schmidt became an invaluable part of the resistance. His duties took him all over Lithuania and a good part of Poland. He had trucks in which to send the strayed German soldiers back to their units. He could requisition new uniforms for them, supply them with travel documents. He put all these to the service of the Jewish fighters, and became an essential link in the Jewish communications network.

No one knows how Schmidt was taken, but taken he was, and brought to Gestapo headquarters on Washaskauer Street in Bialystok where the Security Police commandant himself, SS Major Gustav Friedl, led the interrogation of the fifty-year-old "traitor." Friedl knew what he had, strapped down on the table in the basement torture chamber; he reasoned well enough that a German —a German with Schmidt's position and duties—must have been an important recruit in the Jewish resistance.

For the leaders of the fighting resistance in many of the ghettos, the capture of Anton Schmidt was infinitely threatening. He knew them all; he could betray them all. They knew him as a brave and an honorable man, bound to them by conscience and a practicing humanity. But they were new, then, in the bleak business of a fighting underground, and they did not know how strong such ties might be. Were they as strong, for example, as the mystic bond between Jew and Jew? How much will such a man endure for the Jew, to whom he is not—after all —blood brother?

The questions themselves seemed auguries. So the resistance drew inside itself, and the leaders went down into the sewers to wait. They waited three days. Then the sentries placed on the rooftops saw a dreadful procession coming out of the Gestapo headquarters in Bialystok. First came Major Gustav Friedl; then a squad of SS riflemen; and then, dragged in a cart to the gates of the ghetto, the mangled body of a man still—incredibly—alive. When the SS men hauled Schmidt from the cart, he could not stand on his burned feet, so they tied him to a post at the ghetto gates and there they shot him.

Years later, the West German government was to publish a book honoring the *Germans Against Hitler*. The name of Anton Schmidt does not appear among those who are remembered thus "reverently and gratefully." Since there were so few such Germans against Hitler, it is hard not to feel that the omission is deliberate. Perhaps Schmidt's acts of resistance against Hitler spread over too many Germans besides Hitler, perhaps they cut too close to the bone; perhaps the evidence he gave to Abba Kovner in Vilna that winter's day in 1942 has since helped to hang too many Germans for his name to be popular in his fatherland even after the passage of years. He was a man alone, who worked his way alone through the muck of mass anonymity under which the German people served the Nazis then and by which they are sheltered now. And he, among the very few, did not wait until the "thousand-year Reich" was already crumbling before putting at stake his honor and his life.

Anton Schmidt, who was not a Jew, kept faith with the Jews and kept silence for them. The Jewish fighters learned the first part of a harsh lesson then: that good men in such times are few, and those with strength to match their goodness are rarer still; but when there is such a man—blood brother or no—he will endure what he must.

That was the first part of the lesson. The bitter corollary came months after the death of Anton Schmidt, when they were to learn that a good man, in a lonely hell, may break; and that even the tie binding Jew to Jew unravels when the strength runs out of men and leaves them only terror and bursting pain. In such a time, the sin is not upon the men whose strength proves less than they have need of, but upon those who have made their need so terrible.

The Vilna resistance learned this second part of the lesson when the first commander of the Jewish Fighters' Organization was betrayed by a Jew named Saul Koslowzki.

Koslowzki was eighteen years old, a liaison man carrying messages from the headquarters of the Vilna resistance to its units throughout the ghetto. He was taken secretly and before he was missed, he had already been broken in the basement torture chambers of the Gestapo. The Germans wanted from him the identity of the man they knew only as "the Lion." The boy stood the questioning for nearly a night and when they were careless for a moment, he grabbed the knife they had "questioned" him with and killed himself. But the moment of carelessness had come too late and the boy's act was one of bitter remorse; he had already given them the name of Itzik Wittenberg—who was "the Lion."

The Gestapo went into the ghetto, to the office of Jakob Genns—the head of the Jewish ghetto police— and it was Genns's turn to measure *his* strength. The measure was short of the need and Genns gave them Wittenberg, calling him into Genns's office where the Gestapo men and the SS guards waited. It was four hundred yards from Genns's office to the ghetto gates and the Germans never got that far with their prisoner. Wittenberg hadn't gone out alone when Genns had sent for him, and the Jewish fighters who guarded him were on the Germans and they were dying in the streets and Wittenberg was away; the whole thing took seconds.

After that, the ghetto was quiet. A troop of the SS came in to remove their dead and wounded, and went out again. But the Germans were busy; and when morning came, the armored cars stood at every ghetto gate and the ultimatum was delivered to Jakob Genns: "Give us Wittenberg, or we will raze the ghetto."

By then Wittenberg, dressed in women's clothes, had been taken away by Vitka Kempner and even Abba Kovner and Abram Hornick didn't know his hiding place, so that no amount of pain could force their tongues and they could do what they had decided to do. They went themselves to Genns, each of them offering to take Wittenberg's name and go to the Gestapo in his stead. But by then it was known that Koslowzki had talked, and it wasn't known that the boy was dead; so Genns was afraid Koslowzki might talk again when faced by the bogus Wittenberg, and he wouldn't go along with the stratagem.

Genns sent his police auxiliaries into the streets to tell the Jews of the German ultimatum. He called them together in mass meetings and told them they were all to die because the fighting resistance wouldn't give up one man, one man. And Kovner and the others went into the streets to beg the Jews to stand fast; to tell them that it was not one man who stood between them and life, that the Germans had doomed them anyway, and that all that remained was the bond between Jew and Jew and the chance to die fighting.

So now it was up to the Jews of Vilna to find the strength they needed, and they failed. The Jews turned against the fighters. The leaders of the resistance ordered their men not to draw weapons as their own people—now a frightened mob—fell upon them with stones and clubs, women clawing at their eyes, screaming that they —the fighters—were the butchers of their children, and not the Germans who stood behind the machine guns with the mass graves and the gas chambers behind them! It was dreadfully clear, the Jews were ready to buy an hour of life with the body of Itzik Wittenberg; to sell him for hope, for less—for what the fighters knew was only the hopeless illusion of hope.

Abba Kovner went to Vitka Kempner and she took him to Wittenberg. Kovner tells it this way: "I said to him, 'Look, there are Jews in the streets. We shall have to fight them before we get at the enemy. Give the order and we will fight.' No, he was not prepared to give that order. He was a great man. He gave me his revolver and appointed me as commander of the organization. He went out into the street. We all stood there, we had guns in our hands, the fighters were on one side facing the masses of the Jews. And he went out to the ghetto gate and turned himself over to the Gestapo."[30]

The Jews went into their houses with their burden of shame. The Germans, who had put them to an inhuman test beyond their strength to endure with honor, took "the Lion" of the resistance and killed him secretly in the dark cellars of the Gestapo. And in the streets of Vilna stood the fighters, as they were to stand in other ghettos when the news of Wittenberg's sacrifice was brought to them, wondering bitterly for what it was they fought.

The bitterness passed, was put into perspective within the whole hell of their lives. They did know, after all, why they fought; and no act of rejection and betrayal could affect their purpose. They fought for their people —not perfect, perfectly honorable, perfectly brave—but for their people *as* people. They fought that the Jews should not go to their dreadful deaths without the dignity of resistance, without a Jewish voice raised to cry "Evil!" without a Jewish hand lifted to strike against the evildoer. They had pledged themselves to be, in this sense, the redeemers of their people; and nothing of this had changed. So the fighters took up their guns again. . . .

The months passed, summer to autumn to winter, and it was beginning spring of 1943. The war had begun to change. The armored claws of the Wehrmacht had been blunted at Moscow and broken at Stalingrad; the Allied armies were winning in North Africa. The invasion of Italy was only weeks away, and that of western Europe was now certain to come. Germany was beginning to bleed its strength into the earth, and death was raining down upon it from the skies. None of this had meaning for the Jews, entering the fourth year of their captivity in the fifty-five ghettos of eastern Europe. In the ghettos, they starved and sickened and died and were butchered. The earth around *them* heaved with the gaseous stirrings of hundreds of thousands of their brethren decomposing in the mass graves. The skies above *them* were darkened by the smoke rising from the long chimneys of a dozen death camps where a million Jewish lives had already become only an obscene stench upon the drifting winds. Against the millions of Jews—the unarmed men, the aged, the ill, the women and children—against this enemy, the Germans had been for four years endlessly triumphant. Whatever might happen elsewhere, on this front total victory still seemed possible. Of all Hitler's golden promises, for which the German people had delivered up their iron souls, none seemed any longer likely of fulfillment save only "the annihilation of Jewry"; and even this last might slip from their grasp if they dawdled on the way. So the Germans made haste.

The Oberkommand Wehrmacht might need transport urgently for the fighting war, never mind, priority went to Adolf Eichmann for the trains to go from the ghettos to the "labor camps." Nearly every day, the trains discharged their freight of Jews at the "labor camps" of Treblinka, Sobibor, Mauthausen, Belzec, or at Auschwitz, over whose gates was emblazoned the cheering truism: *Arbeit Macht Frei*—"Work Makes Free." And at all these places the work for the Jews was the same hard labor of choking to death in the gas chambers. Within twelve months of time, beginning in 1943, the Germans were to deport to these camps and others, and there to murder, the Jews of Warsaw, of Sosnowiec, of Bialystok, Minsk, Vilna, Riga, Krakow, Lida, Smolensk, Lublin. Himmler had ordered the liquidation of all the ghettos, and the "final solution" was approaching its final phase.

In this same period, the desperate ghetto fighters changed their tactics to try—as far as their feeble strength would allow—to frustrate the total liquidation of the ghettos. Before 1943, it was mostly the Communists who sent their fighters out of the ghettos to organize partisan bands in the forests and there to await the inevitable arrival of the Red Army guerrillas. The Zionists, who formed the great majority of the Jewish Fighters' Organizations, were determined not to desert their people in the ghettos. They held their ghetto bases and hoped thereby to persuade the hundreds of thousands behind the walls into a massive movement of fighting resistance. But by 1943, it was clear that for the Jews, as for every other people in the whole history of struggle, the underground fighting resistance would remain a minority movement and the Jewish masses—starved and sick, deluded by hope, terrorized by incredible savagery and overwhelming force—would go unresistant to their deaths.

So there were three things left for the fighters to do, or to try to do: the first was to organize new bases from which to fight when the ghettos would no longer exist; the second, to use these bases also as a means to save the lives of Jews; and the third, to organize final acts of resistance within the ghettos to delay the annihilation of the Jews while killing as many Germans as possible.

For the first two of the three objectives, they began to speed the organization of the Jewish partisan brigades, the forest fighters, whom the Germans called "the green men."

Picked units of fighting men went out of every ghetto into the forests to prepare the way. At first, they tried to contact non-Jewish partisan bands that were already operating in a few places. But the first squad from the Vilna ghetto was disarmed by the partisans under General Markov and left to be hunted down and killed by the Lithuanian fascists; and in Poland, the partisan commanders Lemishevski and Czarni mobilized three brigades of the "People's Guard" to slaughter nearly seven hundred Jewish fighters who had come out of the ghettos of Lublin, Krasnik, Lukow, and Wlodawa.[31] Even where the Jewish fighters were welcome—as in the forest areas controlled by Soviet and Polish partisan bands led by Generals Kaputsa, Holod, and Garbaty—even there, the Jewish fighters were welcome if they brought their own guns, but unarmed Jews and those who could not fight were driven out to be killed in the open fields by the Polish peasants who sucked in anti-Semitism with their mothers' milk.[32] So the Jewish partisans, who saw the forests as places of refuge for their people as well as bases from which to fight, were forced—for the most part—to make their hard way in the woods alone.

The fighters came first, in small groups, and built what they called "the family camps." Then they began to take the Jews out of the ghettos. Most of the Jews wouldn't go. It was madness; the way was infinitely dangerous and if, after all, they did reach the forests, how would they survive?

Most would not go, but hundreds did, thousands did. The black resistance took them out of the ghettos in small groups—five, eight, a dozen, twenty at a time— with a couple of the fighters guiding them and more behind them, to die—often—fighting off the German patrols or the armed collaborators. . . . They took them through the sewers; they took them in stolen Wehrmacht trucks, in carts, on foot, at night. They bribed guards, and fought suicidal actions to draw the German patrols away from the escape routes, and killed the anti-Semitic peasants along the roads who otherwise might point the way to the pursuing SS men. . . . They went however they could. They took whoever would go—the children, the women, the ill, the old—whoever would go, whether they could help or only hinder, whether they could fight or not, whether they could survive in the forests or only die there; they were all anyway marked for death and this death was better. . . .

Out of Kovno, Malachi Wald and Chaim Yellin and the others led the Jews sixty miles across the hostile countryside to the Augustava forests and the tangle of the Rudniki swamps. . . . Abba Kovner and Abram Hornick and the girl, Vitka Kempner, took them out of Vilna to the Norocz forest. . . . Far to the east, Dr. Yehezkel Atlas and his men led them from the Wola ghetto, swimming the Zczara River, losing two out of every three on the incredible journey of 142 miles to the Ruda-Jaworska forests. . . .

For months, the fighters went these awful routes, ghetto to forest to ghetto to forest, in a long nightmare of frustration and frantic haste. The Germans were taking the Jews from the ghettos now in the hundreds of thousands, and the way to the gas chambers was quick and short and wonderfully organized. The way to rescue was long, hard, and uncertain, and death waited at the end of the journey for many of the few who went the way. And so many would not go, would not try to go! Night after endless night, the fighters risked their lives and at the last moment —standing at the breached ghetto walls, or down in the stinking sewers, or huddled in the thin shelter of the stubbled fields—at the last moment, later than that! time after time there were those who lost heart, refused to go on, better the hell they knew than the hell they didn't. Then the fighters, their hearts breaking, would lead them back again to the ghetto death—risking their own lives again to do it. Or they would fall upon their frightened brethren, threatening them, beating them, driving them on into the darkness, the fighters themselves knowing that all the painful way might lead only to another kind of death. . . .

Still they did come, out of every ghetto, a thin and spectral trickle of skeletal people, starved for years behind the walls, going out now to a new dark terror, led by men and women, by boys and girls who knew no more of the forests than they did themselves. Despite it all, thousands of Jews came into the forests, and the fighters who brought them organized them into the miserable "family camps," nursed them, fought like wolves to protect them, ravaged the countryside like the Mongol hordes to feed them, buried them when they died. And they died, in the thousands, nearly 50 percent of them came out of the ghettos to die in the woods within three months. . . .

The fighters brought the Jews into the forests, left men behind to protect them, and the others went back into the ghettos for the last desperate battles there. The ghettos were being liquidated and everywhere the Germans came now, there were Jewish fighting groups to meet them. At Riga and Lodz and Sosnowiec, the Jewish Fighters' Organization dynamited the railroad stations from which the deportation trains were leaving every day. . . . A thousand SS men were held outside the Bialystok ghetto for four days, until Mordechai Tennenbaum-Tamaroff and 80 percent of the fighters he led were dead in the ruins of their bunkers. . . . At Tulczin, they fought until they had nothing left to fight with and then they let the Germans in and burned the ghetto down upon them and blew it up around them. The ghetto smoked for eight days and when the Germans came in to bury their dead it was impossible to separate charred Jew from charred übermensch; so the bulldozers turned them all into the earth. . . . In Vilna they fought until the Germans, fearing another Warsaw ghetto debacle, broke off the action and offered the Jewish community "safety" in a labor camp that really was a labor camp. The fighters were opposed to the deal, but the Judenrat accepted it and twenty thousand Jews went out of the ghetto to the camp. (They survived for another year there, until the SS slaughtered them two days before the Russians liberated the camp.) When the twenty thousand had left, the fighters went out of Vilna through the sewers to the forest where Abba Kovner organized them into "The Avengers" Brigade and led them back to take Vilna from the retreating Germans just over a year later. . . . And there was Warsaw. Above all, there was Warsaw. Here there were eight hundred Jewish fighters, and it took three times that many SS troops and a hundred demolition experts, a battery of field artillery, and four tanks to pull the ghetto down. It took them thirty-three days to do it. . . .

Even then, when the ghettos were down in ruins, down in ashes, when the tanks had gone in against the pistols and the soldiers against the boys and girls, even then there was no end to it. The fighters who survived crawled out of the ghettos and into the forests, and in the length of the eastern front there were twenty brigades of Jewish partisans to claw at the Germans from then till the end of the war.

So that Paul Joseph Goebbels himself wrote the tribute down in his diary before he went to his death in the führer's bunker deep in the flaming rubble of the thousand-year Reich—"One sees what the Jews can do when they are armed."

Four

Four from the Furnace

There are no "typical" stories to be told of those who survived the holocaust the Germans loosed upon the Jews of Europe. The word itself comes from the wrong lexicon, it belongs to the statistician; it is too bloodless to be meaningfully applied to the individual human being. So the four stories that follow here are not "typical." They are no more than the stories of four of the people who came out of the Nazi furnace so tempered that they have been able ever since to travel the hard and bitter road with Malachi Wald. . . .

Ben-Issachar Feld—"the Messenger"

In December 1941, there were about four hundred people living in and around the farm village of Sanik in central Poland. Twenty of these were German soldiers who were billeted there. For the most part, the soldiers were an easygoing lot and if the occasional rape or broken head is overlooked, one cannot say that the villagers suffered more than the usual inconveniences imposed by an occupation force. Except, of course, that they starved, for the soldiers were there to guarantee the delivery of 75 percent of the farm produce of Sanik to the Wehrmacht. Starving or not, the villagers were pretty lucky nevertheless because, after all, though Jews, they were allowed to live, while all over Poland at that time Jews were being trodden into the earth like beetles.

One of the lucky Jews of Sanik was a boy not quite fourteen years old, a clownish-looking kid with oversized hands and feet tacked precariously to an undersized body, wearing always a scrap heap of clothes much too large for him, buttoned and tied and pinned so he wouldn't just lose them. Even his name, Ben-Issachar Feld, seemed too big for him and so he was called "Benno." In time to come, the boy would grow big enough for his real name, but by that time he had another name and was famous.

Only six of those who lived in Sanik then are still alive and traceable, and none of these remembers any heavenly light illuminating Benno as he trotted about the village, stumbling over his big feet and clutching at his sleazy rags. In retrospect they wonder at their lack of discernment, for the nimbus must have been there and they know now that the hand of God was on him from day he was born.

If ever a babe was born to his future, Benno was. He was born a blond, with a short straight nose and eyes of a singularly frosty blue—a mutant among the five dark, long-nosed, doe-eyed children of Ruben and Rebecca Feld—and the only boy among them. And he was born prematurely, with so tenuous a hold on life that for nearly two years he was kept swaddled in the cocoon of his crib and his parents and elder sisters took turns watching him, fearful that the light would go out of those strange blue eyes and the baby would die alone and unnoticed. When they named him Ben-Issachar, it seemed a reckless challenge flung in the face of God, for *ben* is the Hebrew word for "son"—Ben-Issachar, the son of Issachar—and the appellation is given among the Jews to guarantee the continuity of the grandfather's name. This infant seemed too frail a reed on which to hang such a hope of genealogy. Still he was the only boy, so there wasn't much choice.

All that, though, is by the way. The essence of the thing is that Benno was born blond and that as a baby he was thought too feeble to bear the shock of the customary circumcision. And after that, in the weight of tragedy that fell upon the family, the ritual was just let slip so that in December 1941, Ben-Issachar Feld was surely one of the very few uncircumcised Jewish boys in all Poland.

When Benno was three years old, his father came home from the fields complaining of a sharp pain in his side and stumbled off to bed without his supper. The village didn't have a doctor, and Mrs. Feld brought her husband the traditional comforts of hot tea and the heated frying pan wrapped in a towel to press against his side. Both these remedies were wrong for him as it happened. Within hours his inflamed appendix had ruptured and by dawn Ruben Feld was dead. The night her father was buried, Rachel—the oldest daughter—clumsy with grief, overturned a lamp in the barn and the splattering kerosene killed her in a terror of blazing straw and crashing timbers.

It was clear then that the place was accursed, so Rebecca Feld sold the farm and moved out of Poland to the town of Guben, just over the border in Germany, where the Felds had some relatives. With the money from the sale of the farm, she opened a small grocery and began life anew. That was early in 1931. As the years went by, the business prospered moderately and Mrs. Feld began to plan for the future of her children. Guben was a backwater town and the storms which rocked Germany at the time eddied out into indiscernible ripples by the time they reached Guben. There were only a handful of Jews in the town, most of them had been born there and their neighbors saw no reason to make any violent changes in the slow placidity of their lives. The swastika flag of the Third Reich went up over the schools in the town, but nobody gave any great regard to the new Aryan educational doctrines. The ponderous Germanic curriculum maintained unchanged and the Feld children—including Benno when he grew old enough—were pupils like any other and regularly won the small awards attendant upon diligence as to conduct and homework.

The thirty or forty Jews in Guben were an assimilated group, speaking German, living as Germans. There was no synagogue and no Jewish community life. Whatever Jewish cohesiveness there was could be discerned only in an adulterated observance of Passover and, occasionally, of the bar mitzvah ceremony by which a Jewish boy at the age of thirteen formally attains man's estate. Once the Feld children began attending school the need to conform, to be as much as possible like the kids around them, was very great. They spoke Yiddish or Polish only with their mother and that reluctantly, mocking her halting German and her "greenhorn" old country ways. For a time, Rebecca Feld tried to maintain some elements of the Jewish character of her home as it had been kept in Poland. But the pressures were too great, the Jewish ceremonial requires a man to conduct it and Benno was too young and disinclined, and the inertia of the other Jews of Guben in time seeped into the Feld's household also. After that, there was left only the mourners' kaddish, the prayer for the dead which Mrs. Feld taught Benno to recite each year on the anniversary of his father's death, to remind the Felds that however they might live in Guben as Germans among Germans, they were ineluctably Jews and strangers among the goyim.

The reminder came somewhat more forcefully during "the night of broken glass" at the beginning of November 1938.

On November 7, 1938, a seventeen-year-old Jewish boy named Herschel Grynszpan waited on the steps of the German legation in Paris, clutching a pistol in his sweaty hand. Two weeks earlier, young Grynszpan's parents—together with ten thousand other Jews of Polish origin living in Germany—had been rounded up by the SS, packed in freight cars to the Polish border and there hustled across the bleak winter fields into Poland, with machine-gun bullets biting at their feet to urge them on their way. In the course of the operation, 437 of the refugees died, some of exposure and the rest of gunfire aimed well or badly, depending on the point of view. Among the dead was Herschel Grynszpan's father.

Young Grynszpan was studying in Paris at the time and when the news reached him, he cast about for some

act of meaningful vengeance. This brought him, thin and
shivering, to stand in the winter sleet on the steps of the
embassy with his coat collar turned up and a newly
bought gun in his pocket, determined to kill the German
ambassador and by this dramatic act to bestir the world's
conscience with regard to the plight of the Jews in Germany. As a political assassin, the boy was entirely inept;
and as a political analyst he was innocent beyond belief.
The man he actually shot that day was not the ambassador, but the legation third secretary—Ernst vom Rath
—a man of goodwill to whom anti-Semitism was repellent
and who was himself under surveillance by the Gestapo
because of his anti-Nazi sentiments; and with regard
to the plight fof the Jews in Germany, the conscience
of the world remained untroubled. The only significant
reaction to Grynszpan's efforts came from the Nazi hierarchy. On the afternoon of November 9, Reinhard Heydrich—the head of the Security Police—sent the following
cable to all regional police officers throughout Germany:

> Because of the attempt on the life of the Legation
> Secretary vom Rath in Paris, demonstrations against the
> Jews are to be expected tonight, November 9th–10th,
> throughout the Reich. The Police Presidents are to get in
> touch with the Gauleiters in order that they may adjust
> their measures to the following conditions.[33]

Heydrich instructed the Nazi district leaders and the police to ensure that in the "expected" demonstrations there
should be no danger to non-Jewish lives or property.
Apart from these precautions, his orders went, "the demonstrations which are going to take place should not be
hindered by the police." The spontaneous reaction of the
outgraged German people against the coreligionists of
young Herschel Grynszpan was, in other words, to be
properly organized. And so it turned out.

In that single night, in the major cities alone, 191
synagogues and 171 Jewish-occupied apartment houses
were burned to the ground; 7,600 shops, stores, and
factories owned by Jews were looted and destroyed; 236
Jews were killed—among these 43 women and 13 children—more than six hundred were maimed, thousands

were badly beaten. Twenty thousand Jews were arrested for "provocative acts in disturbance of the peace"; half of these were sent within three days to the Buchenwald concentration camp where, ultimately, more than eight thousand died.[34]

An estimated million and a half solid German citizens went charging through the streets that night, millions more—less athletically inclined perhaps—looked on. Throughout the country, scores of German Christians were injured when the balconies upon which they had swarmed, heedless of risk in their innocent efforts to obtain a better view of the festivities, collapsed beneath them. There is no record of any similar numbers evincing any comparable disregard of danger in their efforts to rescue some of the embattled Jews. Though it should be set down that twenty-two non-Jews—twelve in Berlin, five in Cologne, four in Frankfurt am Main, and one pitifully alone in Düsseldorf—were arrested for interfering with the orderly process of the "demonstrations."[35] And a decent regard for historical accuracy requires the footnote that five members of the Nazi party were arrested for rape and were expelled from the party for having "dishonored its principles" by the Nazi party court under Major Walther Buch. The court made it clear, however, that it was not the rapes as such that were offensive, but the "violation of the Nuremberg racial laws" which forbade sexual intercourse between Jew and Gentile.[36]

In the years before, Jews had been harried, robbed, tortured, and killed in the streets of Germany by night and by day and in sufficient numbers; but in large part these crimes had been the deeds of a few thousand brutal storm troopers. Now the German government had ordered a vast pogrom and well over a million ordinary German people had rushed to carry it out, while the rest of the millions stood by to watch the crimes committed by their fellow citizens in the name of all of them. And in the next days, in all the thousands of Christian churches in all Germany, there is record of only seven pastors calling from their pulpits for justice, or even penance.

The streets of Germany's major cities were buried under the crystal shards of $3 million worth of broken glass; but more than the streets had been buried, as more than the Jews had been killed. The night of November 9, 1938, marked the death and the burial of the innocence and the conscience of the German people. For the crimes of that night had been done in front of all of them and no living man or woman in all Germany could any longer have remained unaware of the evil that was loose among them.

Measured against what was happening elsewhere in Germany that night, the burghers of Guben were restrained and neighborly toward the Jews of the town. The town council was aware of what their German duty required; but the majority of the councilmen found the task distasteful, not sufficiently odious to impel them to resign their posts, but unpleasant enough to lead them to seek some way out. The solution they hit upon, after some hours of debate, arose out of the comforting theory that one may lose a little bit of one's virginity and still remain pure.

Among the thirty-odd Jews in the town, Rebecca Feld and her children could hardly have expected to be considered by the town councilmen as *unsere Juden*—"our Jews"; they had, after all, arrived in Guben only seven years previously. So they were selected as the scapegoats on whose heads might be heaped the sins of the tiny Jewish community. That night—in the presence of the police, the council, the fire brigade, and the citizenry of Guben—one house and one small grocery store were regretfully but efficiently burned down.

Mrs. Feld, her four daughters, and her son were put on a truck and escorted by two shamefaced policemen along a back road toward the Polish border. And on the way, the ingenious circumlocutions of the Guben councilmen became nonsense and the town lost the rest of its virgin purity. The youngest of the Feld daughters, Esther,

had begun screaming when their home had gone up in
flames and her thin, nerve-racking keening continued as
the truck pulled out of town. Until, finally, one of the
policemen guarding them could stand no more. He struck
the girl. The single blow was delivered, one may assume,
with no particular evil intent. it was launched by the
snapping of frayed nerves of a man engaged in an unpleasant task of which he was ashamed. Esther reeled
back in the lurching truck, the low tailboard caught her
stumbling feet, and by the time the speeding truck was
stopped, the girl lay dead on the road in a welter of blood
and shattered bone.

And so it happened that despite the solicitous care of
the townspeople of Guben, one of the Jews of the town
was killed; one out of less than forty, a proportion—it
might be mentioned—higher than that achieved in any
other community in Germany on that "night of broken
glass."

Well, the thing was done. No sense in making a fuss
about it. Perhaps ten minutes later, a shocked and now
lunatic woman, two girls, a boy, and the broken body of
a dead child were set down in a wood just over the border
in Poland. The town of Guben had solved its Jewish
problem, until August 1940 when a slave-labor camp was
established just outside the town and the rest of the Jews
of Guben were sent there to die.

On November 15, six days after their banishment from
Germany, the three surviving children of Rebecca and
Ruben Feld brought their silent, vacant-eyed mother back
to Sanik. There the villagers gave them a hut and a small
plot of land, and dropped off food and clothing from
time to time. And there they lived, after a fashion, in a
kind of uneasy dream-haunted peace. Until on July 14,
1941, a German army unit marched into Sanik and Rebecca Feld watched them and then went out to the ceme-
tery where her husband and her daughter Rachel were
buried, and hanged herself from a scrubby tree.

The long chain of incident and happenstance was nearly complete now. There was Ben-Issachar Feld, the boy
Benno, with a man's full measure of hate already full

grown inside him; blond, blue-eyed, uncircumcised, German-speaking—a tool, hardened and sharpened and tempered to the work it would do. . . .

For a time then nothing singled out Benno and his sisters from those around them, and it seemed that the moving finger had indeed moved on. They lived a life that qualified, in Sanik, as normal. They stayed out of the way of the German soldiers. They combed their meager belongings for a needle or a book to barter for a scrap of leather or a candle or a piece of soap. They scrabbled for food in the thin patch of land behind the shack in which they lived. They went hungry, always, as did everyone. The Felds were perhaps hungrier than most. They'd been poorer to begin with and had less land; and even so, like everyone else, they had to share what their land did produce with the German army. The tithe of charity the blighted family had been accustomed to receive from their neighbors came to very little indeed when it had to be taken from the 25 percent of the crops the Germans left for the people of Sanik. Still, the Felds survived, and their existence was uneventful in the terms of the time and place, until the day late in December 1941 when Rabbi Yehoshua Moshe Aaronsohn stretched out his hand to the tool that was the boy—Benno—and put him to the work for which he had been crafted.

The rabbi had come to Sanik from Gostynin, some thirty miles further east. For over three hundred years, seven generations of Aaronsohn rabbis had stood for their people against the oppressors: against the Jesuit pogroms in the reign of King Sigismund in 1630; against the Haidamak cossacks in 1768; against Michael Muraviev, who sold the Catholic nobles licenses to hunt the Jews with dogs through the forests of Poland in 1866; against the Black Hundreds of Czar Nicholas II in 1905; against the Jew-killing Polish patriots of Marshal Pilsudski in 1920. And when, in July 1940, the Gestapo came to Gostynin and it was Yehoshua Moshe Aaronsohn's turn, he stood where his fathers had. So the Gestapo came after him in the dark of a night, and the Jews of Gostynin took their protesting rabbi by force and smuggled him away to Sanik. They begged him to stay there quietly, and to live. It was his duty, they said, to live. There were men who had to stay alive to bear witness at some future time, they said, and Rabbi Aaronsohn was a man whose testimony the world would believe. So he lived; through Auschwitz, through Konin, Theresienstadt, Buchenwald. He lived through it all; and wrote it all down and buried his writings in the mass graves with the ashes of the piled dead. After the war, he and his diaries bore witness at the war crimes trials at Nuremberg and Krakow and Poznan and Warsaw. Only after that, in April 1951, could Rabbi Aaronsohn stand down and come to Israel to begin his own life again, to become a member of the Chief Rabbinate in Petah-Tikvah, his duty done, the last of the generations of Aaronsohns—the rabbis of Gostynin.[37]

It was to Rabbi Aaronsohn, hiding in Sanik, that Moshe Podhlebnik was brought on December 18, 1941, when he crawled out of the Chelmno death camp. Podhlebnik, who had been shot, burned, left for dead on a pyre of flaming corpses. He was, indeed, very nearly dead and out of his mind with pain and horror. He was the first man to come out alive from Chelmno, the first witness of what was being done there in the new brick buildings with the "shower rooms" in which the bathers were cleansed forever by the cyanide gas that hissed out of the apertures in the concrete ceilings. For two weeks Rabbi Aaronsohn nursed the tortured man into spells of rational consciousness and wrote down the words that bubbled from his blistered lips.[38]

So there it was. Behind the curtains of illusion—the "security" of the starving ghettos, the "self-government" of the Judenrats and the Jewish ghetto police, the "re-settlement" areas, the "labor" camps where "Arbeit macht frei"—behind all the curtains of illusion the Germans had drawn between the Jews and the fate intended for them, lay the reality of the gas chambers of Chelmno. And if at Chelmno so elsewhere, in other camps with the electrified fences and the guarding SS men and the prowling man-killing dogs.

Aaronsohn had evidence now, but what good was it with him—a bearded, hooknosed, recognizable, and hunted Jew—locked in the tiny village of Sanik? Someone, someone else, had to carry the news to the thirty-five ghettos so the Jews would know that the Germans intended to murder them all. It was forbidden for a Jew to travel; death for him if he was caught. But someone had to go—and not by foot, or by night, or buried under the manure in an ambling cart—the word had to be carried all over Poland and there wasn't time. It had to be someone who could ride the trains, in the full sight of the SS troops and the Gestapo men and the Polish informers.

The rabbi turned for help to the leaders of the small group of Zionist youth in Sanik. They talked it over and made a plan; and there was only one person in the village who had a chance to carry it out. They found Benno digging for edible roots in the frozen fields and asked him if he would go that night, telling no one at all, to Warsaw and from Warsaw thence wherever he might be sent. They told him nothing, save only that it was dangerous, and that it was important to the whole Jewish people and that Rabbi Aaronsohn would vouch it so. The boy agreed and was taken to Aaronsohn. The rabbi told him carefully that what they were asking him to do could bring him death, and that they would tell him nothing of the meaning of his mission for fear that under torture he might reveal it. "Torture" and "death"—the words carried such a dramatic weight of fear that no boy with a boy's dreams of glory could refuse; nor could Benno. Aaronsohn gave him only an address in Warsaw and a message to commit, without comprehension, to memory: "Aunt Esther has turned up again, and is at Megilla Street 7, apartment 4." The rabbi promised that when Benno was safe away, he would tell Benno's sisters what was good for them to know; but that for his sake and theirs, and more than theirs, the boy himself was to tell them nothing.

And so it was. Benno went quietly from his house that

night and lay down under the sacks of a waiting cart and was taken along the dark paths until the town of Gostynin could be seen beyond the fringe of forest. There Benno and the two young men who accompanied him lay waiting for the dawn. Only then did they give him the story he was to tell to the German guards at the railroad station. When the early light began to finger the fields, they sent him out toward the town. Ben-Issachar Feld, blond, blue-eyed uncircumcised, speaking German; a fourteen-year-old boy, frightened and alone. Ben-Issachar Feld, to be known from this day forever as Benno the Messenger, on his way now inevitably to Malachi Wald. . . .

The Wehrmacht corporal who commanded the squad of overage volksdeutsche auxiliaries guarding the railroad station watched, grinning, as the kid came toward them, clutching at his slipping pants, stumbling over his big feet—a typical clumsy, Polack bastard kid.

The boy told the story he'd been given to tell. The corporal said nothing but crooked a thick finger and Benno followed him along the station platform to an office and into the terrifying presence of an SS lieutenant with the skull and crossbones on his black uniform making meaningful and immediate the death and torture Benno had been told about. The lieutenant was used to the fear he engendered, so there was nothing strange that the boy stammered when he told his tale; that his name was Janno Pavel, a Pole, a good Christian Polish boy; that the dirty Russians had killed his parents when they retreated from Gostynin; and that he was sick and tired of grubbing in garbage cans and sleeping in doorways; that, please, would they let him go to Warsaw where he had an aunt who would take care of him, please, sir?

The questioning began then: Where did he learn his German? His mother's parents had been German-born and his grandmother had taught him, until she died. Where had he lived in Gostynin? Behind the factory, where all the buildings had been destroyed in the bombings before the Wehrmacht had arrived. It went on like that for awhile, the boy swallowing his fear, cold blue eyes staring at cold blue eyes, the desk between them, the two blond heads like as peas in the pod of kinship reserved for the Aryans. Finally the lieutenant scribbled an order and gave it to the corporal, get the kid photographed and fingerprinted, give him an identity card and a travel order to Warsaw, and put him on the train. . . . Wait a minute: and here came the last flick of the whip of professional suspicion. The lieutenant came around the desk and stood over the boy: "Take down your pants. Take them down." . . . The too-big pants, down; the ragged shorts, down; the limp penis coldly naked, uncircumcised, the final evident testament to Christianity; the lieutenant satisfied: "All right, get him the things he needs, get him a bath, too, he stinks!"

The train went out of Gostynin for Warsaw that night, with Ben-Issachar Feld on it, Janno Pavel now, with ten German marks of good German charity in his pocket and a legal *Kennkarte*—worth a fortune—carrying his picture and his fingerprints, attesting to his pure and perfect Aryan status; and in his mind, the Warsaw address and the meaningless message.

At Warsaw, the *Kennkarte* got him through the station guards with hardly a glance and a wandering hour brought him to the address he'd been given. And then what? He had an address and no name to go to—that meant no name to have betrayed had things gone badly in Gostynin; but it also meant the blank walls staring down at him from the grubby hallway in which he found himself. The building had a janitor, a man named Sochaczow, and others had come to that building with that same uncertain look in their guarded eyes. He took the boy down to the room next to the furnace, gave him a thick chunk of bread, and asked the two cautious questions: "Where are you from? What do you bring?" Benno told him; the message had no meaning for Sochaczow, but the name of Aaronsohn was known to him. So out they went that night, Benno and Sochaczow, down into the sewers—the boy choking with the stench and the enclosed fear—and up again in the Warsaw ghetto, to the secret place of Hashomer Hatzair, the Zionist Young Guards.

Mordechai Ankilewitz was there, a lean, shock-haired man who had, then, less than two years to go before he was to die in a flaming bunker at the head of the ghetto fighters of Warsaw. Benno repeated his message—"Aunt Esther has turned up again, and is at Megilla Street 7, apartment 4." Ankilewitz sat there for a moment, puzzling it out. Then he reached for the Bible, and there it was, out of another time and another persecution. For chapter 7, verse 4 of the "Megillat Esther"—the biblical story of Esther—reads: "For I and my people are sold to be exterminated, slain and lost; but if we were only being sold as slaves and maidservants, I would have stayed silent."

There it was, the truth, from Moshe Podhlebnik out of Chelmno, from Rabbi Moshe Yehoshua Aaronsohn of Sanik, by way of the boy—Ben-Issachar Feld, Benno the Messenger. The curtain of illusion torn now, and the truth out. The Jews in their millions were being sent to the guarded and secret camps, not, as the Germans told them, to bend their backs in labor for the Third Reich, but to be killed.

At that moment, before an aging janitor and a four-teen-year-old boy, Mordechai Ankilewitz began to plan the Jewish Fighters' Organization of Warsaw and the he-roic revolt of the Warsaw ghetto began to be born. . . .

Out of the ghetto the next night, down through the sewers, and into the Aryan quarter of Warsaw went Ben-no the Messenger. Across Poland he went, going openly as Janno Pavel, carrying the coded centuries-old warning, to Itzik Wittenberg in Vilna, to Mordechai Tennenbaum in Bialystok, to Abba Diskont in Kovno. And behind him everywhere the flames of a Jewish fighting revolt flickered into being. For three years, Benno the Messen-ger, become legendary, carried that blessedly legal *Kennkarte* that opened the roads to him, traveling fast and safely past the German guards, carrying the messages that had to go quickly and had no other way to go from underground to underground. Until in June 1944, Benno the Messenger found himself in Lublin with Malachi Wald. . . .

Judah Klein, the Wigmaker

When Judah Klein was thirteen years old his father apprenticed him to a wigmaker in Warsaw and for the next eleven years Judah made wigs. Not ordinary wigs, worn to ease the balding ego. Judah, one might say, made wigs for the glory of God. He fashioned the sheitels, the coverings of human hair that strictly orthodox Jewish women don when they shave their heads on their wedding day as a symbol of their withdrawal from the vanities of questing maidens and of their submission to God in heaven and their husbands on earth.

Judah was a fine craftsman, and a successful one. By the time he was twenty-four, in February 1942, he had a wife, two children, and a house on the fashionable Genzia Street. By that time, of course, his ownership of the house was pro forma only and the happy memories of his prosperous tenure there were beginning to assume the quality of a distant dream. For the Germans had, by then, been long in Warsaw and Judah's house was occuped by Hans Lautz, the geschäftsführer—or commercial boss—of the Warsaw ghetto. The Germans had packed 445,000 Jews into a ghetto area of 1⅓ square miles, containing just over 61,000 rooms. That made an average of more than seven persons to each room. Judah, his wife and their two children, his parents, and his wife's widowed father were crammed into one small room looking out—if "out" is the word—upon the heaving heap of offal that piled up in the air shaft of a reeking slum at 17 Dzika Street.[39]

As things went, then, Judah Klein and his family were among the fortunate ones in the ghetto. They were alive and together. And every now and then, Judah would climb to the roof of the crumbling tenement and sit there cross-legged, squinting in the bleak winter sunlight, making a wig for some young lady still vibrant enough to love and sufficiently bemused by this and a belief in God to wish to marry according to the precepts of the Law. The wigs weren't what they had been and neither was the pay, being mostly a matter of a few hoarded trinkets.

But the trinkets could at that time be bartered for food, and so the Kleins managed to eat fairly often. There weren't many families managing that in the Warsaw ghetto then.

The conditions in the ghettos of Poland were periodically reported to the German Governor General Hans Frank by an agency euphemistically called the Main Propaganda Division. These reports were secret and were to be destroyed immediately after Frank had seen them, but the one of March 21, 1942, from the Warsaw District survived and was introduced in evidence by the prosecution at the Polish War Crimes Trials in 1946:

> The death figure in the ghetto still hovers around 5,000 per month from starvation. A few days ago, the first case of hunger cannibalism was recorded. In a Jewish family the man and his three children died within a few days. From the flesh of the child who died last (a twelve year old boy) the mother ate a piece. To be sure, this could not save her either and she herself died two days later.[40]

In such circumstances, keeping oneself alive was a conspicuous achievement, and to manage this also for one's dependents involved a miraculous combination of luck, energy, and devotion. When Judah had no wigs to make, he searched for any other kind of work. When he could find no work, he stole. He had always been small, and now he was thin, there was no weight to him at all, and he could slip through a window opened upon the fetid air and move like a wraith in the dark. Judah Klein, an honest man, became a burglar. And, becoming this, he —who had always before had a strong sense of community responsibility—became a man concerned with his family, himself, and no others. He worked and stole and risked his life, and he had neither energy nor inclination to engage in activities that did not directly help to keep himself and his family alive. He took no part in the Jewish community organization of the ghetto, he held aloof from the white resistance that attempted to provide food and medical care to the whole ghetto. All this was

quixotic lunacy. He took care of his own; that was
enough—and hard enough—for a man to do. Judah did
this until August 1942.

On the second of August, the Germans took twenty
thousand Jews out of the Warsaw ghetto to the Treblinka
extermination camp and within five days most of them
had been efficiently processed up to and including the
ultimate gas chambers; and what remained of them, Judah's wife, children, and parents included, consisted of
so many pounds of potentially usable commodities carefully collected. For in the midst of all the martial maxims
of "blood and iron," "race and Reich," by which the
German people lived, some of the more innocent hom-
ilies still survived—albeit somewhat adapted to the curious exigencies of the times—and among these, the ancient adage, "Waste not, want not." Under this clarion
call to patriotic economy, the frugal Germans stripped
the Jews arriving in the camps of their clothes, shoes,
spectacles, glass eyes, artificial limbs. Even the toys, the
rag dolls—battered symbols of a lost security—that the
children carried, were taken away. All of it was counted,
collated, stored, entered in the meticulous ledgers. And
after the gas chambers, the mute voyagers were halted on
their way to the nearby crematoria while the gold teeth
were hammered out of dead mouths, fixed conveniently
agape by the frozen last gasp of the dying effort to breathe
just once more. SS Major Gustav Melmer, a certified bastard from Frankfurt-am-Main who worked in the finance
department of the Reich Main Security Office, had the
responsibility of delivering the teeth in padlocked cases
—like any other gold—to the Reichsbank in Berlin, until
Reichsbankdirektor Otto Wilhelm's outraged protest that
"the Reichsbank is not a dealer in second-hand goods."[41]
After that the gold teeth were rendered more acceptable
to the Reichsbank by being first sent to the Prussian State
Mint where they were melted down into ordinary gold
bars whose rectangular anonymity concealed their somewhat unusual origin.

In this atmosphere of careful husbandry it was not
to be expected that the Germans, who even probed for

hidden wealth in the body apertures of their victims, would overlook the treasures more easily accessible. All arrivals at the camps had their heads shaved. The long hair of the women was collected and sent from all the camps in Poland to Treblinka. It was this that saved the life of Judah Klein.

By the time Judah arrived at Treblinka, the hair had piled up until it filled seven warehouses. There was a factory to steam and process the raw material, and cunning machines to weave it into bolts of cloth. Very useful cloth it was, light and warm, and with an attractive luster. Coat linings of the stuff were much in demand, for example, among the German officers suffering the severe winters along the eastern front. There was a room in the factory where twenty workers filled special orders. What was it you wanted, Herr Brigadeführer?—a blanket for your bed, or your friend's bed?—a woven dress of bright red hair to delight your wife back home?—a coat of many colors for your little girl, to show that daddy loves her? Whatever you wanted, if you were a German of sufficient status or had money in lieu thereof, and if you didn't mind such things as *Jewish* hair, you could get it at Treblinka.

For such projects, Judah Klein—bringing the skills of eleven years as a wigmaker—was a positive godsend. He quickly became a kind of foreman, with his own handicraft limited to the really special requests arising out of the more errant flights of German fancy. When, for example, Irma Greise, the beautiful "angel of Birkenau," had a birthday coming and Dr. Josef Mengele was at his wit's end for a present to give the lady whose passionate loins he shared with several others—male and female—at the Auschwitz-Birkenau camp, he brought his problem to his friend SS Sturmbannführer Karl Mummenthey, who ran the Treblinka workshops. Mummenthey, sweet Cupid's aide, had an idea and ordered Judah Klein to translate inspiration into reality. So Judah crafted a whip of choice tresses—brilliant black, at Mummenthey's tasteful insistence, to contrast with Miss Greise's own blond hair—and tipped it with tiny knots of plaited silver

wire. It made a wonderfully thoughtful gift, considering
the deviant nature of the lady's proclivities, and she was
never without it. Witnesses at her war crimes trial in
1945 testified that the whip went into bed with Miss
Greise and her partners; and that she used it more publicly to rip open the breasts of young Jewish women who
were brought to Birkenau. For this latter activity, the
British tribunal had her hanged.[42]

Treblinka had the hair factory, and a small stone-
crushing plant, but these were incidental dividends: the
camp existed solely to house the assembly line that ran
from the railroad siding just inside the fences to the gas
chambers and the crematoria. The Jews were dragged—
stupefied and half-asphyxiated—from the window-
less freight cars, whipped along the barbed-wire runways
to an enclosed pen where they were stripped, their heads
shorn, their bodies searched with wire probes. Then they
were clubbed into the ten gas chambers, two thousand
at a time. The steel doors slammed, the vents opened.
Fifteen minutes later, the interior blowers were turned
on. Ten minutes after that, the doors were opened and
the sonderkommandos—the Jewish inmate corpse handlers
—were sent in under the guns of the SS guards to haul
out the bodies, covered with the vomit and the filth that
voided from mouth and rectum and bladder with the
agonizing retching spasms of their smothering death. Out
into the open, then, the dead tossed on the ground, six
men of the sonderkommandos to wrench the gold teeth
out of their mouths with pliers, SS men watching closely
to see that the Third Reich was not cheated of its just
gains. The bodies hauled up again, thrown onto carts,
dragged across the yard to the crematoria, and shoveled
off into the open-hearth furnaces, the flesh blistering
away, the eyeballs crackling, the blood and body juices
hissing in the flames. Five hours it took, a little more
sometimes, to transmute two thousand humans beings into
a dirty cloud of greasy smoke. Another hour or so to
rake the ashes, clear the ovens, hose out the gas chambers
and the yards. Time for the SS men to have lunch, smoke
a cigarette, write a letter home—except for a few to

stand with machine guns guarding the knot of sweating, half-naked, half-starved, brutalized, empty-eyed Jews of the sonderkommandos who had nothing now to do until the next transport arrived.

Two transports a day, during the good months, and that's how they all went until more than three hundred thousand people were killed there. Treblinka was one of the first of the death camps. It had none of the refinements of camouflage and concealment developed later at Auschwitz and other places. No pleasant gardens blooming around the square anonymous buildings that housed the gas chambers. Inside the buildings themselves, there were none of the sly, reassuring signs: "To the Showers," "Families—Keep Together," "Mothers—Watch Your Children." At Treblinka it was speed that was counted on to keep the victims numbed and docile, speed and the armed guards, and above all the numbing shock of confronted horror.

Auschwitz, Birkenau, Ravensbrück, Dachau—these and other "combination" camps where the Jews were worked as slaves before they were turned into carrion—were huge places, with great sprawling barracks housing "permanent" inmate populations of over sixty thousand each, with thousands of guards and administrative personnel. The Auschwitz complex covered over forty square miles, it was guarded by five thousand Germans together with Polish and Ukrainian auxiliaries and 250 killer dogs. At Auschwitz alone, the I. G. Farbenindustrie profited from the labor of more than ten thousand Jewish slaves at a time.[43]

There was none of this at Treblinka, or at Chelmno, Belzec, or Sobibor. These places were killing grounds, merchandising only a single product—death. A hundred thousand persons were brought to Treblinka each year, but the inmate population was kept at a steady seven hundred Jews; the rest were killed within hours of their arrival. Of the seven hundred, four hundred worked on the sonderkommandos. Half of these were killed off every month and replaced, generally from among the new arrivals. The other three hundred worked on maintenance, or in the hair factory, or at the rockcrusher. These could live for a few weeks, a month, sometimes as much as two months, until their work capacity was so reduced by starvation or disease or insanity that the Germans were compelled to regard their continued existence as inconvenient and unprofitable. For the changing population of seven hundred Jews who were allowed to tarry thus in the vestibule of the gas chambers, the maximum life expectancy was no more than two months.

The only exceptions to this inexorable shift to the gas chambers were a handful of men whom the Germans kept alive because their skills were particularly valuable. Among them were two doctors, a master electrician, three machinists who kept the rockcrushing plant and the hairweaving machinery functioning, and Judah Klein, the wigmaker, and those who worked with him. Inevitably these more-or-less permanent residents became an elite group; their relative longevity alone binding them together and setting them apart from their fellow Jews. Only they could maintain, in terms of the slaughterhouse in which they existed, the concept of a future stretching a bit beyond the next ration of watery soup, the next scrap of moldering potato, the next selection for the gas chamber. And since they had this much future, they were able to plan to extend it.

The plan for a mass escape from Treblinka began with one of the "permanent" inmates, Dr. Julian Chorazyski. Chorazyski was a surgeon, a former captain in the medical corps of the Polish army; a tough man, with that rare cartilaginous tenacity that is a quality of mind that has nothing to do with the muscles of the body. So that when Judah Klein met him—though five months in Treblinka had worn the doctor down to a shambling, big-boned skeleton in a sack of graying skin—the toughness was still there, limitless.

The meeting occurred three days after Judah's arrival at the camp, and the circumstances—in any other time and place—might have been considered unusual. Judah was trying to kill himself.

Thousands of Jews were seeking suicide in those days.

In the ghettos and the camps, horror unhinged their minds, tragedy broke them. They killed themselves out of sorrow, in desperation, from a desire somehow to choose the manner of their dying, out of the unbearable guilt of being themselves alive when those with whom their lives had been intertwined—and for whom they were responsible—were dead. It was this last that motivated Judah when he'd been three days at Treblinka and the shock of recognition stirred his numbed mind into the realization that the ashes that drifted down upon from the nearby chimneys—the dirty dust that he blinked out of his eyes and wiped from his face—were what remained of his wife and his children.

So he sat down in a corner of the barracks and sawed away at the veins in his wrist with a piece of rusty tin.

In a place like Treblinka, one didn't interfere with a man bent on suicide. One merely waited. It was a matter of a combination of timing and a nice estimate of distance so that one would wait long enough for the man to die and far enough away to give him a decent privacy, but not wait too long or at such a distance as to deprive oneself of the opportunity to inherit—by the process of a scrambling grab—whatever might be useful among his clothes and his possessions. In such a situation it was important that the contestants exercise a proper self-discipline, so there was some grumbling among the onlookers in the barracks when Dr. Chorazyski came closer to Judah than seemed to the others to be fair. But as a doctor, Chorazyski had status in the community and all of them lived so close to the need of his skill that there were none who would choose to make him their enemy. So they grumbled, but softly, and they didn't move.

Chorazyski squatted down beside Judah and whispered to him: "You're doing it wrong. I'm a doctor and I know, you'll never get it done that way."

Picture it! The two creatures crouched on the filthy floor, one trying with trembling fingers to let his life out through his veins and the other—a doctor—telling him gently how to go about it, until the one gives the piece of tin to the other and says—"Here, please, help me. Do it for me."

"Me?" says Chorazyski. "Why should I help you? You don't help anyone. What will you do for me?"

Judah looks up at him, and begins fumbling at the laces of his worn shoes. "I'll give you my shoes; please, you can have my clothes."

"I don't want your clothes, I'll tell you what I want, I want a German. You can give me a German. Listen, I'll explain it to you. You want to die, it's a good idea. Go out and jump on a German, fasten your teeth in his throat and tear out his jugular vein, put out his eyes with your thumbs. With luck you'll kill him for us and for those he's killed. You want to die? Good, take one with you."

For a moment, Judah stares, then he gets up and starts for the door, and he's changed, now, now he belongs to Chorazyski. The doctor goes with him, an arm around the little man's shoulders. And just inside the door, "Wait a minute. You want to kill a German? Why only one? Wait a little bit longer," Chorazyski whispers, "and I'll show you how to kill a lot of them. Only wait a little bit."

The waiting took a year; but Judah Klein was no longer a man alone thinking only of himself and with only guilt and self-hate to keep him company. Now he had a friend, and others besides himself to hate, and with these—a man can wait. . . .

For the year that it was planned and prepared, the Treblinka revolt depended on half a dozen men. There were Dr. Julian Chorazyski; Dr. Marius Leichert, like Chorazyski a former Polish army officer; Samuel Rajzman and Yosef Gross, who were machinists; a maintenance electrician named Eliahu Grinsbach; and Judah Klein. Others came in later and lived through certain stages of the project, but these formed the core. It wasn't only a matter of limiting the conspiracy for reasons of security. More important was the fact that there were not more than these few whose work gave them a life expectancy long enough for them to function with some continuity.

The difficulties were incredible. Though Treblinka was a small camp, so many thousands of Jews were being processed to death there that the Germans maintained a relatively large guard detachment. The German and Ukrainian personnel totalled seven hundred men and thirty Helferinnen, the SS women's auxiliaries. There were twelve killer dogs. It was clear that the conspirators could hope for, but not really count on, support from whatever thousands of Jews might be en route from the freight cars to the gas chambers at the moment the revolt burst. But these transients were always in a state of such catatonic terror during their brief journey through the barbed-wire corridors from their arrival to their death that they were an unpredictable factor. So the only dependable allies were to be found among the seven hundred of the "steady" inmate population. That made a rough numerical equality between those who might join the revolt and those who would crush it. Seven hundred diseased and starving Jews penned behind double rows of barbed wire against seven hundred SS men trained as a military force, armed with pistols, rifles, machine guns, grenades. Assuming some Jews got past the guards and through the wire, there was the leveled and scorched earth that stretched in a perimeter four hundred yards deep all around the camp; they had this to cross with the machine guns in the guard towers at their backs before they reached the sheltering forest. And the forest—miles of swamp and underbrush, with no paths that they knew and no food they could get. And all of it in the rear-echelon areas of the German army.

Under such circumstances, to hope for the success of the revolt would have been a manic fantasy. It seems unlikely that the Jews so indulged themselves. What they did hope for—and even this was wildly optimistic—was, as Chorazyski put it to Judah Klein, "to kill a lot" of Germans. From the nature of the preparations they made, it seems clear that *killing* was the aim. They made little effort to collect civilian clothes, or to forge identity papers,

though these were vital if they were to pass among the
Polish population outside the camp. What they did in
their year of preparation was to collect weapons and,
slowly and with great caution, to sound out the people
who might use them. The men who cleaned the camp
saved every scrap of metal they found and passed it on.
Dud bullets and ejected cartridge cases were stolen from
the SS target range. The powder was taken from the de-
fective bullets and packed with the cartridge cases and
other scraps into hoarded tin cans, fused with bits of cloth.
These, hopefully, became bombs. Knives were fashioned
out of other metal garbage and surreptitiously honed to
some kind of edge by scraping them for hours on bits
of stone. In the hair factory, Judah Klein plaited short
strangling nooses, and longer ropes tipped with stones.
They made blackjacks by stuffing stones into small cloth
sacks. All of these had to be hidden from the guards,
buried under ground, hung into the fecal mess of the
latrines. They agonized over the fear of informers, they
sweated blood during the flash searches of the camp. Little by little, the hoard of "weapons" grew, and they shut
their eyes to the fact that it all amounted to nothing.

Then, in July 1943, Arbeitsführer Carl Gustav Farfi—
the labor boss of Treblinka—came down with a case of
bleeding hemorrhoids and this ridiculous happenstance
took on the aspect of a miracle.

Farfi was, presumably still is—since he is alive
in Düsseldorf—an ignorant and superstitious man. An old-
line Nazi, stuffed full with all the racial abracadabra of
his kind, Farfi nonetheless clung to the medieval idea that
the Jew—by virtue of his Jewishness—had certain special talents, and among these the gift of healing. So that
when pain came in its particular fashion to this stupid
butchering übermensch, he took his embarrassing troubles
not to the SS doctors, but to the Jew—Dr. Julian Chorazyski.

Farfi made all the arrangements, and there he was—
on that bright summer's day—stretched out on his stomach, his fat buttocks bare, on a table pulled close to the
sunlit window, with his trousers draped over a chair and

a key to the iron door of the arms arsenal in his pocket, and his eyes clamped shut against the terrifying sight of the scalpels and the hypodermic needles. It all went well. Chorazyski covered his patient's head and upper body with a sheet—important to keep things sterile, you know —slid the novocaine into Farfi's behind, and moved around with a great clattering of the frightening instruments while he slipped the keys from Farfi's trousers and tossed them to Yosef Gross who came wandering past the window at the properly planned moment. It was perhaps the longest hemorrhoid operation in history; long enough for Gross, the machinist, to go and file a duplicate key out of a scrap of brass and get the original back to Chorazyski before Farfi was permitted to raise his head and wipe the tears from his eyes.

So now they had a key; and weapons, real weapons, were within their reach. The miracle had happened, but there was a sting in it. The next day, there was a selection for the gas chambers and Dr. Julian Chorazyski was taken to his death. No one really knows whether Farfi arranged this, fearing the word would get around that he had gone to a Jewish doctor—and with so unheroic a complaint—and had even wept at the sight of the surgical knives. In any case, Chorazyski, who had been one of the camp's "immortals" and had survived scores of these selections, was this time taken.

For a flashing instant it seemed the revolt would be born abortively then, when SS Dr. August Wilhelm Mitter pointed his finger at Chorazyski. But Chorazyski put a restraining hand on Judah Klein's arm and shook his head at the others who moved to group about him. Clearly this unprepared, unarmed moment was not the time. So Chorazyski, who was a fighting man, went in this way and for this reason submissively to his death.

The leader was gone. They had paid for their miracle.

There were forty of them in the plot by then, and the loss of Chorazyski nearly broke them. He had recruited each of them; he had been for them iron and rock and father and friend. There are leaders like this and when they go, they leave a hole and those who have followed them tend to slide down into it. This happens even to normal men. These men in Treblinka were not normal. They were sick, starved, they stumbled when they walked, their minds quivered on the edge of madness. It was Judah Klein and Marius Leichert who found the strength to pull the group together again. Judah out of the hate that drove him, and Leichert because he had something of Chorazyski's iron in him. But both of them knew they could not hold their people long.

They decided to stage the revolt when the Germans brought in the next transport of Jews to be executed, and they revised their plans to fit the fact that they now had a chance at getting weapons. It was all very complicated. They couldn't simply steal the guns and hide them away until they were ready, for the theft would certainly be noticed very quickly. So it was decided that Leichert and four others would sneak into the arsenal just before the revolt was to start and be ready to hand guns and grenades to the Jews who would rush to the arsenal when the signal was given. Leichert's group would then remain in the concrete blockhouse and hold it against the off-duty SS men who would undoubtedly run there to arm themselves when the revolt broke out. This meant that as long as the Jews held the arsenal, the Germans would be compelled to concentrate substantial forces against them; it also meant that the five men would certainly be killed.

The timing of the revolt posed another problem. The guards were always busiest during the time when the thousands of Jews in a transport were massed with the whole length of the six-hundred-yard barbed-wire corridor that led from the railroad to the gas-chamber compound; and it was important also that these thousands of newcomers be given a chance to join the revolt. But since the sonderkommandos were at such times already isolated within the fences of the gas-chamber area, some weapons would somehow have to be gotten to them before they went into the special compound. These could only be grenades and pistols, capable of concealment within the clothes of the sonderkommandos. These would have to

be stolen earlier, and only a few could be taken to minimize the risk of a premature discovery. And, most important of all, the uprising would have to break at once,
all over the camp.

It was decided that Yosef Gross, who as a maintenance
worker had more freedom of movement than most, would
touch off the revolt. He would be given a couple of hand
grenades and would get down to the railroad junction and
throw them at the guards who massed there when a transport came in. He was to wait for the critical moment
when the Jews were out of the freight cars and the guards
were busy driving them to the gas chambers. The explosion of Gross's grenades would be the signal for the revolt. In the hair factory, Klein and his men would start
to kill the guards and call on the other Jews working
there to join them. Samuel Rajzman and his group would
do the same at the rockcrushing plant. Others were to
rush the perimeter fence and try to blow up the guard
towers just beyond with homemade bombs; still others
would try to tear down the fence in as many places as
possible; the sonderkommandos would attack the SS men
within the gas-chamber compound. Each of the groups
was to mobilize as many of the Jews as would join them,
as the revolt broke, for the specific task assigned to
each group. The idea was to keep going, in an explosion
of speed and violence, to do as much damage and as much
killing as possible, and to keep moving, those who could
get out of the camp to head for the woods beyond; and
beyond that, there was no plan. . . .

On the evening of August 1, 1943, they learned that
a transport of four thousand Jews would arrive early
the next afternoon, and D day was settled for them. That
night, Eliahu Grinsbach smeared his body with garbage
to help hide his scent from the patrolling dogs. It took
him nearly an hour, sweating with fear, to get across the
floodlit yard from the barracks to the arsenal and back
again with the three pistols and ten hand grenades which
was all he had dared to take.

In the barracks, the makeshift bombs and blackjacks

and the hair nooses that Judah Klein had woven were dug up out of the filth of the latrines and distributed among the conspirators. Five of the grenades and two pistols were given to the sonderkommandos, the other pistol went to Leichert's group. Yosef Gross got his two grenades, two others were given to the men who cleaned the guards' barracks with instructions to throw them into the hall where the off-duty guards slept. The remaining three grenades were wrangled over—like gold, like bread —until Leichert decided to give them to three men who would try to blow up the main gate of the camp. All this done in the dark of the night, in the sleeping barracks—an insane charade performed by a clutch of half-dead, whispering zombies.

Then it was over; and they climbed up into their tiered bunks, forcing their skeletal bodies to lie still on the bare boards, the weapons hidden in their filthy rags, their eyes gleaming like splintered glass in the dark—forty men, waiting for morning. . . .

August 2, 1943, and the seven hundred inmates of the Treblinka camp up, as always, in the first thin flicker of dawn and out of the barracks for the morning *Appell;* the three or four who had died in the night lay on the ground, as usual, to be counted with those who were still alive. There were the customary curses, the accustomed casual brutality, the kick in the groin for the man who moved, the spittle in the face for nothing at all. And among the seven hundred, there were forty men who stood like rock, desperately careful to catch no guard's eyes. . . .

The hours dragged across their strung nerves, fear milking sweat out of their juiceless bodies. In the hair factory, Judah Klein and the others fought their trembling fingers as they sat at the looms, guiding the light plastic shuttles —specially crafted for this unique task—along the strange silken woven strands of hair that represented all the dead women whose suffocating agony was enshrined now only in the brief memory of the clattering looms. . . . Samuel Rajzman and his men at the rockcrushing plant, the boils on their bodies leaking pus, the crusted chancres breaking open with each rupturing effort to heave the laden wheelbarrows along to the moving belt that carried the rocks to the crusher overhead. . . . At the inmate hospital, Dr. Marius Leichert—former professor of pathology at the University of Krakow—and his helpers, working with long-handled rakes, scraping up the week's collection of bones and skulls which was all that remained of the Jews who had come that past week to SS Dr. August Wilhelm Mitter with ailments too ordinary to be interesting or too troublesome for his limited skill. For such as these, Dr. Mitter kept the lime pit in the courtyard of his neat brick building with the big red cross painted on its walls and roof.[44]

The hours dragged, and it was noon; it was one o'clock; it was two; it was three fifteen.

At the corner where the barbed-wire corridor from the gas chambers opened to enclose the railroad depot, the tower guard climbed his ladder, and fitted the heavy belt of cartridges into the machine gun that snouted down toward the tracks fifteen feet below. The guards with the rifles and the machine pistols and the clubs drifted along the platform and squinted along the tracks and waited impatiently, cursing the heat and the glare. Twenty feet from the tower, Yosef Gross kept his head down and tried to make himself invisible in the thin shadow of an electric pylon as he fumbled among the corded wires of the junction box and shrank, suddenly, into himself as Kurt Franz passed by, the black dog panting at his side and slavering in the heat. SS Obersturmbannführer Kurt Franz, commandant of Treblinka, the Knight's Cross of Gold gleaming on the black uniform, the death's head like bleached bone on the black cap, the face beneath it blond, open, innocent as a medieval choirboy, reflecting nothing of the maniac who took young Jewish girls to his bed and strangled them at the moment of his orgasm and stuffed the naked bodies under his bed until morning or, sometimes, until the festering corpses swelled and stank.[45] Gross watched the commandant pass and swore to kill him before the day was out, but this

Franz is a lucky man and a tough one, with the instinct for self-preservation of a hyena. Gross was to miss him on that day, and in the years to come Judah Klein was to fail four times, so that Kurt Franz is alive today and was free as a lark until April 1961 when the persistent pressure of the Israeli police finally compelled the West German government to put him in jail "to await trial."[46]

It was three thirty now, and looking down from the depot at Treblinka one could see the line of smoke advancing from the horizon. It was almost time. The guards tossed away their cigarettes, the bored chatter dribbled to an end. Yosef Gross tensed, and fumbled surreptitiously at the hard unaccustomed spheres of the grenades beneath his shirt. It was almost time.

Suddenly the rusting locomotive was there; behind it, the twenty boxcars, the wooden walls of each containing —crushing in on—two hundred parched, starving, and bewildered Jews, four thousand frightened Jews in twenty filthy freight cars. It began then, all at once: the harsh shouted guttural German commands the doors slamming open the Jews bulging out spilling out the hard hands throwing them on their way the clubs beating them into the barbed-wire corridor the first hundred already driven past the compound and into the brick building that housed the gas chambers. And then, too soon, Yosef Gross forgot it all, forgot that he was to wait until the gas chambers were full and the corridors full and the guards strung the whole length of the six hundred yards between the depot and the gas chambers. Gross didn't wait, couldn't wait. He came whirling away from the pylon, tearing the grenades out of his shirt, the first one to blow apart the tower guard and send the machine gun hurtling down; the second grenade thrown at Kurt Franz, killing the six SS men near him and wounding Dr. Mitter, but missing Franz. And then Gross, screaming, flinging himself like a dog at Franz's throat, tearing at him like a dog; but a real dog was there, Franz's dog, and Gross was down and dead, the blood bubbling out of the hole where his face had been.

The Treblinka revolt had begun!

All over the camp, guards and inmates stood fixed in the one instant of paralysis at the crash of the first grenade. Then it began and by the time the second explosion came they were already in movement, the fighting gaining speed and space, spreading like a landslide. . . . Judah Klein flung himself backward from the bench of the loom, rolling like a cat, and up with the strangler's cord of hair taut between his hands and on to the back of the guard, tripped and down with two of the others trying to kill him and the noose hissing beneath his head, biting into his neck as Judah thrust his hands across and heaved upward, the snap of bone clean and sharp, Judah up and away, pausing to rip the guard's pistol from his holster, that instant saving him as another guard came in the doorway, his machine pistol swung in a stuttering arc that killed four men before Judah had the gun and cut him down. . . . Elsewhere in the hair factory, other guards died, blinded by hair blankets flung over their heads and beaten to death, strangled by the hair nooses, thrown through the second-floor windows to the ground below and kicked to death when the men came rushing out into the yard. . . . Marius Leichert tore out of the clinic courtyard, leaving a guard behind him screaming, his hands fluttering at his face where Leichart's terrible rake had clawed out his eyes and ripped off the flesh; Leichert and his men away, racing for the arsenal, to be thrown off their feet as the wall of the guards' barracks was blown apart when the two Jews who cleaned there hurled their grenades in among the sleeping SS men. Leichert came up, clutching his broken shoulder, and was off again, the others behind him, in a stumbling run; a frantic second with the key rattling in the lock of the iron door and they were in the arsenal, ripping the guns from the racks as Samuel Rajzman and his men, those that were left of them, the first away, came tearing in shouting for guns, screaming for guns. . . . Eighty Jews were down and dead already in the packed mass of the gas-chamber compound and the men of the sonderkommandos had killed seven guards and were tearing themselves to bits on the cruel barbs of the fences, trying to get out of the sight of the SS man on the roof of the building who was up there with a submachine gun knocking them over as though they were wooden ducks at a target range. . . . In the fenced corridor from the railroad siding to the gas chambers, at the railroad depot itself, the four thousand Jews who had just arrived were a seething, screaming, hysterical mob of men and women and children, trampling each other underfoot, some of them fighting to get back into the freight cars, clawing for shelter under the train, trying to get away from the searching leaden hail that tore their lives out, that smashed through body and brain and bone. . . . The main gate was down already, blown by the grenades of the three men who had this job, and two hundred of the Treblinka Jews had rushed the broken gate, most of them to pile up in a heaving clump of dead and dying, trapped in the cross fire of two machine guns the skilled and disciplined SS men had rushed to the gate in the first moments of the revolt. . . . All along the fence, men had died tearing at the barbed wire and other men were after them, dying there, and only some of them out, through the few—the terribly few—gaps, out and away and racing across the stubbled fields for the sheltering woods beyond; Judah Klein among them, and Samuel Rajzman, and 180 others. But not Leichert, not the men with him, not any of those who had rushed to the arsenal—a few of them to get the guns and all of them to die under the machine gun they hadn't known about, the gun that was hidden always in a corner room of the nearby administration building, that commanded the front of the arsenal, and under gunfire from the tower that covered the back of the arsenal, and under the rifle grenades of a squad of SS men sheltered in a storehouse across the way who killed them calmly, skillfully, with trained precision. . . .

It was three forty-six in the afternoon, and it was over. The Treblinka revolt had lasted eleven minutes and it was over. Of the SS men, 117 were dead and wounded; 1100 Jews were dead, the rest of the thousands lying face down in the seeping marsh of dirt and blood within the barbed-wire corridor and the railroad depot, lying still, the lifted head, the slightest movement bringing a volley from the tense and hating guards who ringed them about. And 180 Jews, only a few of them armed, into the woods like animals, to be hunted down like animals by the Treblinka guards and a task force of a thousand SS men and soldiers of the regular German army sent in by Heinrich Himmler himself.

For four days, the Germans prowled the forest, tracing the Jews with packs of hunting dogs, spotting them with helicopters, burning them out of the underbrush with flamethrowers, killing them on the spot, wherever they were found. Of the 180 Jews in the forest, only 18 survived, to find their way in time—maddened and starved and hardly human—to a group of Jewish partisans, survivors of the Warsaw ghetto revolt.

And among these few, Judah Klein the wigmaker, on his way to Malachi Wald—and vengeance. . . .

The Little Sister of Rachel Baum

Of all the "teaching myths" that have come down through the ages of organized societies to instruct and inspirit the hesitant gentleness of man, none is more appealing than the cycle of beast-marriage tales. The legend has variations according to the time and the place of its telling, but the basic elements are these: There is a prince or young chieftain transformed by witchcraft into a beast of hideous aspect and condemned by the same spell to a life of terrifying violence against the people of his domain. One day, the beast kidnaps (or receives as appeasing sacrifice) a maiden of such purity and transcendent beauty that he falls in love with her and keeps her in solicitous bondage within the confines of a magic garden. There the maiden, seeing the beast with the perceptive vision of an empathetic heart, grows unafraid, and is able to give the trapped and tortured monster tender courtesy and, in time, the beginnings of love. The spell is broken, the cloak of evil falls away, the beast sheds his terrible guise and stands before her, regal, handsome, loving. Prince and maiden wed. Rejoicing fills the land. Beast-prince, captive maiden, and burdened people are thus alike redeemed by the pure understanding of a gentle heart.

The story is old enough and sufficiently gratifying to have earned its place in cultures spread throughout the world, and the emendations of the passing ages are nowhere basic. The North Americans and the French have it now from Mme. Leprince de Beaumont's hundred-year-old "Beauty and the Beast," and here the beast is a kind of huge horned bull. About the same time, the brothers Grimm, tracing the archetypal myths, gave their version to the Dutch, the Scandinavians, and the German-speaking peoples in their tale "The Frog-Prince." Centuries before, the Basque shepherds had their beautiful youth changed into a serpent; and the Magyar nomads of the lands that became Hungary knew him as a wild boar. When the Briton tribesmen raised the monoliths of Stonehenge, the tale of "The Beast from the Waters" was already old. The cannibal bushmen of the islands now called the Philippines handed down through their generations the story of the young chief bewitched into a great ape. For the pygmies in the African rain forest, the beast-prince was a crocodile.

But within the pattern of the culture and the age, the message remained essentially the same, its meaning clear, the extension of its application comforting: Return ye good for evil, things are not always what they seem, none is bestial beyond redemption by the intercession of the pure and gentle heart.

And such was the tale's meaning also in Ciechanow, in central Poland, where Rachel Baum was born on July 6, 1921, and where the enchanted beast is considered capable of many guises, sometimes a white wolf or bear, sometimes a huge and hideously ugly man.

Those who remember Rachel Baum when she was a child tell that her beauty then was of a radiance so illuminating that people were stilled in the streets when the girl walked by, and that when the onlookers could move again, they went smiling in a warm glow of well-being. And there are others who saw her, years later, go to her violent death in the Birkenau camp, blinded and beaten and tortured beyond belief, who swear that even on that terrible day, the battered face was somehow glorious and the brute men who grouped about her on the gallows platform stood stunned and mute, even as men like them had stood long ago about another saintly fighting maiden whom they knew as the Maid of Orleans, and we call Joan of Arc.

In the twenty-three years of her journey from birth to martyrdom, Rachel Baum earned her place in the sober recitations of history. And when the generation of those who lived in her time has gone, and the years have veiled the distinctions between fact and fantasy and have eroded the limiting boundaries of reality, this Jewish maid of Ciechanow, Poland, will surely have grown larger than life and will have become part of the eternal myths that sustain her people.

It began for Rachel when she was ten years old. In August 1931, a maniac pederast named Jan Mielecz broke his previous pattern of furtive cellar fumblings, and raped and killed a child on a farm near Ciechanow. For a day and part of a night, fear gripped every parent in the town and bands of armed men joined the police in searching for the aberrant giant. Then the word came that Rachel was missing. The whole town knew the girl, at least by sight, and the thought of such innocent beauty so dreadfully endangered sent them out with clubs in their hands, a raging mob of vigilantes. And then at dawn the girl came up from a cellar, leading by the hand the shambling Frankensteinian thing that had snatched her from the streets but had not, in the long hours since then, done more than stroke her hair and sit before her, a monster awed. Rachel Baum and Jan Mielecz, Beauty —and the Beast.

The legend of Rachel Baum began that day. In Poland, as elsewhere, the men and women who live bent close to the earth—who are peasants, not farmers—are quick to read the secret signs and hear the hidden stirrings of those they call "the Folk," whom they may no longer openly worship but whose mysteries lie deep in the dark collec-

tive unconscious of man. For such people, myth and
reality are intermingled components of ultimate truth; and
from that day in August 1931, for the peasants around
Ciechanow, the girl Rachel was a person set apart, "under the protection."

Except for the incident with Jan Mielecz, and for whatever transcendental interpretation one chooses to assign
to the special quality of Rachel's luminous beauty, there
seems to be no other evidence of this "protection." And indeed, if it did exist, it was finally to fail her terribly
at a time when men bloodied the earth under an enchant-
ment so ferocious that—unlike the beast of the ageless
fable—they were, in their scores of thousands, unmoved
by love or pity. But it is in times of pain and fear that
man seeks comfort beyond the normal ken; and when the
times are those of terror absolute, the myth becomes belief and is clung to as the only guarantor of hope and
sanity. And so the myth of Rachel Baum, "under the
protection," survived even her special pain and her awful
death; survived even the beasts beyond redemption. . . .

Little is known of the first years of Rachel's life. Until
she was six, she was an only child and lived with her
parents, Hirsz and Malka Baum, on a farm her father's
family had owned and worked for three generations. Then
her sister, Hannah, was born and soon after that her
father sold the farm and the family moved to the nearby
village of Ciechanow. It seems probable that it was the
mother's wish that impelled the move. Malka was city-
bred, she'd been born in Radom and had lived there until she was nineteen (when the marriage with Hirsz had
been arranged) and she didn't take easily to the rigors
of Polish farm life. In any case, the Baums came to
Ciechanow in the winter of 1927 and there Hirsz set
himself up as a grain merchant. His business prospered
and he soon became a substantial figure in the village
and a leading member of the Jewish community which
comprised about a fifth of Ciechanow's eight thousand
inhabitants. So from about that period, the record of the
Baum family—and of Rachel—becomes more detailed.
Surviving neighbors and friends remember them well; and

there are the childhood reminiscences that Hannah Baum told to Malachi Wald and the others in his group when she joined them at the Lublin displaced persons camp in 1944.

As far as the record shows, only two occurrences roiled the prosperous placidity of the family's early years in Ciechanow, and both concerned Rachel. The first was the incident with the lunatic Jan Mielecz in August 1931. The second arose later that same year when the children in Rachel's school, perhaps bewitched by the mystery of her earlier deliverance from violence or simply charmed by her happy beauty, selected her to play the role of the Virgin Mary in the school's Christmas playlet. The instinctive emotional reaction that on that earlier occasion had sent the people combing the village beside Rachel's terrified parents this time did not apply. The school children announced their decision in mid-November and there was, therefore, time for the leisured beneficence of reasoned thought. The headmaster of the school, a civilized and careful man, consulted both the village priest and the village rabbi. The community leadership thus joined in common cause, the rest was simple. Rachel's parents were persuaded that it ill befitted a Jewish child to participate at the commemoration of the false redeemer; and the parents of the other children were reminded, in case the Baums proved uncooperative, of the necessity of keeping the Jews in their place. So when Christmas came, some other child—possibly less radiant but certainly more suitable—played the role of the Virgin; and Rachel, sitting at home, was presumably contented by the residual benefit of having learned early the vital natural law that Jew and Gentile are born to apartheid. It is pleasant to record that even in a community so primitive as Ciechanow, there was no one tasteless enough to mar the enthusiastic enshrinement of eternal truth by referring to the historic embarrassment that the Holy Mother of Christ had indeed been, alas, a Jewess.

The years that followed were the early ones of Hitler's rise to power, and Rachel would sit modestly during the long evenings and listen to her parents and their friends endlessly discussing the impact that the turbulence beyond the borders might have upon the always tenuous security of the Polish Jews. Rachel kept her own counsel, as was proper for a youngster, but in 1936—when she was fifteen—she joined the Zionist youth group in the village. Her parents raised no objection as long as this new activity didn't interfere with either her lessons or her household duties. Chief among these chores was taking care of her younger sister Hannah, and this became something of a problem. Hannah was a healthy and energetic child, imbued with wanderlust that led her—from the time she could toddle—to go journeying forth into the wide world. Given an instant's inattention, she would go charging along the dusty village roads until some passerby would recognize her and, dangling a candy or a piece of fruit before her as one tempts a straying foal, would coax her back to her home again. When Rachel began attending the Zionist meetings, she had perforce to drag Hannah along, even to those larger gatherings in adjacent villages to which Rachel drove in her father's pony cart. There, with a doll to keep her company and a stick of sugar candy to keep her quiet, the little sister of Rachel Baum sat in a corner while her elders studied Hebrew and talked of the future they would someday carve out of the deserts of Palestine. So that Hannah took it all in, as it were, by osmosis, and became a Zionist that way.

Zionism gradually became the central reality of Rachel's life and when she had completed the limited schooling offered by the facilities in Ciechanow, she devoted herself almost entirely to Zionist activity. When the German Wehrmacht thundered into Poland on September 1, 1939, Rachel was eighteen years old and she was by then a delegate from the youth movements of the Ciechanow region to the Zionist General Council of Poland. On the heels of the invasion, the council called an emergency meeting in Warsaw and there declared the loyal allegiance of the Polish Zionists to the Polish government. The Zionists, like all the Jews of Poland, stood solidly with all the Polish people in this time of heroic trial. In the corridors of the meeting place, the delegates could even be heard expressing their convictions that good would come out of all this evil since, at last, the western world would surely rise and together with the valiant Polish army would crush the Nazis. Even the anti-Semitic government, now needing all possible support, would certainly extend the hand of brotherhood to the Jewish citizens of the threatened homeland. This was the majority opinion, and the small doubting minority—including, as the records show, Rachel Baum and three of the six other youth delegates—was stilled. Out of the crucible would come the new Polish nation, granting equality to all.

This general optimism lasted only hours. All over Poland, even in the areas far beyond the initial German penetrations, pogroms broke out in almost every town with Jewish inhabitants from the very first day of invasion. When the Jew-killers of the German SS and SD came into Poland in the wake of the panzers, Polish soldiers who had thrown down their rifles picked up clubs and joined their erstwhile conquerors in beating the brains out of nearly three thousand of their Jewish fellow citizens within the first three days of the war's beginning. So much for Polish unity. As for the rest of the romantic dream of the triumph of right over might, it died under the Stuka dive bombers and perished beneath the weight of the German tanks crushing the beautiful horses and men of the pitiful nineteenth-century Polish cavalry. Of all the optimistic predictions, then, there was left only the vision of a succoring western world, as represented by France and the British Commonwealth. This world roused itself indeed, as predicted, and declared war in clarion tones of clearest virtue; and then settled down to an impotent year behind the metaled and concrete fantasy of the Maginot line.

In November 1939, two months after the German-Russian partition of Poland, Reichsminister Hermann Göring established an organization called the Main Trusteeship Office East (Haupttreuhandstelle Ost—HTO). The HTO was to be "the only authorized agent to order con-

fiscation, to appoint and dismiss administrative commis-
sionioners" in the occupied territories, and the German
police were ordered to be at its disposal "for the forcible
execution of its measures."[47] The HTO was to strip that
part of Poland controlled by Germany of ". . . all raw
materials, scrap, machines, etc., which are of any use for
the German economy. Enterprises which are not absolute-
ly necessary for the meagre maintenance of the bare existence of the population must be transferred to Germany."[48]

As director of the HTO, Göring picked one Max Winkler, then Nazi mayor of Grudenz, and during the next
three years this clerkly vandal robbed the Polish people
of $2 billion worth of industrial assets, raw materials,
and foodstuffs. To accomplish this piracy with proper
efficiency, Winkler divided the occupied territory into four
administrative regions and set up a headquarters in each.
The regional headquarters for central Poland was Ciechanow.[49] The selection of the village as a headquarters
was surely only an accident of geography; but as a result of this circumstance a man named Fritz Bracht came
to Ciechanow, murder and rape were visited on the
Baum family, and seven years later Hannah—the little
sister of Rachel Baum—tied this man, Bracht, to a chair
and beat him to death.

Fritz Bracht was a Neanderthal negation of the Nazi
Aryan stereotype. He was dark, fat, squat, hirsute, and
sly. In Nazi party circles he was called *der Affe*—"the
ape." His position of moderate prominence in the party
was commonly reputed to have resulted from the judicious
use of contacts arising out of the practice of his prewar
profession. He'd been a whoremaster, specializing in the
organization of lewd performances at some of the more
exclusive Nazi gatherings in Hamburg. That Bracht had
been a pimp was a matter of record in the files of the
Hamburg police; but it must be admitted the rumor that
grateful clients saw to his political advancement remains
only a rumor, perhaps arising from the fact that he had
no apparent qualifications for the eminence he achieved
in the winter of 1942 when he was appointed gauleiter—
or Nazi party boss—in central Poland.

Soon after his appointment, in the early spring of 1943, Bracht began a tour of inspection. His purpose was to ensure that the thousands of SS men and other functionaries in German administrative centers in Poland did not forget, in the course of their labors so far from the homeland, that it was the Nazi party from which sprang this magnificent resurgence of the German nation. And so Bracht came ultimately to the administrative headquarters of the HTO in Ciechanow. And there on the street in front of the building he saw Rachel Baum, waiting for her father who was inside settling the seasonal delivery of grain from his warehouse to the confiscating agents of the HTO. Bracht stopped, asked the girl her name, demanded to see her identity card, and went into the building. That was all that happened then, but knowing what is known of *der Affe,* it is now obvious that the rest of what was to occur followed from that chance meeting as inevitably as does the night the day.

That night Bracht addressed a meeting of the German personnel stationed in the Ciechanow area. He spent an hour or two after that doing some convivial drinking with his compatriots. Then, together with his chauffeur-bodyguard Martin Krause, he came to the Baums' home. And there Fritz Bracht raped Rachel Baum and when her father came at him with a knife snatched from the kitchen, Bracht shot and killed him.

All passion spent, there was time then for Bracht to contemplate the shambles wrought in the course of his night's amusement and to consider the possibility, remote but worrisome, that some embarrassment might arise therefrom. Bracht seems to have had all the characteristic German concern for *Ordnung* usefully wedded to the cagey ingenuity of the professional pimp, and so in due course a solution that would leave everything all neat and tidy suggested itself. While Martin Krause remained behind to watch the weeping women in the Baum home, Bracht paid a call on Arpad Wigand, the Gestapo commander for the Ciechanow area. The nature of Wigand's job rendered him unshockable and in any case he was not one to make difficulties for a party comrade simply because the poor unfortunate had been tempted from the paths of absolute rectitude. Matters progressed satisfactorily. Hirsz Baum's name was put on an arrest warrant charging him with sabotage. The fact that he had been killed resisting the arrest was then set down on the proper form and under the required seal and became, thereby, recorded truth. Then the deportation order was made out against the survivors of the Baum family as a normal warning to other would-be saboteurs. This much was merely an act of glowing brotherhood undertaken to solve Bracht's personal problem. No one knows which of the two buddies thought of expanding this into an aktion to deport a hundred other people, or whether this was intended to cover the matter of the Baums, or whether it was—simply—that the bureaucratic mind was offended at the inefficiency of wasting manpower and transport on the deportation of only three women. Whatever the motive, by the time Fritz Bracht left Ciechanow that afternoon, presumably with a relieved mind and a clear conscience, Hirsz Baum's body had been shoved into the Polish earth; and Malka Baum, her raped daughter Rachel, and the child—Hannah—not yet sixteen, together with a hundred other women of Ciechanow, were all on their way to Birkenau, which contained the women's camp at Auschwitz.

So it happened that the evil that had passed by Rachel Baum in August 1931, when her beauty so entranced the mad Jan Mielecz that he could do her no harm, came to her in April 1943 at the hands of a beast less enchanted —the Nazi ape, *der Affe* Fritz Bracht. And the girl, whom her neighbors in their peasant imaginings had thought of as "under the protection," was thrust from the shelter of such benign and primitive fantasy, shoved out into the real world of nightmare fashioned for the Jews of Europe by the advanced thinkers of the Third German Reich. . . .

On the morning of April 14, the people deported from Ciechanow arrived at the Auschwitz-Birkenau camp as part of a transport of a thousand Jews packed into ten freight cars. Enroute they had been shunted aside to make way for Wehrmacht trains, and what with this and other wartime confusions they'd been zigzagging down through Poland for three days and nights. There were no sanitary facilities and very little air in the sealed freight cars. There was no room to rest, no room to move, they stood all this time in their own filth, clawing at each other— the stronger ones—in the claustrophobic fight to get a little space or to win a place close to the sides of the freight cars where the cracks let in a little air. And during these three days and nights they had, of course, been given no food or water. So when the doors were slid open inside the fenced station at Auschwitz, a good part of the cargo of stinking wretches consisted of people dead or dying or vomitously ill.

The dead were no problem. A line of carts, with camp inmates harnessed to them, was waiting at the siding and the SS guards compelled the newcomers to dump their dead companions on the carts which were then dragged out of sight behind the station wall and some distance to a line of open pits. The corpses were thrown into the pits, sprayed with kerosene, and set on fire.

The dead were no problem, but the sick and the dying required a slightly different procedure, a humane intermediary stage. The people were all ordered to stand. Those unable to do so unaided were helped to their feet by another squad of veteran inmates and, accompanied by a few guards, were led away "to the hospital." The phrase was the first the new arrivals heard of those comforting euphemisms that comprised the special glossary of the death camps. The stumbling invalids were then led to the same burning pits and were there shot. That made them dead and they could then be processed in the normal fashion.

Among those so processed was Malka Baum, not sick so much as numbed and drained of life-force by the shock of her sudden and violent widowhood.

After the essential preliminaries, the rest of the reception procedure went smoothly and very quickly. The people were lined up for a "medical inspection" that would determine their "work assignments" at the camp. There was no difficulty. The machine gunners in the towers and the armed guards who moved among them were enough to discourage any recalcitrants within the bewildered mob. And though it was all pretty frightening, the inspection for work assignments seemed reasonable enough under the big sign that spanned the camp gateway and spelled out the placid homily: *Arbeit Macht Frei*— "Work Creates Freedom." There were five inspectors: Josef Mengele, Heinz Thilo, Bruno Kitt, Edmund König, Friedrich Entress, and they were indeed all doctors— although any comfort the patients may have taken from the doctors' presumed adherence to the Hippocratic oath was probably vitiated by the fact that the five physicians all wore the black uniforms and the Death's Head emblems of the dreaded SS. Nevertheless, no one was in a position to protest, and the newcomers passed before the five doctors in under fifteen minutes. The young ones and those in pretty good condition were kept in the lines. The others were sent to one side, gathered into groups, told they were fit "for light work only" and were then led off "to the showers." Everyone now knows that these shower rooms were the gas chambers where Zyklon B sprayed down from the deceptive nozzles as the victims strangled, fell, and lay befouled by the spasms of their profane and agonizing death until they were dragged off to the final searing cleansing of the cremating ovens. The whole world knows this now, but Rachel Baum and Hannah and the rest of them huddled in the Auschwitz station didn't know it, not then; and those who were sent "to the showers" went willingly enough, only uneasy about whatever delay there might be before they would be permitted to rejoin parent or child or husband or wife.

When the dead and the dying and those fit "for light work only" had been cared for, there remained on the long platform about six or seven hundred of the thousand who had arrived at Auschwitz not more than an hour before. These were counted and divided again, male and female set apart, and marched off through the camp to the barracks sheds.

One may assume they gawked about them, affrighted,

There was fear enough to be drawn from the quick-caught glimpses of the inmates past whom they marched—men clothed in crusted rags, their eyes sick and sunken in faces starved down to the fundamental bone, shambling and skeletal, reeking with dysentery, filthy, their sackings of loose skin leaking pus from boils and ulcerating sores— the sturdy SS guards, even the hungry newcomers themselves, a ripple of obscene well-being in this ocean of pain.

The setting, too, was suited to the store of human misery it contained. Auschwitz-Birkenau squatted within a soggy neck of unhealthy marshland between the Sola and Vistula rivers. Thirty-four thousand slaves had begun building the camp in June 1940. Within six months a third of these had sweated their lives away, dead of malnutrition and malaria, dead and buried where they had fallen, mixed with the thousands of tons of crushed rock used to fill in the pestilent swamps. By the time Rachel and Hannah Baum were taken to Auschwitz, the three main camps spread over more than twenty square miles and the work of expansion was still going on so that in 1943 the construction program took another 2,976,380 man-days worked and another four thousand lives.[50]

The entire camp area was surrounded by an electrified barbed-wire fence twelve feet high. A pole topped by a floodlight stood by every hundred yards. Every four hundred yards there was a guard tower with a machine gun snouting down. Beyond the fence, outside the twenty square miles, was a bleak perimeter a quarter mile deep, bulldozed flat, offering no shadow of scrub that might shelter an escaping prisoner. At the western edge of this blasted area there was a fringe of trees marking the SS picnic grounds, a mirage of green paradise encircled by barbed wire and seen from hell. The only other things that relieved the murky gray were the red brick walls of the crematoria and the formal flower beds, fertilized by an experimental mash of human blood and ground bone, that surrounded the commandant's home and two other buildings. One of these was the hospital for the administrative and guard personnel. The other contained

the headquarters of the Politische Abteilung, the Political
Department run by SS Untersturmführer Ernst Grabner
who was in charge of rooting out any resistance plots
within the camp. It was pleasant for Grabner's men, working in the underground interrogation chambers, to be able
to relax for a moment and smell the scent of roses drifting through the slit windows from the flower beds outside. No doubt it was also pleasant for the prisoners, once
they had been released for a time from the iron boot
and the thumbscrew.

These flashes of relieving color apart, all else at Auschwitz was gray: the fog seeping in from the swamps, the
greasy smoke curling up from the crematoria chimneys,
the weathered wood of the barracks sheds, the gray stone
and concrete of the factories. And the prisoners, too, were
gray; their faces ashen, bleached by fear, by hunger and
fatigue, by the creeping death that was upon them all.

In 1943, the Auschwitz-Birkenau complex contained a
quarter of a million prisoners. For most of that year and
the next about eight thousand people were killed at
Auschwitz every day; but the trains dragging the packed
freight cars came in day and night and the inmate population remained roughly constant. Guarding this shifting
mass were 5800 of the SS, including 400 of the Helferinnen—the armed women's auxiliaries. There were
850 Polish and Ukrainian fascists, and 250 dogs. Counting the four-footed killers, this made a guard total of only
6900 to hold down a quarter of a million people. In all
truth it was a difficult task, though not quite as bad as the
statistics alone would indicate. The electrified fence that
killed on contact was a big help in preventing escapes.
The prisoners were a mob, and diseased, starved, afraid.
The guards suffered none of these disabilities and they
were disciplined and armed. The machine gun, the pistol,
the club, are great instruments for cutting down the odds.
And the guards had help inside the fences.

There were five thousand German professional criminals serving sentences at Auschwitz, a group apart. Pimps,
perverts, thieves, murderers, they were nevertheless all

FOUR FROM THE FURNACE

geborene Übermenschen—born members of the master race—and the rest of the imprisoned quarter of a million were to their twisted minds as dirt beneath their Aryan feet. By profession, inclination, and birth, these were allies of the SS; and they helped run the camp. It was from among the German criminals that the SS appointed most of the Block Älteste and the Capos who worked as camp police, supervised the inmates' barracks. Under the 180 German civilian employees of the I. G. Farbenindustrie and Krupp and the Bunawerke Rubber Company, the Älteste and the Capos controlled the thousands of prisoners who worked as slaves to the mutual profit of these pillars of present-day German industry and of the SS which collected payment for the slave labor.[51] The Älteste and the Capos were hyenas only—carrion eaters to the killing SS—but like the hyena, themselves capable of killing when the prey was weak and the risk nonexistent; and in Auschwitz the prey was plentiful and helpless. There were many ways these hyenas could contrive the death of a man. They could club him to death; they could put him on the punishment list and have him whipped to death, or gassed or shot; they could report him to the Politische Abteilung and have him tortured to death as a member of the resistance; they could deprive him of his rations and he would starve to death; they could assign him to the construction gangs where no man lasted more than two months; they could send him to the crews filling in the swamps and malaria would kill him.

And then, finally, the SS could count on many hundreds of prisoners who were wicked or weak, and who would, out of fear or for the reward of easier work or an extra day of life or an extra piece of bread, be Judases to their fellows.

But despite the fear of death, the leaden apathy imposed by disease and hunger, by isolation and the absence of hope, despite all the terrible apparatus of oppression and betrayal—in all the history of Auschwitz there was no single day without some act or movement of resistance glimmering in the brutal dark as testimony to the awesome dignity of man.

It began at Auschwitz before there was an Auschwitz, when the place was only a cluster of Polish cavalry stables—long abandoned—rotting at the edge of the swamps beyond the village whose Polish name is Oswiecim. On June 14, 1940, the first consignment of 700 slaves arrived from Krakow to build the camp. Filthy and confused and hungry, they filed past Rudolf Franz Ferdinand Hoess—the camp commandant, and past SS Brigadier General Erich von dem Bach-Zelewski—the Prussian nobleman whose inspired vision had birthed the concept of Auschwitz. As the story is handed down in the unwritten record, one of the slaves—his name unknown—stumbled and fell against Bach-Zelewski, who struck him. The man staggered, pulled himself erect and spat in Bach-Zelewski's face; and was shot on the spot. Bach-Zelewski is alive and respected in West Germany and peacefully cultivates the rose gardens that surround his villa at Lauffenau; and the other man is dead and long part of the Oswiecim swamps. But one is a murdering dog, and the other—nameless—is the first of the heroes of Auschwitz.

In the same group from Krakow was a man whose name we know—Tadeusz Wiejowski, a shoemaker, fifty-one years old. Nothing in Wiejowski's life before had fitted him for leadership, but within three weeks he had a plant and people, and on July 6—under cover of a stage riot—Wiejowski and twenty-four others pulled down a section of the temporary stockade and disappeared into the Polish countryside.[52] Hoess and Bach-Zelewski put five hundred men into the area and for two weeks they tortured everyone in and out of the camp who might possibly have had a hand in the escape. Neither Wiejowski nor any of the others was taken, and all that was left for the SS was reprisal. On July 22, 1940, Bach-Zelewski ordered the execution of eighty-five of the Auschwitz prisoners and the deportation of every Pole living within a 2½-mile radius of the camp.[53] After that, the guards were increased and later the electrified fence went up and there were no more successful group escapes. But by then resistance was alive in the minds of the Auschwitz slaves and there were always to be men and women there who were unwilling just to hold still and die.

For a long time, the most effective of the continuing resistance groups was that of the Communists, led by Heinz Dirmeyer. Dirmeyer had been an observant Catholic and a Social Democrat in Vienna, where he was born. But on February 12, 1934, the fascist Catholic Chancellor Engelbert Dollfuss joined together 17,000 government troops and 3000 Austrian Nazis and they attacked the workers' housing projects which were the center of Social Democratic strength in Vienna. Five thousand citizens were killed or wounded that day, the Social Democrats were smashed, and the road was opened to the inevitable Austro-German Anschluss. In all this destruction, the Austrian Catholic hierarchy saw only the triumph of godliness over the forces of radical atheism. That day marked the end of Austrian democracy and it marked, also, the end of Heinz Dirmeyer's adherence to the Church and to political moderation. Two years later he was a Communist and a major in the International Brigade of volunteers fighting for Republican Spain. In the battles for University Hill outside Madrid he was taken prisoner by the Franco forces and turned over to the German Condor Legion that fought for the fascists.

Nothing more was heard of Dirmeyer until he showed up in the Dachau concentration camp in September 1938. By then the Gestapo had held him for more than six months and he was almost unrecognizable. For the next two years he was in and out of the punishment cells at Dachau and Sachsenhausen, but they didn't kill him and that was a mistake. In mid-1941 he was brought to Auschwitz, and he, Josef Cyrankiewicz (who later was to become a premier of Poland), and the Jewish Communist Bruno Baum began to build the Communist underground.

And about this time, too, the Jews began to organize.

In those early days, Auschwitz was not a killing ground. It was a slave-labor camp, established to fill the expanding needs of Krupp's Union Fuse & Explosives Company and the I. G. Farben factories. Men and women did die there, by the thousands every month, but this was only

incidental to the camp's purpose. As in the ghettos, so
in the camps, the German aim was not yet openly defined as the annihilation of millions. It appeared to be
merely—if so diminutive a term can be used—the enslavement of millions. So in this period of resistance, for
Jews and Communists alike, there was the "white resistance" of the ghettos. The clandestine organizations in
the camps struggled to keep their people alive, and human. They stole extra rations from the camp storehouses.
They stole medicines. They hid the sick who would otherwise be automatically executed as no longer economically
exploitable. They bribed the SS men and the Älteste
and the Capos to assign their people to work that would
not so quickly kill them. They jockeyed and conspired
for such positions of minor influence as were open to
inmates and could be used to protect others. They organized clandestine lectures, smuggled in radios or built
them with stolen parts, so they might keep open some listening post to the world beyond the fences.

Jews and Communists, each in their own way, did what
they could to delay the inevitable decline of human beings into what the Germans wanted them to become:
cattle, numb, brutalized, without purpose or hope.

The risk for both the underground organizations was,
as it was everywhere, very great. The punishment was
death.

The punishment for resistance was the same for Jews
and Communists. The kind of risk was the same and the
same heroism was required to accept it. But there were
differences in degree, and the percentage of risk was higher for the Jews. In part, this disparity arose from the
divergence of their backgrounds. The Communists in
Auschwitz came from countries in which, by 1941, they'd
had long experience as outlaws; they knew how to organize clandestine activity. Dirmeyer and his associates
built their organization according to the established Communist pattern, in cells of not more than ten members
each, with only trusted and experienced comrades assigned to the liaison work between groups, and with only
the few top leaders holding ultimate knowledge of the

whole organization. The Jews were less disciplined and less experienced. These factors alone increased the risk. But the major element of difference between the Jewish and the Communist undergrounds lay within their differing concepts of the role of resistance. The Communist leaders saw their task within the framework of political fraternity, they worked with and for the *Communists* within the camp, then numbering less than four thousand. The resistant Jews identified themselves with *all* their co-religionists, they worked for and with all their people; and nearly two-thirds of the 67,000 prisoners at Auschwitz in 1941 were Jews. And so, inevitably, the Jewish organization was the more exposed, and suffered more. Within the final three months of 1941, for example, informers twice betrayed parts of the Jewish underground to Ernst Grabner's *Politische Abteilung*. Finally, on December 12, 1941, Grabner's men took thirty Jews into the main camp compound and hanged them. Among this thirty were all the leaders of the Jewish resistance group, and the organization was broken.

Until June 1942.

In June 1942, the German armies of the east held a line across Russia from Leningrad and the Gulf of Finland in the north to within reach of the Caspian Sea. Behind this line, sixty million Russians and all the peoples of eastern Europe lay captive to the Third Reich. Within this helpless and surrendered territory there were six million Jews, and the Germans had been busy killing them. Although a quarter of a million Jews had been murdered in wild pogroms within the ghettos, most of the work of slaughter was done outside the ghettos by the four Einsatzgruppen, the special commando forces that roamed all the eastern areas under the protection of the Wehrmacht and whose diligence had by then accounted for a million Jewish dead.

Despite this considerable accomplishment, and despite the sustained and selfless devotion of all the men engaged in killing the Jews, it had long been evident that the methods used were not commensurate to the task and that they were wasteful of manpower, ammunition, and other resources which could otherwise contribute even more directly to winning the war. There seems to have been no disagreement within the German hierarchy as to the paramount necessity for butchering the Jews—indeed, in mid-summer 1941, the Germans had officially embarked upon what they called "the final solution of the Jewish problem" (which was total extermination)—the problem was merely a technical one of ways and means. By August of that year, the problem had yielded to German national genius. The name of the hero who first thought of reversing the previous system and of bringing the victims to the killers is unknown and he remains, alas, unrewarded. But the man who followed this conceptual breakthrough with the idea of building special camps in which to kill the Jews by poison gas was the chief physician of the SS, Gruppenführer Dr. Ernst Grawitz, who was persuaded to commit suicide in 1945 by Hannah Baum, Rachel's little sister.

Dr. Grawitz's idea was welcomed by all those burdened with the civilizing task of rendering Europe *Judenrein* (Jew-free) and by June 1942 there were six such death camps operating in Poland alone: Chelmno, Belzec, Treblinka, Lublin, Sobibor, and—the largest of them all —Auschwitz. In these camps nearly four million Jews were ultimately gathered together, stripped of everything conceivably useful to the German economy (quite literally from the hair on their heads to the shoes on their feet, or their artificial limbs), and killed by Zyklon B gas— a derivative of hydrogen cyanide which, out of patriotism and for profit, was manufactured and sold to the concentration camp administration of the SS at the rate of 150 tons a year by subsidiaries of the I. G. Farben, Degussa, Goldschmidt, and Tesch und Stabenow Internationale consortium.[54] While awaiting their turn in the gas chambers, the Jews worked as slaves for the enrichment of the nation that was killing them; and even after their death, the fat was rendered from the bodies of many of them for soap and industrial lubricants and their bones were mashed for chemical fertilizer. It was a miracle of maximum utilization unsurpassed in the history of even the German people, justly famed as they are for energy and efficiency.

There were, it is true, some disadvantages to the system but these must be accounted as relatively minor. Most important, perhaps, was the irritating inconvenience that once the killing centers were fully operative it proved impossible to maintain the illusion and camouflage that had masked the full meaning of Germany's "final solution of the Jewish problem" and had helped keep the Jews largely docile while awaiting their deaths. The Einsatzgruppen, which had previously done most of the killing, had worked deep in the forests or in the hinterlands and —except for the killers themselves—few witnesses survived, and fewer still of these remained sane enough to bring credible testimony to alert the ghettos. There had already been thousands of Jews killed in the ghettos themselves, but these killings had been at least partly explained away by the Germans as spontaneous pogroms or acts of harsh reprisal. With the death camps functioning, the Jews finally understood the unbelievable truth that what they faced was not mindless savagery, not the slavery of the "work camps," but planned and pitiless extinction. This realization changed the structure of Jewish resistance. The clandestine organizations that smuggled food and medicines and tried to keep alive the Jewish identity in the ghettos and the camps did continue. They were never to stop until the collapse of the Third Reich, but for many Jews this protective "white resistance" was no longer the front line of struggle. The "black resistance" emerged, having as its aims the raising of revolts and the killing of Germans. For this new work a new Jewish leadership came into being. Men and women—for the most part young and for the most part Zionist—began to take the places that had for centuries been reserved to the elders, the teachers, the revered rabbis. It was they who built the loose confederation they called the Jewish Fighters' Organization.

During the spring and summer of 1942, the Jewish Fighters' Organization decided to send some of their people into the very mouths of the furnaces, to the death camps themselves. The men who volunteered for this task arranged to be included within the deportations from the ghettos to the camps. The theory was that these people, being young and strong and able to work hard, would not soon be selected for the gas chambers and that, therefore, they would have time to organize a fighting resistance within the camps. And so, indeed, it did happen.

The volunteers came into Auschwitz during the early months of 1942—Mordechai Bielowicz-Hilleli, Leibel Braun, and Noah Zablodowicz. They began rebuilding the Jewish resistance organization which had been destroyed when its betrayed leaders were executed on December 12, 1941. By June, these three men—together with Israel Guttman and Judah Laufer—headed a group of three hundred men. Soon after, the Jews made the first hesitant contacts—through the Jewish Communist Bruno Baum—with the commanders of the Communist resistance. In July, the Jews and the Communists joined together to form the General Underground Organization, and to plan a mass revolt at Auschwitz.

It was all very difficult. The leaders were scattered throughout the whole vast complex of the Auschwitz camps and even minimal contact involved great risk. The German spy system among the inmates was well organized, and though some informers were ferreted out and isolated and accidental deaths arranged for the most dangerous ones, this critical problem could never be completely solved. Little by little, by bribery and maneuvering, the organization's command group got a few of its people into useful positions within the camp administration. Men working as tally clerks, recording the statistics of death, recruited men within the sonderkommandos—the isolated groups of inmates who staffed the gas chambers and the crematoria under SS supervision. Others infiltrated the labor gangs clearing the malarial swamps outside the camps and were finally able to establish a tenuous contact with a small band of partisans in the neighboring forest. From the partisans they got parts for a radio, seven pistols, two hundred rounds of ammunition. At night, in burrows dug secretly under the stinking latrines, they made clubs, sandbags, crude knives of scrap metal, crafting all those primitive tools which are the weaponry of an underground without resources. Three attempts to burglarize the SS arsenals failed and the men involved were taken into the cellars of Ernst Grabner's *Politische Abteilung* and managed, somehow, to keep their mouths shut until they were released by death.

It was so slow. With all the painful, dangerous effort, the miserable pile of junk that was their weapons grew hardly at all. And all the time, there were a thousand inmates—all of them Jews—who every day handled enough explosives to blow up Auschwitz.

Just across the railroad track from the main Auschwitz camps was Birkenau, fenced and guarded as was Auschwitz itself. Isolated within Birkenau, behind its own fence and the patrols of the Helferinnen—the SS armed women's auxiliary—was the women's camp, with forty thousand inmates. And inside that, another fence—this one patrolled by SS men—and beyond all that stood the squat, ugly buildings of Krupp's Union Fuse Company in which a thousand women inmates, under heavy guard, mixed and packed high explosive for the Wehrmacht.

For nearly a year the weaponless men of the resistance gazed at the Union as men dying of thirst watch the river just beyond their reach. But there was no contact between the men and women at Auschwitz, and even among the women those who worked at the Union were kept separate. There was no way. And if there were? If a message could be sent to the women behind the fences and the guards, then send it to whom? Who among these separated, unknown, unknowable and nameless women could be trusted, trusted automatically, without previous contact, without discussion, without checking?

And so it stood. Until at last someone remembered recognizing Rachel Baum among the women of Ciechanow who had been marched—that day in April 1943—through the main Auschwitz camp into Birkenau.

Noah Zablodowicz, in the Jewish command, knew Rachel—they'd been delegates to the Zionist General

Council of Poland from the Zionist youth movement, Hashomer Hatzair, the Young Guards. Zablodowicz knew Rachel; they had someone now, among the unknown women, who was known and could be trusted. They had an address, now, for a message—if they could get it through.

They got it through. It was easy. Zablodowicz went to an SS Oberleutnant whose soft heart could be moved to grant small favors for large bribes. This time the bribe was a handful of gold teeth, concealed by the men of the sonderkommandos whose job it was to wrench them from the mouths of the corpses before they shoveled them into the ovens. And the favor? So small. Only to see that this hoarded tin of sardines got to Zablodowicz's fiancée, Rachel Baum, somewhere in Birkenau. And if, from time to time, there were other messages, other innocent tokens that passed between the despairing lovers, why the man who passed them would profit greatly—there were other gold teeth to be gotten, perhaps a watch, maybe even a diamond ring; and what was the harm?

And so it was done, the coded Hebrew writing under the label. Rachel could be depended upon to find it and to understand. Back came a message, there were more bribes, and a way was open. Rachel Baum began to organize the women in Birkenau, and her little sister Hannah, who worked at the Union, began to smuggle out explosives—a handful at a time, in small sacks slung in her armpits, or between her legs. A little at a time, and that little growing as Hannah organized the women in the powder-mixing room. So now they had gunpowder and some of the new plastic explosive in the women's section of Birkenau; and it had to be gotten out from there to the underground command group in Auschwitz. This, too, was easy. Rachel's women stole cloth from the tailor shop in which they made uniforms for the SS and holiday dresses for the Helferinnen. Out of this they made caps for their "men friends" across the way. The caps went an established route—a few at a time—via the woman in the SS Helferinnen who was the Oberleutnant's girl, and from him to Noah Zablodowicz for "distribution." And each of these little morale builders carried in its folds a few precious grams of explosive. Did the SS man know? He knew or chose not to know. By then he was caught, he'd been taking bribes for a long time and his neck was as much in the hands of the Jews as theirs were in his. And, besides, he was getting rich.

With what they got from Rachel and Hannah Baum's women, with hoarded tin cans and a curious collection of metal scraps, the underground organization made bombs and even grenades—out of a section of sewage pipe "liberated" by some enterprising ganef—three crude bangalore torpedoes which they thought would be useful in blowing out the gates.

The months went by, it all took time, and they had no time. It was beginning winter of 1944 and the gas chambers were spewing out six thousand corpses a day and among these, every day, were some of the members of the resistance. The pressure upon the organization's leaders was very great; the men in the underground didn't want to die that way, they wanted to die fighting. They had joined the organization to kill Germans. Well, wasn't it time?

No, it wasn't time, not yet. The partisans in the forest had agreed to coordinate a flash raid on the camp when the revolt was triggered; but the partisans weren't ready, and the underground command in the camp waited for them and held against the pressure from below. . . .

And then it all fell apart.

Early in the morning of October 26, 1944, the six hundred sonderkommandos who worked in the enclosed area of the gas chambers and the crematoria learned that two-thirds of their number were to be included in the next day's gassing. In a flare of desperation they rose then, that same day, thinking to force the command group's hand and start the general revolt. They had no way to get a message through quickly, but they had a way to let the whole underground know. Long before, the sonderkommandos had mined the crematorium buildings; now they touched them off. Crematorium no. 4 was totally destroyed, and 2 and 3 partly so; and within minutes six hundred men were killing the SS guards and the seared bodies piled up as the prisoners tried to pull down the electrified fence that separated the killing area from the rest of the camp.

The explosion roused the camp and nearly a thousand men of the underground risked their lives to race for the places where the weapons were hidden, but the guards were shooting at every moving man and the arcs of machine-gun fire set bullet fences across the camp compounds. Six members of the command group were killed where they ran and the others decided in desperate haste that the revolt, raised thus unprepared, could only fail in a massive slaughter. This hard judgment made, they sent back their men and watched in shuddering pain the terrible result of their agonized decision.

The sonderkommandos were butchered. Two thousand SS men swarmed into the camps. In the confusion, a hundred or so prisoners managed their individual escapes. And at the end of the day, there were 1100 inmates dead, killed by the raging SS men in a wild revenge for their thirty casualties.

Now the wolves descended upon the women of Birkenau.

For the SS the question was: Where did the explosives come from that the sonderkommandos had used? And with the arsenals intact, there could be only one obvious answer. So Untersturmführer Ernst Grabner went into the Birkenau camp, behind the three isolating fences, to the women who slaved in Baron Krupp's Union Fuse Company—Ernst Grabner and the talented men of his Politische Abteilung, that innocently named "Political Department" whose research techniques were those of the Spanish Inquisition.

Eighty women were selected at random from the thousand who worked in the factory, were taken into the cellars of the *Politische Abteilung*, and there put to the rack—no euphemism, this, they were put to the rack. And among these—what wonder?—there were those who knew something and who, their bodies broken, their bones pulled from the sockets, told what they knew.

There were five names gasped out or screamed out of the torn mouths, five named as leaders of the women's underground at Birkenau. Miraculously not "the little sister"—Hannah; but the miracle didn't extend to Rachel Baum who was no longer, as of old, "under the protection."

They took Rachel then, and the other four, to the dungeons beneath Block 2 of Auschwitz Lager I and left them there overnight. They brought them out in the winter dawn, stripped them naked, and whipped them past the thousands of men standing for the morning roll call to where Ernst Grabner was waiting for them.

What happened to the five of them is known,[55] and the world has no right not to know. This is what happened:

On the first day, two women died; one when she sucked in the flames of the blowtorch held, for a careless second, too near her face. The others, that day, were not tortured, but one died of heart failure as she watched. At the evening roll call, the three women were marched back again—past the inmate thousands—to their dungeons.

On the second morning it was the same, the women naked under the whips, past the watchers, to the waiting torturers. No one died that second day, and the women came back—all three of them, staggering now, holding before them their bloody hands, crushed.

And on the third morning . . . nothing. The thousands formed, and were made to wait. But no one came from the dungeons, and the prisoners were sent to work, to wonder: Were they dead? Or had they broken? Ernst Grabner was a clever, subtle man, but his cleverness was to earn him nothing that day. What he earned, he was given; but that was later.

The women weren't dead and they hadn't broken. They were there the next morning, for the same savage parade.

Only Rachel returned that fourth evening. Not walking. Dragged by the SS men, her mangled foot dribbling blood on the frozen ground.

From the time the women had first been taken,

the underground command had tried to reach them, using the now-terrified SS Lieutenant as intermediary between them and the dungeon guards they had to bribe. On the fourth night, it was arranged. Mordechai Bielowicz-Hilleli went out with another man, carrying knives, and the orders to help Rachel to an easier death. Whether they got there, and what happened if they did, is not of record. They didn't get back. The SS men who dragged Rachel out of the dungeons the next morning also carried two stiffening bodies and flung them on the ground so the prisoners could see the wounds the dogs had torn.

That evening, the prisoners stood again with their eyes fixed in dreadful anticipation upon the iron doors behind which the torturers worked. The doors didn't open. No one came. Then, from among the now-weeping thousands, there came a shuddering sigh of dreadful release, and after this—first the whisper and then the full-throated, somehow defiant chant: *Yis-gah-dahl, v'yis-kah-dahsh, shemay rah-boh*—"Be great and be holy, O Lord, our God." . . . The mourners' lament, in Aramaic, older even than the ancient Hebrew tongue itself, the ageless unquenchable adoration given by the Jew—in the presence of death, on behalf of the loved dead—to the living God. . . .

But it was too soon. The thing was not yet done.

On the morning of the sixth day, when they came out of the tiered hovels in which they slept, there was a gallows in the broad bare yard; a gallows, and in front of it—machine guns and a line of SS riflemen. The prisoners knew then that it was not yet finished, it would be finished now.

The distant iron door opened then and out she came, on a litter, carried carefully, the burden was fragile and had to serve their final instructive purpose. They carried her up to the gallows platform and set her down on it, the tramping boots and the warning snick of rifle bolts the only sound in that cold damned dawn.

She stood. This torn body stood. Raised on the strength of her *own* purpose, Rachel Baum stood and looked out over the massed prisoners, seeking a face she could not find nor—finding—see. And called out: "Hannah! Little sister! Avenge me!"

They hanged her then.

And they forgot Hannah, the little sister of Rachel Baum; forgot and left her alive. To join, one day—with Malachi Wald. . . .

Arnie Berg and the Silver Spoon

Arnold David Berg was in trouble from the beginning—he was born to a family of maiden aunts. He had a father and mother, of course. It made no difference. That was only an accident of sex and status; in all psychological and behavioral traits his parents, too, could qualify as maiden aunts. In addition, his father had two unmarried sisters. His mother's sister had been married, but only briefly. The misadventure had had little affect on her and was, in the loving atmosphere that enveloped them all, never mentioned.

The boy was born to another burden: the Bergs were rich. The money came originally from an ancestor who had shipped as a surgeon with the American privateer Joshua Barney, and had proved so talented a bloodletter that he'd set up in the business for himself. Dr. Solomon Bergsturm collected enough loot so that the quantity, in due course, obscured the origins; and by the time Arnold was born, this somewhat violent chapter in the family history was so overlaid by the patina of age and discretion that only the glint of gold showed through. In time, also, the family name was shortened to Berg. This act of obscurantism apparently exhausted the energies of the original hell raiser's descendants, for nothing else that they did seems to have been deserving of note—until Arnie arrived.

Arnie was conceived during what must be described as an excess of emotion attendant upon his father's return from the wars. The war was the First World War and Mr. Berg had spent four difficult months as a welfare officer attached to the Paris headquarters of the American Expeditionary Forces, then he was sent home to recuperate. By the time Arnie was old enough to toddle about under the watchful eyes of his mother, his French governess, and three doting aunts, things were back to normal and in the Poughkeepsie mansion no sounds were heard more passionate than the tinkle of feminine laughter and the occasional chortles emitted by Papa Berg as he sat in the library and gloated over his stamp collection.

Somehow, within these pastel surroundings, Arnie developed into a shocking throwback to his cutlass-wielding ancestor. By the age of sixteen, he was six-foot-one and had a frame like a standing oak and a face to match. In due course his appearance, already regrettable, was rendered even more inelegant by the bent nose and sundry scars he acquired on the football fields and in the wrestling rings of the fancy schools he attended; and his voice developed into a rumble that sounded, in his home, like an out-of-tune tuba smuggled into a chamber-music recital. He was clearly a misfit and his family knew it, but he was theirs and they did their best with him.

Each year, from the time Arnie was nine years old, the Berg entourage trundled off on the accustomed grand tour of Europe. Their time abroad was spent in a series of hushed pilgrimages to the usual art centers and the accepted watering places and, of course, to the great cathedrals. They didn't get to any synagogues; it was not the fashion; the Bergs were Jewish, but not very; and in any case, they were unaware of any Jewish equivalent of the Sistine Chapel and what they reverenced was Culture, not God. Whatever piety was involved in their annual hegira was contained in the pious hope that some refinement might rub off on the overgrown oaf they had sired. They were continuously disappointed. Arnie bore it all with an impatience that increased each year, and hurried home to the bone-crushing tackles and the elbows in the groin and all the other pleasures of close-combat sports from which he derived his uncomplicated satisfactions.

It went on like this until Arnie was eighteen. Then there was a change.

In the quiet of Mr. Berg's library, the sounds of distress occasioned by the 1929 stock-market debacle and the resultant depression had passed unheard; and it wasn't until 1935 that the family noticed that, comparatively speaking, they were short of money. It was a disaster kept, in accordance with the Berg tradition, within genteel proportions. The mansion was sold; the family moved into a somewhat smaller house with a considerably reduced staff; Mr. Berg disposed of the more valuable items in his stamp collection; and life continued. Even in these straitened circumstances they were managing pretty well and there was no suggestion of anybody going to work. So when Arnie announced his determination to find a job during his school vacation, his parents were opposed. His father developed the interesting thesis that if Arnie went to work he would be depriving someone who really needed the paycheck and that, therefore, his project was essentially unpatriotic; but the argument fell on deaf ears and they had what passed in their quiet household for a terrible quarrel.

Arnie stormed out of the house and in the classic tradition of the American runaway headed for the golden west.

There were about twelve million unemployed in America in those days, and a lot of them were also beating their way to California, but Arnie didn't see them. Those who took the train, as he did, sneaked into freight cars or rode the rods under the coaches, and they kept wary eyes peeled for the railroad police. Arnie traveled first class and looked at the pretty girls.

In the 1930s there was an established routine for handling the hordes of migrants drifting across America in pursuit of the will-o'-the-wisp of work. Each state shunted them across to the next state which moved them to the next one and so, by the natural law of drift, they ultimately piled up in the peripheral areas of the eastern, southern, and western seaboards, like sand against a seawall. Once there, they were rounded up by the police at the railroad yards or the various city limits and booted into shanty towns. These were festering communities which sprang up outside the larger cities and were usually located in the midst of the municipal garbage dumps.

So it was that the train bringing Arnie Berg to Los Angeles, that June day in 1936, also brought the customary complement of freeloaders. By the time he was snuggled in at the Hollywood-Knickerbocker Hotel, the bellhops provided by the sheriff's office had escorted his erstwhile fellow travelers to their accommodations some twelve miles from where Arnie slept. The distance between them was to be spanned in three weeks.

In that amount of time, Arnie exhausted the employment possibilities in Los Angeles, and had slid down the hotel scale from the Hollywood-Knickerbocker to the "hot-bed" joints on Skid Row—where for fifteen cents he was entitled to provide eight hours' sustenance in a twenty-four-hour meal enjoyed by the bedbugs. He had also considered, and stubbornly rejected, the possibility of amending the optimistic fiction of his letters home and sending a straightforward appeal for help. He was left then with two possibilities—panhandling or stealing. In the area in which he found himself, though, the competition was keen in both professions and the pickings lean; so he headed back toward the more prosperous sections of the city, thinking that he could argue out the ethics for himself en route. This was a mistake he would not have made had he not been, at the time, still an amateur. It was the unwritten law everywhere in America then that the poor were to be meek and the destitute invisible, and like most unwritten laws this was enforced more rigorously than any on the statute books. In Los Angeles the line at which the invisible became visible—and thus offensive—was drawn north of Main Street and west of Figueroa. As soon as Arnie shuffled over the border there were two policemen to help him count his money and, when this took an insufficient amount of time, to escort him to a night's residence in the city clink. There he was given a no-mattress bunk and plate of beans and he said to himself gleefully, "How long has this been going on?!" He figured he now had it made; he could stand it as long as they could, and he was saving money every day. . . . Silly boy.

The next morning, he was fingerprinted, mugged, taken

before a judge paralyzed with boredom, pleaded guilty
to vagrancy, happily received a sentence of thirty days
in jail, indignantly heard the sentence suspended, and
within two hours was escorted—bitterly demanding his
rights of incarceration—to the city limits. There he was
told that if he crossed the city line again it would earn
him nothing but lumps on the head. The cops pointed
him down the slope in the right direction and leaned on
him enough to assist him on his way and when Arnie
picked himself up and looked about him, there were
the garbage dump and the shacks and the other bums,
and he knew he was home.

Everything in this new community was pared down to
the essentials. It offered a pressure-cooker survival course
that would have taxed a Sioux Indian. Arnie had his
pockets picked, his shoes exchanged for a more suitable
pair while he slept, his jacket bargained away from him
by two persuasive gentlemen equipped with broken beer
bottles and noses to match. He'd been conned, short-
changed, cheated at cards, and otherwise educated within
the first three days and since, by then, he had nothing
left worth separating him from, he was considered to have
graduated from the sheep to the wolves and could set
out on his own. With this instruction behind him, and
his own more than adequate physical resources, he might
have done pretty well in the jungle, but then the Messiah
arrived.

Other states had other Redeemers, but in the California
shantytowns the Messiah was usually one of a team of
labor contractors who picked up seasonal workers for the
huge cotton and fruit ranches that sprawled through the
San Joaquin and Imperial valleys. They collected so
much per head from the farmers for every able-bodied
man they delivered who was willing to work under conditions that had not been seen in America since John
Brown's body stood on its own two feet. The contractors
were one up on the ancient slavers because they were not
only paid by the farmers, but they also gouged a dollar
out of every man they graciously permitted to indenture
himself to this latter-day form of peonage. Arnie had a

dollar he had somehow cunningly withheld from his shantytown tuition fee, and he paid it over and was on his way.

Arnie and the other lucky ones spent the next few hours clattering about in the back of a truck hurtling from Los Angeles up into the sunbaked bowl of the San Joaquin valley. Then the truck stopped and they were spilled out and could blink about them at the metropolis of Pixley, a blistered hole inhabited by two thousand bleak-eyed Kallikaks which then qualified—and still does —as the cloaca of the western world. The citizens' reception committee consisted of the overseer of the farm for which they were hired and his praetorian guard of half a dozen armed thugs whose guns and special deputy badges had been issued to them by a state blindingly benevolent toward the needs of the large corporate land-owners.

The overseer spelled out the terms of their employment: They would get twelve cents per sack of picked cotton, they could average about thirty-six cents an hour. Housing would be provided by their employer and fifty cents a day would be deducted from their wages to pay for it— in advance. Water would be generously available, at ten cents a pailful. Food and anything else they needed could be purchased at their employer's store at prices only 20 percent above normal. Anybody who didn't like it could leave now or quit later—so long as he paid the two dollars cost of transportation to Pixley now or, if he exercised a later option, so long as he wasn't in debt to the employer.

Considering their economic circumstances, they had about as much choice as a rabbit with myxomatosis. Nobody fell out of line. The overseer sluiced a stream of tobacco juice into the sizzling dust, the deputies hitched up their gun belts, and the happy throng trotted off.

Arnie was a young giant in peak condition, he'd been an offensive guard of such power that his tackles had left any number of well-conditioned athletes unconscious on the football fields and thereafter fit only for the most sedentary occupations; but he'd never before done "stoop labor" and for the next two weeks his spine was just one long curve of segmented agony. At the end of each day, several of his dried-up little coworkers who outaged him by two to one and underweighed him in the same proportion would help him stumble off the field and massage his bent back until he could straighten into something approximating his normal height.

This passed. The sun, the work, and the living conditions pared him so that like his fellows he was down to the irreducible bone and sinew, and in time he was as sweat-stinking and filthy as any of the others; but he was still different. For one thing, the dirt was *on* him, not blown into him by the winds that had made a dust bowl of the Midwest farms from which most of the others had come. For another, he wasn't as hungry as they—not nearly—they'd had years of near-starvation behind them. And finally, he still had a home to go back to, and the others had only the corroding memory of their homes bulldozed flat when the sheriffs had come to evict them from the farms that had been theirs for generations and now belonged to the banks that foreclosed their mortgages. The others accepted him and liked him. He was a good-natured kid and he did a man's work; and though he used pretty fancy words in their endless political discussions of an evening, he didn't put on airs and he wasn't a know-it-all. They liked him, but he wasn't one of them; not until the day a deputy sheriff shot him in the belly with a tear-gas shell fired at close range.

The strains of years of depression had torn the fabric of American society and exposed the existing system as criminally inadequate to the needs of the people. By 1936 the twelve million unemployed were violently unwilling that the crumbling ruin of the status quo should continue to be patched up at the expense of their uprooted families and their starving children. By then, too, they had leaders who rejected as obscene the philosophy that poverty was ordained by God and that recurrent misery was a condition of man governed by laws as immutable as those determining the fall of a leaf. Franklin Roosevelt

was in the White House railing against "the malefactors
of great wealth," and the fabulous John L. Lewis had a
Bible in his hand and in his mouth the thunderous call
to "organize the unorganized." The people had reached
bottom and found revealed there the revolutionary truth
that rights are God-given and privilege not, and they were
on the move, and would move with whoever was going
their way—white or black or deep-dyed red. The miners
struck in Harlan County and were suppressed with
bloody violence, and struck again, and won. The steel-
workers struck in Illinois and were shot down in the fields
and clubbed in their homes, and still they won. In San
Francisco, the massacre of the longshoremen on their
picket lines led to the general strike during which a hundred thousand workers escorted their martyred dead
through streets emptied of police, and the city teetered
on the brink of revolution. Everywhere the thick crust of
a rotten society refused to give until it was broken and the
workers broke it.

Some of this breaking began on a hot summer's day in
Pixley, California. As part of this, and on that day,
Arnie Berg crossed that invisible, individual border be-
tween the youth and the man. . . .

There was a crowd of about three hundred of these
red-necked dust-bowl refugees blocking the main street of
Pixley that Sunday morning. They could not have been
in church, the churches of the town weren't open to the
migratory workers who flooded the area, but the saloons
were, and they could have been there getting innocently
drunk. Instead, they were out in the street, listening to
some Communist rabble-rouser preaching hell and revolution, telling them about civil rights and how they ought
to join a union and all that kind of stuff. So the sheriff
and his deputies decided it was time to enforce the peace.

There weren't more than twenty or thirty deputies and
all they had were pistols and tear gas and riot guns, so
they were pretty nervous (understandably so, since most
of them were new to the business, having been recruited
only recently by the Associated Farmers in San Francis-

co). The deputies had little choice, there was no doubt the crowd was breaking the law.

The deputies ordered the crowd to move on and formed a wedge to break through and collar the anarchist who was inciting them. Arnie happened to be in the deputies' path. He was quite probably the most conspicuous thing in the way and one of the excited peace officers clobbered him over the head with the barrel of his gas gun. This normally persuasive argument failed of its purpose. Arnie rocked, but stood, and struck back. The deputy went down and, wafted beyond the borders of patience by a combination of righteous indignation and the pain of a broken jaw, aimed his gun at Arnie and fired. The tear-gas shell caught Arnie in the belly, driving his belt buckle halfway toward his spine and dumping him in the dust beside his victim. The crowd looked at him lying there dead, and became a mob. In a flash, noses were bloodied and eyes blackened, gas guns exploded spreading the acrid gas over the innocent and the guilty alike so that tears fell like God's rain. And in the midst of it all, Arnie surged up again—miraculously resurrected—with the fallen deputy's gun clubbed in his hands, laying about him like Samson among the Philistines.

The deputies broke free and ran. They re-formed at the end of the street and when the crowd started after them, they drew their pistols and fired warning shots into the air. The angry workers hesitated before the menace of pistol and riot gun. Everything stopped, suspended on the trembling point of sudden death.

The moment held, neither side willing to initiate carnage. Then the crowd gathered up its wounded and slowly withdrew. Sullen defiance hung between the two groups, the antagonists denying defeat. And then there was only the cluster of bruised deputies, and the roiled dust beginning to settle in the quiet street.

All during the day, word of what happened at Pixley went out to the migratory workers' camps throughout the San Joaquin and the Imperial valleys. The news grew more dramatic in direct proportion to the distance it traveled, and within hours there were caravans of vintage flivvers clattering toward the scene of the reported massacre, each battered car loaded to its collapsing fenders with hard and angry men. By nightfall there were nearly two thousand men at the outskirts of Pixley, piled up against a line of several hundred deputies and armed townsfolk brought in from the nearby communities by the Pixley sheriff when he smelled the trouble brewing. The stage was set for blood.

The sheriff had a truck equipped with a loudspeaker and his opening gambit was to call upon the crowd not to listen to foreign troublemakers and to go quietly to their homes. Since nearly everyone there counted three or four generations of forebears born in America, and since they had no homes to go to, it's possible each of them thought the sheriff's remarks were addressed elsewhere. In any case, they didn't budge, and the growling grew louder. The sheriff's next idea proved somewhat more felicitous. He invited the leaders to step forward and discuss matters, promising that no one would be harmed or arrested. This was a happy stratagem; there were no leaders and in the processing of selecting some and formulating demands, time passed and the crowd calmed. Finally six men were pushed forward: four whose names are now unknown, and Arnie Berg, and a man named James MacGowan from Madera. MacGowan had been sent to California by John L. Lewis's Committee for Industrial Organization to get the migratory workers into the newborn United Cannery, Agricultural, Packing, and Allied Workers of America—a catchall trade union which came to be known in its short fighting history as "the UCAPAWA" or, simply and lovingly, "the union."

There in the strip between the armed deputies and the watchful crowd, the six men and the sheriff talked. The sheriff pointed out that he could do nothing about their demands. But he did offer to set up a meeting with a group of employers that coming morning, and to get the ball rolling that way. It seemed reasonable. Arnie was chosen to tell the crowd and he got up on the loudspeaker truck, his size and his scorched shirt helping to identify him as the hero of "the Pixley massacre," and he told them what had been arranged, this, and more, not knowing then *why* he told them more. He told them who he was and of the rich life he'd lived, unearned by him or his father or his father's father, wealth growing without toil from the loot snatched by a murdering pirate nearly two hundred years before. What kind of a world where idle men grew fat and and working men hungered? He told them, and in the telling threw away the silver spoon he'd been born with, and joined them. Having joined them, being one of them, he could tell them then to wait a little longer. There was, he said, a time to fight and a time to talk. The talking time was now, would they trust the men they had chosen to lead them, and go in peace?

They trusted Arnie Berg.

He'd made the first speech in his life, and found that he could move men. The power had come unbidden, from some till-then concealed source of passionate understanding, some reflex of instinctive purpose and knowing which was never after to fail him and which set him on his way from that night—undeviating as a landslide —until it brought him inevitably to Malachi Wald.

The talking time proved brief. The employers' representatives, organized into the antilabor Associated Farmers and instructed by the banks and corporations that held ultimate ownership of the land, would yield nothing at all. They would have to be forced. Arnie and James MacGowan and the others went out from Pixley that day and began to organize the forcing.

John L. Lewis's Committee for Industrial Organization sent some money, and ten men to help them. For four months the organizers roamed the valleys, bringing small groups to meetings held in the dark of night, building the base of the union. They were hounded and jailed by the police, beaten and tarred-and-feathered, and two of them lynched by vigilantes. The law in the valleys was the employers' law and there was none other. When at last they felt strong enough to call the migratory workers from the fields and the orchards and out of every cotton mill and packing shed, the naked force of fascism was brought against them and men and women died.

With the strike endangered by hunger and violence, Arnie and others went storming through the cities as far east as Detroit to spread the story of what was happening in the feudal fiefs of the California valleys, and to organize support. Money poured in from everywhere. Arnie came back to the valleys leading two hundred volunteers from the great industrial unions to help the migratory workers hold their picket lines. Roosevelt sent the federal marshals in to protect the strikers. The National Labor Relations Board held hearings in Los Angeles and attorney David Sokol there proved the Associated Farmers to be a criminal conspiracy.[56] Deputies in the towns of Tulare, Visalia, Madera, and Corcoran were indicted in the federal courts. The pressure grew, the cotton withered in the fields, and the fruit rotted on the trees. Until the powerful landowners, who would yield nothing when a little would have been enough, were broken; and the settlement brought the migratory workers of California out of peonage. The union had won; and the union was—or nearly was, or so it then seemed—Arnie Berg.

He stayed with it for another five months, operating from the newly established headquarters in Bakersfield, the youngest secretary of a statewide trade union in America—he was not yet twenty-one.

It was the cold winter of 1936–37, and all over America as elsewhere in the world millions of people warmed themselves in the passionate brotherhood of the liberal left. It was a time of wonderful, purposeful clarity; the shape of the bright future hung before the young in heart like a vision of the holy grail. It was there, and attainable. All it required was the great crusade against the sons of darkness. The crucial point was in Spain where the forces of Nazi Germany and Fascist Italy had gone to armor the spearhead Francisco Franco had thrust into the heart of the republic. The Abraham Lincoln Battalion of the International Brigades (the volunteers who fought for Republican Spain) was being organized in New York. Arnie went there.

He'd been a year away from home, and he stopped en route. It was a sad meeting of loving strangers. What did they know of him at home? They had raised him gently and intended him for the quiet harmless life they knew; and he came to them like a winter's gale, hard and fierce and bent on battle.

America abided by the "nonintervention pact" whereby Great Britain, France, Germany, and Italy undertook to give aid to neither side in the Spanish War. The democracies thus denied to Republican Spain the assistance a legitimate and freely elected government might claim— or at least buy—in order to defend itself against a fascist revolt. Having swallowed this, the rest of the dose of massive hypocrisy went down more easily, and the governments of France, England, and the United States accepted with little visible amazement the curious appearance of Italian tanks and German Stuka dive bombers and artillery accompanied by the requisite manpower together with two brigades of Italian infantry and the German Condor Legion. All of which thousands of men and masses of equipment, armor, and airplanes were enlisted in support of the Spanish fascists and arrived in Spain by a process so entrancingly invisible as to leave the German and Italian rulers in total ignorance and the western democracies so bemused that they could see in this martial legerdemain no reason whatever for considering the nonintervention pact an abrogated nullity. The Frenchmen, the Englishmen, the Americans who volunteered for the International Brigades on the side of Republican Spain were therefore at least technically violating the law of their lands and they went an underground route; without documents, or with passports obtained by subterfuge, all of this subjecting them to possible imprisonment. The unit of the Lincoln Battalion of which Arnie Berg was part sailed from New York under the guise of a group tour of Europe and went from Paris, with guides supplied by the French trade unions, over the Pyrenees and into Spain that way.

The battle Arnie sought he found within three days of his arrival in Spain.

Generalissimo Francisco Franco had three columns advancing on Madrid along an arc ranging from south to northwest of the city. Early in March he formed a fourth column consisting of an Italian tank regiment and infantry brigade, two regiments of Moorish infantry, and a supporting squadron of the German-supplied, German-piloted Stuka dive bombers. This conglomerate triumph of "nonintervention" Franco hurled at Guadalajara, which barred the eastern approaches to Madrid. The battle was joined on March 11 and the Republican defenders were soon forced from the hill positions and, without tanks, artillery, or air cover, found themselves dug into the bombed rubble of the town itself. On March 16, the Spanish government scraped together just over a thousand men and mounted a flank attack southeast of Guadalajara. Among these thousand were 220 Americans of the Lincoln Battalion who'd been taken from the arrival depot, given rifles, and thrown—thus untrained—into the battle. At Guadalajara, Arnie Berg killed for the first time. By March 20, when the mauled fascists had retreated, nearly half the American volunteers were dead or wounded, and Arnie had become a platoon leader by virtue of the heavy casualties among the officers. Six months later, largely through the same process, he was a captain; and two months after that he was back in Madrid with the doctors picking shrapnel out of his thigh and abdomen and wondering whether to cut off his leg. The leg stayed on, and in January 1938 Arnie was ready to fight again. But by then Constancia de la Mora was running the Republican propaganda organization and needed someone to try to rouse the American people; so Arnie went to do the job.

For over a year, until Spain fell to Franco and his German and Italian allies, Arnie organized committees and raised money and smuggled weapons into Spain past the "nonintervention" blockade whereby Britain and France—with America as accomplice—betrayed the Spanish republic and opened the way to World War II.

The fall of the Spanish republic shook the earth Arnie stood upon.

In Spain as in the California valleys, he'd been a warrior in love. He'd fought for and been in love with a young man's clean and innocent concept of justice. It was right that men should eat, that they should share in the fruits of their labor, that they should live without fear in their own lands. Decent men would help them do it, and it would come to pass. Meanwhile, there was fighting. One went where the fighting was, and helped; but the fighting was only part of the passage from dark to day, an act of faith, an act of love; and the enemies were shadows in the passageway.

So it was for Arnie until Spain was betrayed, and he saw that even in the democracies most men cared not at all. Thereafter, he fought no longer *for,* but *against.* He had learned the positive power of hate.

Spain was then only the latest victim of an international policy of crawling self-abasement matched only by that of the Untouchables in India. During the shameful decade of appeasement, the record read like this: Japan's invasion of Manchuria was followed by Hitler's re-creation of the banned German army, which was followed by the illegal remilitarization of the Rhineland, which was followed by Italy's conquest of Ethiopia, then there was Spain, which was followed by the Nazi troops marching into Austria, which was followed by the Munich treachery that delivered up Czechoslovakia. These successive betrayals were acclaimed as the achievement of "peace in our time" and there were only the noisy "premature antifascists" to warn that the fruits of appeasement would yet taste of blood, and that the lesson of cause and effect taught to children in the fable of the house that Jack built might be usefully absorbed also by the mature leaders of men.

Of the premature antifascists in America at that time, Arnie Berg was among the noisiest and the least inclined to sail before the winds of high policy. With the impatience of his youth and his own hot-eyed view of the world, he condemned the circumlocutions of politics on all sides of the right and left of his own position which was, simply, that he hated fascism of every color and kind and would leave nothing undone that might destroy it, and anyone who made peace with it at any time and for any reason was his enemy.

This plunging directness brought him difficulties. At the time of the Soviet-Nazi pact, the Communists in the left-wing organizations within which he was by then importantly placed found him nettlesome and undisciplined, and they passed the word around that he was certainly a Trotskyite and quite possibly a police spy. There wasn't much more they could do about him for within the mass organizations the members trusted him and an open split would have been troublesome. So they were limited to a whispered campaign of character assassination. Meanwhile, the FBI, the congressional Committee on Un-American Activities, and other groupings less augustly enthroned on the right of the American scene considered him a Stalinist agent or a nineteenth-century bomb-throwing anarchist, and denounced him as one or the other, and often—uniquely—as both. Arnie spat upon Scylla and Charybdis and went his own stormy way until, on December 7, 1941, the narrow straits he traveled became suddenly populous; everyone was a pure antifascist and the crusade was on.

During the two years before Pearl Harbor, Arnie had supervised a large-scale undercover investigation of Nazi activity in North and South Ameica. The funds and the volunteer agents came mostly from the Hollywood Anti-Nazi League, the United Anti-Nazi Conference, Labor's Non-Partisan League, and the Spanish-speaking Peoples' Congress, as well as from the CIO. Working thus with trade unions and left-wing organizations where the FBI was not precisely popular, Arnie and his investigators collected material not easily available to government agencies. Early in December 1941, he offered this to Johnson Hayes at the Los Angeles field office of the FBI, and the work he was to do during the war was a result of this demonstration of expertise in a field in which there were—at the time—all too few experts.

In February 1942, the FBI and army and navy intelligence created an informal joint counterespionage group. Soon after, an understanding was reached with the Canadian authorities and—much less officially—with some of the law-enforcement agencies in Mexico, which was then neutral in the war. The result of all this was an inter-American hush-hush effort to dig out and immobilize suspected Nazi and Japanese agents from Canada south to the Panama Canal Zone. Arnie was among a small number of civilian experts, some of them left-wingers, who were coopted to the group.

Arnie was first assigned to a field unit operating back and forth along the U.S.-Canadian border. Either because he was then too unskilled to be temperate, or because he had a flaming hate for the men he hunted, he proved exceptionally violent. Within a month he had killed the Nazi agent Walter Haag in Toronto and had beaten Erich Schaeffer half to death in Seattle when that spy refused to give information Arnie thought he had to have quickly. Arnie's unit boss asked that he be transferred to another territory. It was decided to make use of the contacts Arnie had made during his prewar work with the Spanish-speaking Peoples' Congress, and he was sent into Mexico to join the hunt for spies and saboteurs within the large Japanese communities. The search focused first on the Japanese owners of various fishing vessels which worked the waters off the coasts of Mexico and California. A series of flash raids turned up Japanese naval code books on two such ships, the *Minatu Maru* and the *Saro Maru*, berthed at Guaymas. Both vessels were equipped with exceptionally powerful radio transmitters and both were owned by the Nippon Suisan Kaisha Company which was, in turn, owned by Kokatura Maeahama. Maeahama was a respected businessman who'd lived in Hermosillo since 1929. He was also, as it turned out, a commander in Japanese naval intelligence and an experienced agent, so that when Arnie and his men came quietly to his home they found that he had left quietly some hours before.

As has been mentioned, Mexico was a neutral country, and when Arnie caught up with Commander Maeahama and shot him down in the streets of San Luis Potosi the Japanese ambassador quite properly raised hell and the Mexican government was, to put it minimally, displeased. Maeahama had been shooting at Arnie at the time, so it proved possible to have the incident reported as an act of self-defense in the course of a personal quarrel; but Arnie had to be transferred once more. He was sent to the Panama Canal Zone where, awkwardly, he did it again.

One of Germany's spy masters in South America was a man named Hans Wilhelm Koehn, an Argentine citizen living in Buenos Aires. In June 1942, Koehn slipped into the Panama Canal Zone with an Argentine passport describing him as Hernando Blaine and checked into the Tivoli Hotel where an alert agent recognized him. The agent was alert but not smart, and he tried to arrest Koehn who gave him a knife for his pains and was back across the Colombian border before the alarm was out. Koehn was wanted badly; it seemed that it might be easier to get him in Colombia than to snatch him from Buenos Aires, and Arnie was sent after him. The guess was that, since Koehn had had no time to do whatever he'd come to Panama for, he might not go far. So Arnie flew down to Bogotá and combed the hotels where—indeed—he found his man apparently comforted by the illusion that he was safe on neutral Colombian soil. Arnie offered Koehn his choice of coming with him back to American territory where he could legitimately be arrested or of staying where he was, dead. Koehn elected to travel, but at the Bogotá airport he changed his mind and slugged Arnie, who then killed him.

There are very few places more public than an airport and it was impossible to keep the incident quiet. Everybody was upset—the Colombians, whose neutrality was thus noisily violated; the Argentine government, whose citizen had been killed; and Arnie's superiors, who thought the whole thing pretty clumsily handled. The American authorities, of course, never admitted that Arnie was other than a murderous tourist; and Arnie sat in the Bogotá prison for a month before a deal was made to get him out.

Once back in Los Angeles, he was bluntly told that since he couldn't seem to arrange his assassinations in a manner private enough to qualify as clandestine, he ought to find some other line of work, and he was discharged—as the phrase goes—"for the good of the service."

By that time, though, another wild man—this one in Washington, D.C.—had collected a bunch of intellectual rowdies into a department of dirty tricks called the Office of Strategic Services and it was suggested to Arnie that he might find those surroundings somewhat more congenial. Arnie went east to present his credentials to Brigadier General William J. "Wild Bill" Donovan.

The OSS took Arnie in and sent him to school to round out his education. He was an apt and diligent scholar and by the time he was graduated and commissioned a lieutenant, he had learned a number of worthwhile skills. He could jump from airplanes, blow bridges and buildings, he could kill a man with grace and speed using only his hands or such innocent appurtenances of everyday life as might be readily available anywhere—matchboxes and pencils, for example. He was, in short, ready to go out into the world and he expected to be sent to England and thence promptly parachuted into France to kill Germans. His superiors had other ideas.

The OSS had been organized to fulfill a special espionage-activist function—to gather intelligence information in the German-occupied countries, to train resistance movements, to kill. The nature of this work required the OSS to recruit its personnel largely among people of superior intelligence and education who had a knowledge of foreign countries, customs, languages. Most of the recruits had led easy and cultured lives, many of them came from scholarly and relatively sheltered professions. They could be taught how to kill, it was necessary also—and more difficult—to teach them to want to kill. In such company, Arnie was a rare rough jewel. He hated the enemy, and was at the same time informed, articulate, and communicative. So they used him to teach hatred.

Arnie had not envisioned spending his war years as an indoctrination officer at OSS headquarters in Washington and he wasn't happy. But as it turned out, because that's what he was and where he was, he came to participate in a drawn-out battle more significant by far than any he had known or would ever know. And though in this battle the antagonists shed no blood of their own, the casualty list was a long one.

It developed this way:

Early in August 1942 an agent of the World Jewish Congress in Switzerland named Gerhard Riegner brought a report to the American legation at Berne. Ambassador Harrison authenticated the report and on August 17 sent a cable to the State Department which read in part:

> . . . at the Fuehrer's headquarters, a plan has been discovered and is under consideration according to which all Jews in countries occupied or controlled by Germany, numbering three and a half to four millions, should after deportation and concentration in the east be at one blow exterminated. . . . Action is reputed to be planned for the autumn. Ways of execution are still being discussed, including the use of prussic acid. . . . Our informant is known to have close contact with the highest German authorities and his reports are generally reliable. . . .[57]

This was the first such reliable report to reach the Allies concerning Germany's planned "final solution to the Jewish problem." Considering the shocking nature of the news, the State Department reacted with notable calm. They suppressed the report until the World Jewish Congress broke the story to the press on November 2, accompanying the publication with documents proving that the Germans had by then already killed well over a million Jews on a sort of formless ad hoc basis. The publication brought quick action, of a kind. The United Nations* formally announced that "racial and political murder"

*Twenty-six nations signed *The United Nations Declaration* on January 1, 1942, in Washington, D.C. In this document, the signatories are referred to as the "United Nations."

would be punished. The British House of Commons stood for two minutes of silence. That seems to have set the pattern. The silence spread, nothing more was done.

On January 21, 1943, another cable arrived from Riegner via Ambassador Harrison in Switzerland. It reported that the Germans were then killing Jews at the rate of six thousand a day and that the Jews of Rumania were being starved to death. The report circulated in the upper echelons of the Department until it came to Assistant Secretary Breckinridge Long, who decided there was no reason to trouble any of his superiors in government who were already overburdened with matters of greater weight than the lives or deaths of a few million Jews. He had the report put on the secret list and tucked away. This admirable demonstration of diplomatic phlegm apparently did cause Mr. Long some measure of anxiety and to spare himself future pain, he caused State Department cable 354/43 to be sent to Ambassador Harrison in Berne warning the ambassador against transmitting any more of Riegner's reports or any similar "such private messages."[58]

Harrison cabled back a protest, arguing somewhat plaintively that even if no action were to be taken, reports such as those from Riegner constituted "authentic intelligence that should be in State Department hands." This, too, was confined to the files.[59] And then all these careful and intelligent precautions were brought to naught by an anonymous underling.

In the days before America entered the war, an interdepartmental decision had been taken to the effect that the Treasury's foreign funds control division was to receive copies of all State Department cables relating to "refugee matters." This was a fiscal arrangement intended solely to inform the Treasury concerning capital transfers in cases of individual refugees. The Jews in Europe didn't come under this arrangement, they weren't refugees since they hadn't gotten anywhere; they were only victims and as such, clearly, no one's concern. And in any case, the interdepartmental decision was never intended to touch matters of policy. Neither Mr. Long nor his associates could therefore predict that some minor official, either bumbling or malicious, would forward a copy of Harrison's protest to the Treasury and thus bring the skeleton clattering out of the closet marked "secret." But that's what happened.

Even so, the mishap need not have been troublesome had the Secretary of the Treasury, Henry J. Morgenthau, had any normal regard for proper procedure. He hadn't. With Harrison's protest cable in his possession, Morgenthau asked for the previous correspondence and State quite properly refused, pointing out it was all none of the Treasury's business. The matter ought to have ended there, but Morgenthau nosed around until he had ferreted out the rest of the Riegner-Harrison file and he went crashing in to Secretary of State Cordell Hull. Morgenthau charged that State Department officials, and Breckinridge Long in particular, had "dodged their grim responsibility . . . and even suppressed information about atrocities in order to prevent an outraged public opinion from forcing their hand."[60] This was a tactical error. Hull was a man of great integrity, but he had an incandescent temper and a fondness for Long which was—as Morgenthau saw it— "one of the Secretary's major weaknesses." Hull allowed the Riegner report to be released to the public, but he refused to go along with Morgenthau's demand that a rescue policy be explored and he told Morgenthau to mind his own business—which was money, not people.

No one in those days fought the prestigious Cordell Hull directly and Morgenthau awaited the furor he was sure would be aroused when the atrocity reports were released. There was, indeed, a certain amount of public disquiet. The American Jewish Congress called a mass meeting in Madison Square Garden to which President Roosevelt and Prime Minister Churchill sent messages of sincere concern; there were indignant editorials in the newspapers for nearly a full week. But other matters were pressing and the Allied governments murmured vaguely about "steps being taken" and emphasized that the thing to do was to get on with the war. "Victory," the leaders said, "would save the European Jewry from the Nazi terror."[61] It was not true, of course, that anything was being done to save the Jews. Nor was it true that victory would save them. The argument might be made that this latter statement is hindsight, but in view of the fact that it was known at the time that six thousand Jews were being killed daily, it seems awkward to argue that anyone able to count on his fingers could really have believed that victory would come in time to prevent millions of Jewish deaths. Whatever protest still rose—almost entirely from Jewish organizations—to cloud the pleasant atmosphere of wartime unanimity was crushed by postulating the paramount necessity of getting on with the war. The reluctance of appearing to interfere with this laudable project seems to have prevented anyone from publicly inquiring why an exploration of the possibilities of rescuing some of the Jews was necessarily incompatible with winning the war. One explanation at least seems to suffice —very few people cared.

Morgenthau cared. Defeated both privately and publicly, he nevertheless kept tilting at the windmills of indifference. He knew by then that he would get no help from the State Department officials within whose jurisdiction the problem properly lay and who had, as he put it conservatively, "small personal sympathy for the humble and the downtrodden."[62] So he sought his allies elsewhere.

He went to Brigadier General William Donovan, the man who was the creator and director of the Office of Strategic Services. Donovan was a mutant within the subtle tribe of Washington officialdom. He had a roaring contempt for the stately sarabands of diplomacy and a willingness to pursue his objectives without regard to the bleating protests of those around whom the crockery crashed. This directness, and a simple decency equally unfashionable for the time and place, caused him to be nicknamed "Wild Bill." For what Morgenthau had in mind, he was an excellent choice.

Morgenthau put his proposal bluntly. He wanted Donovan to help him bypass the official policy of frozen inaction and to try to organize some kind of rescue machinery in Europe. The Jews faced total obliteration and Morgenthau knew that no large numbers of them could be rescued without a massive effort by the Allied governments. This would not be forthcoming; but what Morgenthau hoped for was "to get a few of them out—a few women, perhaps, a few children and babies—before the gates of the concentration camps and the doors of the gas chambers clanked shut."[63]

Donovan agreed, and he and Morgenthau and a few others sat down to analyze the problem. It was complicated enough. The normal intelligence channels were closed by the necessity to keep the operation secret until those who would oppose it within the Allied governments could be faced by a fait accompli. There were other inherent difficulties. Germany's "final solution of the Jewish problem" was being worked out deep within eastern Europe, in areas under German control, and where the Allies' channels of communication led through the London-based governments-in-exile to resistance movements for the most part reactionary and themselves deeply anti-Semitic. There was no contact at all with the Jewish resistance groups. And if contact could be made, what then? The Jewish underground in the ghettos and the forests and in the death camps had learned by bitter experience that the anti-Nazi non-Jews around them were at best indifferent and, more often, actively hostile. They would hardly be likely to greet with open arms and expansive trust an unknown agent bearing glad tidings from the west.

As Donovan saw the project against this difficult background, it required someone who could not be considered reactionary, preferably a Jew, and ideally one trained in cloak-and-dagger work who would have—as it were—a professional rapport with the men of the Jewish resistance. Donovan found his ideal agent right under his hand, in the I & E section at OSS headquarters. Arnie Berg was young, tough, trained; he knew Europe well and spoke French and German; he had been an officer in the International Brigades fighting for Republican Spain and had the contacts and the political reputation that came with this. Arnie Berg—bright Fortune's gift—born a Jew and bred a leftist, perfect.

Arnie was called in, briefed, given money and passports of various kinds, and told to waste no time. He went via Portugal and Italy, traveling as a Swiss citizen and an official of the International Red Cross. Within two days he was in Geneva with Gerhard Riegner. Three days later he was riding the trains east, equipped with German priority travel documents and in the company of a pudgy nondescript Spanish diplomat whose passport bore the name of Jesús Federico Costa. The name was false as was the passport: Arnie's companion was Moses Mandel-Mantello, an Italian Jew and a courier who linked the Jewish communities in Europe.

It was Mandel-Mantello who moved Arnie along the secret roads and contacted those agents of the Jewish underground who could be reached at all. It was he who persuaded these tense and suspicious men that Arnie was what he claimed to be, and that he was neither agent-provocateur nor anti-Semite. And so they talked to Arnie. They handed over to him the terrible reports and the photographs smuggled out of the ghettos and the extermination camps by the Jewish underground. And they talked to him of what they themselves had seen, until horror stood within him like spears of glass and haunted his eyes as it haunted theirs.

What happened to Arnie then neither he nor they had planned. Arnie was a Jew, that is he'd been born of a Jewish father to a Jewish mother; and that had been the end of it, the connection with Jewishness confined to this happenstance of birth and cut when the umbilical cord was cut. Now it was like being born again—of a *people,* to a *people;* with the birth creating an identity that stretched beyond him, that made him component and compounded of those stranger-millions who were unknown to him, who lived elsewhere, lived differently, died as he would not die, but were as he was—born Jewish.

This is a thing that pulses in every Jew—recognized or not, but always there, always—to bind him, as no one else is bound, to all others born unto his people and to the history and the time and the pain of each and all of them. It is set forth in the Passover service that commemorates the deliverance of the Jews from Pharaoh's Egypt: "This is because of what the Lord did for me when I went forth from Egypt, from the land of bondage." The Jews says "for *me* when *I* went forth," and he speaks the truth that lies beyond reality. No other thing than this, however it came about, explains the mystical unity of the Jew. It is perhaps beyond comprehension, but it is so, and no one who does not accept it can know the Jew.

It was recognized by Arnie Berg in Cluj, Rumania, in those first days of March 1943, when he was twenty-five years old. And he would live with it in pride and in pain for the rest of his life.

Only a handful of men met with Arnie and Mandel-Mantello in Cluj. They came from Bulgaria, Rumania, and Hungary; there was one, even, who came out of the forests of Poland. They came to sit before Arnie Berg and say: "We're here now, what will you do to help us?"

"I don't know," said Arnie. "I am sent to begin the work of rescue and it is for you to tell me how."

The Pole spoke first. "You begin too late," he said. "We are the center of it and the wolves have been among us for years, they are all around us and there are no ways out. For us in Poland it is too late to think of rescue, what we think of is the different ways there are of dying. There may be rescue in it," he said then, "a little rescue in a lot of dying; but that comes second. First is the way we have chosen to go, and for that we need guns. Give us guns; you can drop them in the forests, we'll work it out."

"I'll tell them in Washington," Arnie said. "You understand? This is not in my hands; this is not what I was sent for."

"Tell them," said the Pole. "Nothing else is any good to us now; except this other thing—bomb the camps and the railroads to the camps. Send the airplanes and wipe them out."

And when Arnie cried—"It is your own people who will be slaughter then," the Pole answered—"My

God, what do you think is happening to them now!"

It was the turn then of Aaron Keppler, who had come from Bucharest representing Chief Rabbi Alexander Saffran. This was a man buckled close in bitterness, and he yielded none of it when he spoke to Arnie Berg:

"Of Rumania's five hundred thousand Jews nearly half are already dead and the rest would die and ask nothing for themselves of the Americans. But there is a way to save seventy thousand children, if it is done quickly; and for the children I have come to Cluj. It can be done this way:

"The Gestapo chief in Bucharest, SS Colonel Karl Richter, and Rumanian Premier Ion Antonescu are willing to ship seventy thousand Jewish children under the age of fourteen to any country that will take them. An act of tender mercy, this, but with conditions. The first condition is financial—a hundred thousand dollars to be deposited to the accounts of Antonescu and Richter before the children leave, and another four hundred thousand afterward. The money to go to Swiss banks with the agreement that it cannot be touched until after the war. The second condition is cautionary—the children have to have a place to go before they leave. Richter and Antonescu don't want them returning to Rumania, or traveling around the world attracting attention. Secrecy is essential. Secrecy and money."

"You'll have the money," said Mandel-Mantello. "I speak for the World Jewish Congress, and I promise you."

"And the place of asylum?" asked Keppler of Arnie. "What country will take our children in?"

"That will not be a problem," said Arnie. "There's my country. There's America, and England, the British dominions, Canada; there's the whole free world beyond the seas. It cannot be a problem—seventy thousand children!"

"Can it not?" asked Keppler. "I hope you are right, but I know you are wrong. But it is not for me to teach you history, though someone should," he said bitterly.

They went on then, discussing arrangements, communi-

cations, but it all came back to the Rumanian children
and Arnie knew that the Jews of Europe would wait for
this rescue to be accomplished—or at least attempted. If
this were done the men who sat before him, and those
who sent him, would have hope and trust, and only then.
He pledged himself, and went away from Cluj with Moses
Mandel-Mantello.

It was on the Turkish plane to Ankara that Arnie asked:
"What did he mean, this Keppler? What is the history?"
And this is what Mandel-Mantello told him:

Since June 25, 1941, when the Iron Guard butchered
the seven thousand Jews at Jassy, the Jews had been
trying to get out of Rumania. In those early days it was
possible; the Germans weren't in control then and Premier
Antonescu was eager to let them out, to solve Rumania's
Jewish problem at one stroke. The plan was to move
three hundred thousand of them first, across Turkey to
Palestine. The Turks were willing to grant them transit
but they wanted guarantees that the Jews would not be
turned back into Turkey by the British when they reached
the borders of Palestine. There was no British embassy
in Rumania, the countries were at war; but America was
neutral in mid-1941 and there was an American embassy. So the Turkish ambassador, and Rabbi Saffran,
and Monsignor Balan who was the metropolitan of the
Eastern Church, brought the plan to the American ambassador and asked him to have it transmitted to the
British government.

The American ambassador cabled to the State Department, asking that the plan be forwarded to London.

In Washington, Cavendish W. Cannon of the European
division took the cable to his acting chief, James Clement
Dunn, and to Ray Atherton, the State Department's political advisor. All three of them thought the project was a
tricky one, full of hidden dangers. For, as Cannon pointed
out, the three hundred thousand Jews couldn't stay in
Palestine—the Arabs wouldn't like it. So they would have
to go elsewhere, to England, or Canada, or even to
America. And if they did get out of Rumania, there
would be others coming after them; there would be "pres-

sure for an asylum in the western hemisphere," there would be requests for similar treatment from the Hungarian Jews and "by extension [from] all countries where there has been intense persecution." All those Jews out of Hitler's Europe, alive, and looking for a place in which to live! And there would be demands, of course, for America to take its share. Dunn and Atherton and Cannon all agreed this difficulty had to be averted, and so the State Department averted it. Perhaps these high officials felt their colleagues in the British Foreign Office could not be trusted to act with equal wisdom; perhaps they wished to spare them the pain of decision. In any case, the British government was not then compelled to decide because the request of the Rumanian Jews was not passed on to London.[64]

What was left for the Rumanian government then was that other solution being urged upon them by their German allies, a solution made easier to accept by the clear inference that no one really cared what happened to the Jews. And so the Rumanians began murdering them by the thousands every week.

Six months later, in December 1941, the Rumanian Jewish community tried again. The Germans were in closer control by then and one could no longer think of rescuing hundreds of thousands, besides it had been made clear that there was no place for hundreds of thousands of Jews to go. But if not that many, then less, then a very few; maybe that would be acceptable to the western world. This time they bribed the Gestapo chief in Bucharest, SS Colonel Karl Richter, and he agreed to let one shipload out. The Jews got a ship for the voyage, one filthy little ancient hulk called the *Struma,* that they chartered for the equivalent of $70,000 raised by community contributions. It would carry about a hundred people. There were 769 Jews crowded onto it—volunteers, because this was an experiment and no one knew that it wasn't some deadly Gestapo trick. If this one went without notice and without trouble, well—the good Colonel Richter had a soft heart and deep pockets and perhaps there could be other ships.

On the night of December 14, 1941, the *Struma* crept out of Constanta harbor, bound for the Mediterranean and thence—anywhere. It got nowhere. It was an old and rotten ship, and it wallowed 150 miles to the Turkish coast and there the engines failed finally. For nine weeks the *Struma* lay in the Bosphorus with her seams open and the pumps only just keeping her afloat and her passengers kept alive by the food donated by the Jewish community of Ankara. Nine weeks was too long to keep the story out of the newspapers; the whole world knew and the whole world watched. The Turks wouldn't let the Jews land unless they could cross Turkey into Palestine, and the British refused to admit them there. No other country offered refuge. In all the wide beautiful world there was no resting place for them, except in Germany's beckoning gas chambers. So at last the Turks towed the *Struma* out to sea and cast her adrift and six miles off the Turkish coast she sank. The sea alone gave its asylum to the 769 Jews, 70 of them children.[65]

"That is the history Keppler meant," Mandel-Mantello whispered, sitting next to Arnie Berg in the plane to Ankara. "And there were other ships," he said, "before the *Struma,* carrying other hundreds of Jews—the *Pacific,* the *Milos,* the *Alsina,* the *Atlantic,* the *Darien,* the *Petria,* the *Pencho,* the *Salvador;* out of Rumania, out of Hungary, out of Greece, and Italy, and Bulgaria, even Germany. All down in the same only safe refuge that welcomed the *Struma.*

"It's history," said Moses Mandel-Mantello. "It's all part of the record, but who reads the record? Who cares? . . . Only be patient with us if we are now bitter, and skeptical of the decency of your countrymen or any other people."

Arnie sat a long time, silent; and then he said: "We'll get the children out this time, all seventy thousand of them, out and safe." And he went from Ankara to Washington.

On March 12, 1943, Arnie reported to General Donovan and Secretary of the Treasury Morgenthau, and Morgenthau called in Stephen Wise, president of the American Jewish Congress. Within five days, Wise had raised the half a million dollars ransom money demanded by Premier Ion Antonescu and SS Colonel Richter. Hours later, the Treasury approved the transfer of the money to Switzerland and the Treasury's economic advisor, Dr. Herbert Feis, brought the approval to the State Department for the rest of the governmental processing required for transferring money in wartime. There the matter stalled for two months and it could not be shaken loose until Dr. Feis stormed in to Sumner Welles, the undersecretary of state. On May 25, the State Department cabled Berne for "information," and two months later vetoed the project on the grounds that it would be "putting American dollars into German hands." On July 24, Dr. Wise brought the matter to President Roosevelt, pointing out that the Swiss banks and the Swiss government were prepared to guarantee that the ransom could not be collected until after the war. Roosevelt ordered the State Department to go ahead. But by then someone at State decided the advice of the British government had to be sought. The British, of course, had to study the matter anew. The study was careful, it was all very complicated, it took time. It took five months.[66]

By December 1943, the British had completed their deliberate and careful study and had arrived, unsurprisingly, at a negative conclusion. "The Foreign Office," said the government's position paper from London, "is concerned with the difficulty of disposing of any considerable number of Jews should they be released from enemy territory."[67] Apparently there was still no asylum for Jews in the free world; not even for children, who take up less room.

Meanwhile, though, Jewish leaders had been besieging President Roosevelt; Mrs. Roosevelt's aid had been enlisted. The Jews pointed out that their organizations could not be expected—even in the interests of wartime unity—to remain discreetly silent. The pressure mounted. On December 20, Secretary of State Cordell Hull called in Morgenthau, told him of the British reaction, and handed

Morgenthau his proposed reply. The British message, Hull's note said, has been read "with astonishment" and the State Department "is unable to agree with the point of view set forth [which is] incompatible with the policy of the United States government . . ."[68]

After nine months, the State Department had been worn down and the American government was now on the side of the angels. Better late, it is said, than never. Only, for the seventy thousand Rumanian children it was too late —it was never. In all Rumania there were left only five thousand Jewish children alive to be rescued.

There was a scandal then—late, and small, confined to the inner circle of government. Refugee matters were taken out of the hands of the State Department and given over to a newly constituted War Refugee Board, the agents of which did difficult and dangerous work and managed to save some few thousands of Jews. But this was piecemeal, done by dedicated individuals in the dark. When, in May 1944, the chief of the Gestapo's Bureau for Jewish Affairs, Adolf Eichmann, offered the lives of a million Hungarian Jews against ransom, the prospect of so large a rescue again proved too terrible to contemplate. Joel Brandt, the Hungarian Jew who brought Eichmann's offer to the British in Palestine, was sent by them to a prison in Cairo. The American War Refugee Board "made it clear . . . that ransom transactions could not be entered into or authorized by the United States Government . . ."[69] The Hungarian Jews, too, went off to the gas chambers and the crematoria of Auschwitz, and the pain of their dying troubled only a few.

Years later, a time before he was hanged in Israel, Adolf Eichmann wrote the final summation of the long long record. "The plain fact was," said this plain mass murderer truthfully, "that there was no place on earth that would have been ready to acept the Jews. . . ."[70]

For three of those fateful nine months from March 1943, Arnie Berg watched while men highly placed in Washington and London, having—in this matter of the Jews—ill will or no will, by sins of omission and commission kept the seventy thousand Jewish children of Rumania within the path of the juggernaut until it reached and crushed them. For those three months he raged and watched and thought about the children and about the haunted, bitter men who had come to meet him in Cluj, and of the promises he had made to them.

Then General Donovan took pity upon him and gave him an outlet for the pain and hate that choked him. In July 1943, he was promoted to captain and parachuted into France as part of a "Jedburgh team" (two officers and a radio operator) assigned to coordinate and lead partisan units of the French Armée Secrète in the Aisne-Ardennes area. There he stayed until the Normandy invasion reached him, killing Germans with an implacable ferocity that has become folklore in the region.

In May 1945, at his request, he was transferred to the staff of Colonel John Harlan Amen, who headed the interrogation division of the American Office of Chief of Counsel, preparing the war-crimes trials at Nuremberg. For a year he worked at this, hunting down the hiding men who had murdered millions. In that hunter's year, in the last Nazi ramparts at Alt-Aussee in the Austrian Alps, Arnie met Ben-Issachar Feld—Benno the Messenger—who took him to the others, to Judah Klein and Avraham Becker and Hannah Baum—the Little Sister—and to Malachi Wald.

They hunted in different ways, that year; Arnie for the blind goddess of justice and those others for that surer retribution of the rope, the knife, and the gun. So their paths met, and went a little way together, and diverged. To come together again, after the war, when Arnie Berg saw the nations that had stood by while his people were slaughtered stand by again while the surviving remnant were endangered.

"Nobody but the Jew cares about the Jew," said Arnie Berg; and went to look for Malachi Wald. . . .

Five /

/ **The Roads**

In the first part of 1944, the largest armies ever
to fight on the face of the earth were engaged along a
front that stretched for a thousand miles across eastern
Europe. The Russian winter offensive was driving the
German Wehrmacht back upon the borders of Poland and
Rumania. For this titanic struggle the Soviet Union mar-
shaled every resource of manpower and equipment.
Everything that could be used to kill or to trouble the
German armies was thrown into the conflict. Orders went
out from the Red Army's Partisan High Command in Moscow to the "green men" in the forests within German-
occupied territory to begin a new phase in their guerrilla
warfare. Until then, the partisans had been organized into
the traditional small bands and had limited themselves
to such actions of sabotage and ambush as did not endanger their survival as fighting groups. Now they were
told to combine into brigade groups of up to eight hundred men, fighting formations capable of disrupting the
Wehrmacht's rear areas and of significant action against
the German lines of communication and supply.

Although the orders of the Red Army controlled only
the Communist partisans, the increasing tempo and the
changing nature of the fighting brought about by the
Russian offensive affected the non-Communist resistance
movements as well. The amalgamation of these non-Communist groups was also motivated by political considerations. In London the Polish government-in-exile—watching the westward sweep of the Red Army—tried to build

180

its underground Armia Krajowa into a territorial force-in-being capable of bolstering their claims to postwar authority over a reunified Poland which would, they hoped, be independent and western-oriented. The Churchill government did what it could to support this forlorn effort. The RAF shuttled across Europe dropping arms, equipment, and staff officers to resistance groups which gave allegiance to the London Poles. The Soviet Union gave the same aid to the Communist underground.

Amid all this high policy, no one gave any thought to the Jewish resistance. Where the Jews fought, they fought alone; and where they died, they died alone; as they had for years been fighting and dying, and alone. But though the policy makers ignored them, the Jewish resistance leaders were actuated by the same twin necessities that pressed upon the others. It was necessary for the Jewish partisan bands to join together in order to fight effectively under the new conditions of the war. And it was necessary to establish the unity of the Jewish underground in order to claim the right to speak for the surviving remnant of the Jewish people in eastern Europe at war's end.

So the runners threaded the deep forests of Latvia, Lithuania, and Poland, calling together the scattered units of the Jewish fighting resistance. When Dr. Yehezkel Atlas was killed in the fighting against the antipartisan battalions of SS Major General Oskar Dirlewanger, Elik Lipszowicz brought the two hundred men of Atlas's band to join the partisans from the Dereczyn and Zhatel ghettos in the Lipiczany forests. Abram Hornick's men came out of the Norecz swamps to Abba Kovner near Vilna, so that Kovner had five hundred men in his command. Israel Kagonovitch gathered four hundred in the Polesie woods; Ben-Zev Borochov had nearly six hundred at Novogrudok. In Lithuania, Malachi Wald and Chaim Yellin joined forces in the Augustava forests and then set out for the Rudniki woods where Abba Diskont had taken his section of the men who had broken out of the Ninth Fort at Kovno. Wald and Yellin and their men went 140 miles, traveling at night behind the German lines,

and when they got to Rudniki it was to find Diskont
dead, thirty others dead, the band cut to pieces by a
marauding battalion of the Polish exile government's
Armia Krajowa which even in 1944 still lightened its
arduous task of killing Germans by an occasional joyful
pogrom. Wald and Yellin gathered in the survivors of
Diskont's band and the six hundred men formed the
partisan brigade group they called "Death to the In-
vaders."[71]

On March 15 armored spearheads of the Red Army
forced crossings of the Bug River and fanned out into
Poland and the reorganized Jewish partisans burst into
activity. Berek Joselewicz's band infiltrated the suburbs of
Lublin and sucked two thousand men of the German
garrison out after them and spent the next two weeks
cutting them to ribbons in forest ambushes. Kagonovich
pinned down part of an armored battalion and two battalions of infantry by incessant raids on the German
supply roads around Polesie. Two battalions of Major
General Oskar Dirlewanger's special SS antipartisan formations spent their time chasing Elik Lipszowicz's band
through the Lipiczany marshes. Four volksdeutsche battalions came out of the German lines to deal with Borochov's men at Novogrudok. Wald raided as far as Narotch
and Kapoli and the Germans there were never able to
clear the western roads. Kovner's "Avengers" tore at the
German communications network around Vilna and when
the Red Army stormed the city, it was the Jews who led
the first assault group.[72]

All this is but a fragment of the record of Jewish
resistance. Thousands of Jews fought as individual volunteers within the ranks of the Soviet partisans. More than
five hundred of them received decorations for outstand-
ing bravery ranging up to the supreme "Order of Lenin"
and "Hero of the Soviet Union." Ninety-two of the Soviet
partisan formations had Jewish commanders. One out of
every four of the Jewish partisans in eastern Europe was
killed in those first four months of 1944, but they helped
to keep the German rear areas in flame from the Baltic
to the Rumanian border.[73]

In May 1944, delegates of the Jewish partisan groups demanded of the Red Army Partisan High Command that the Jewish Fighters' Organization be recognized as an integrated "Jewish National Army," to fight under their own field commanders within the Russian staff command. The Jews argued thus: Their people had shared the special fate of mass extermination reserved by the Germans for them alone. As Jews, they had been slaughtered; they had fought as Jews. Added now to the centuries of Jewish history, this latest special crucible of mass pain had now indissolubly fused this persecuted people and it was now a nation, demanding national recognition!

The demand was refused. The Russians saw the Jewish Fighters' Organization as a collection of Jewish separatists consituting a dissident national splinter group which would complicate the Soviet plans for a reorganization of eastern Europe. A real and effective Jewish nationalism was no part of Soviet policy. The Russians ordered the Jewish Fighters' Organization to disband and to send its men into the general Red Army partisan formations. Delegates representing about a third of the Jewish resistance groups bowed to the Red Army dictate. The rest—Malachi Wald, Israel Lapidus, and others—refused. So back into the forests they went, fighting the Germans still, but now hiding also from the Red Army partisans who had orders to disband them by force, by whatever force. And from May 1944, the heroic history of the Soviet partisans— as with the Polish underground Armia Krajowa before that time and after—was all too often shamed and bloodied by the killing of hundreds of brave men who were also fighting the common German enemy, but who were fighting—as Jews.[74]

It depended on how you looked at the world, and what you looked at, and where you stood to do the looking.

It was September 1944. The Allies were fighting up from Rome, had broken out of the Normandy beachheads, had taken Paris, and were hammering at the borders of Germany. Minsk had fallen, and Vilna and Lvov, and the Red Army was driving toward Warsaw. It would take almost another year, but it was clear already—the Wehrmacht was beaten, the thousand-year Reich was beginning to crumble. The long night over Europe was beginning to withdraw from a brightening world. If you stood tall on a mountain peak, if you had the world view, you could see the brightness coming.

But if you had something less than the world view, if you stood still in the dark, what then?

Malachi Wald stood in the dark Rudniki woods, and what he saw was different.

Minsk was liberated, and Vilna and Lvov; Krakow too, and Odessa, Kiev, Kharkov, Lublin, and Bialystok; and Warsaw soon. But the Jews of all these places were dead. The partisans ran wild and triumphant in the miles of eastern Europe. But the Jewish partisans were hunted in the woods. Diskont was dead, and the Belski brothers, Tema Schneidermann, Sars Gross and Moshe Sherman, Shlomo Frenkel, and so many others of those who had led the fighting Jews—dead, all dead. And how dead? Not at the hands of the Germans; not by the Latvians, or the Rumanians, or the Lithuanians, or any of the thousands of jackals that ran with the Nazi übermenschen. Killed by the Polish patriots and the Russian patriots. Killed by those who would have been their allies had they —the dead—only not been Jews.

Seen from the dark of the Rudniki woods, for the Jew —Malachi Wald—the night was endless. The heart goes out of a man, even out of a fighting man. The heart goes out, leaving only the empty anguished need to find somewhere some common warmth of love, to bring together the band of brothers scattered on the long roads to this denied victory. Who in this black hell is yet alive? Who is left that walks this earth that stinks of the dead and the deserted Jew?

Avraham Becker had gone east from the Ninth Fort at Kovno; gone with the Russian Vasilienko, in the days they thought the Red Army would help the new Jewish partisans. Perhaps he was still alive? So Malachi sent Mira Lan six hundred miles east through the contending armies to Moscow. And found him! He having come a thousand miles from Soviet Kazakhstan where the Russians had sent him to get him out of the way. Avraham Becker, coming westward with the same mad longing purpose—to seek the band of brothers. . . . Benno the Messenger was found in Crainu, sick with dysentery, was healed and sent west and south to Warsaw and beyond to the burned shell of Trcblinka where Judah Klein the wig-maker had gathered thirty of the survivors of the Treblinka revolt. . . . Malachi himself went in again to the dangerous graveyard of Kovno, once his home, to bring out those few friends—the ghetto fighters who were still alive, living like starving hounds in the ruins and the ashes. . . .

Malachi Wald, and those others who saw as he did, looked out on the endless night of the Jew and sent the messengers all over eastern Europe. The Russians were gathering the Jewish survivors within the reconquered territory into camps at Lublin, and the messengers took the word to the scattered leaders of the Jewish fighting resistance, to the band of brothers: "For us this fight is over, *this* one is. Come to Lublin. We meet at Lublin. . . ."

Lublin was famous. For five hundred years it had been a center of Jewish learning. In 1939, the Germans came and for five years from then they had turned the city into a shining model of their own superior brand of Kultur. In November 1939, the Germans declared Lublin a *Judenreservat*—a "Jew reservation"—and in the years they held the city they made it into the center of a ring of fifty-one slave-labor camps and three death camps: Trcblinka, in which more than half a million Jews were gassed; Sobibor, which claimed a quarter of a million; and Maidenek, where 360,000 were murdered.[75] More Jews than these were killed at Auschwitz, of course, but the record in the Lublin area was adequate. Maidenek itself claimed the highest total number of Jews ever to be killed anywhere on a single day. The Polish Prince Christopher Radziwill, who'd been a prisoner of war at

Maidenek, revealed this to the world when he told the newsmen at Nuremberg:

> I shall never forget the day the Nazis killed 17,000 Jews at Majdenek while I was in another part of the concentration camp. That evening many of my Polish fellow-prisoners got drunk to celebrate. That is terrible but it is true.[76]

That was on November 3, 1943, and SS Lieutenant Georg Kurt Mussfeld, who was in charge of the day's work, boasted to the SS Judge Konrad Morgen that on that day "the ashes of the Jews I roasted floated like dust over all of Lublin."[77] On the strength of that day's notable achievement, Mussfeld was sent—coals to Newcastle—to be an efficiency expert at Auschwitz. He regretted it all later, or so he said in 1958 when Benno Feld and Hannah Baum found him—fat and prosperous—and hanged him in the kitchen of the pilgrims' inn Mussfeld kept in Oberammergau, where every ten years the devout Germans reenact the Passion of Christ.

They came to Lublin, what was left of the band of brothers.

There were fifty thousand Jews in the stockades of Lublin then, still behind the barbed-wire fences that had closed them in for years. But now the guards were Russians, and nobody was killing them. Now the Jews were killing themselves; hanging themselves; tearing their veins open; sixty to ninety suicides a week. Freed of the binding pressure of the murdering Germans, they embraced the death that had passed them by. They could not live in the now-leisured memory of what their years had been. For they were burdened with the terrible, innocent guilt of being yet alive with brother and sister, husband and wife and parents and children long gone before them to tortured death. And they alive, haunted witnesses to their own impotence and to the evil of God and man. So they said to the familiar ghosts, "Wait!" and they took themselves along the dark well-traveled road.

The Russians did their best. Especially with the children: feeding them carefully, giving them clothes and care and schoolrooms and toys; the big, laughing soldiers bringing chocolate, playing games; the Russian women smiling down at them, hugging them close to bosom warmth and sympathy. But not a morning came to kindergarten or play yard without the lengthening shadow of some broken child swinging from a bit of stolen rope in the bright sun.

Never less than sixty suicides a week; and those many more who sat in the corners of the camp hospitals and died, just died. Loneliness and despair and dreadful memory, all these of themselves, can kill.

And there were those who did not die but neither did they live, they breathed, they existed in the numb limbo between life and death, no more than this.

There was no health to be found in the Lublin stockades, no beginning. So the band of brothers went out of the camps, taking with them those few in whom there was sufficient life-force flickering to guide them to some other road. It was against the rules for the Jews to live outside the wire, but the Russian guards were human and not immune to another's pain. Within a week there were nearly two hundred of them, mostly members of Hashomer Hatzair—the Zionist "Young Guards," living cooperatively in a crumbling warehouse. The Russians shut their eyes to the rules, dropped off food, and gave them work cards; and throughout Lublin the warehouse was known as "the kibbutz."

They worked, and shared what they had, and talked. Talked. Each of them told of his particular hell and so they pieced it all together, bit by bit, ghetto by ghetto, camp by camp, murder after murder after murder; what they themselves had seen, what others had seen and reported. Until they had it all, the whole tragedy of the European Jews, from Drancy in France east to Babi Yar and the mass grave at Kiev. Until it was clear that all Europe was a graveyard and there would be no step in Europe a Jew could take that would not leave him standing on his brother Jew, dead and burned and shoved underground.

And so they sought another road, and revived the ancient Zionist dream—Palestine.

They left Lublin then, with the distant guns still roaring westward. Two hundred of them, more, led by Wald and Becker and the rest—out of Lublin toward Palestine. They moved at night, in small groups, by different paths, with a rendezvous point set every five days ahead. They went in zigzags, like men in a maze, turned back at every checkpoint and finding some other place to cross. They went the secret, partisan roads; barred from the towns, turned back from the combat areas, rounded up and shunted off by the military administrations that wanted civilians to stay in one place and out of the way. And out again, gathering the scattered Jews, streams of them that separated, converged, separated again. On across Poland, sliding along the barred border of Czechoslovakia, moving south into Hungary and Rumania, or west into Germany itself, infiltrating through the Russian lines, through the shattered and disintegrating German armies. Until they were spread over the miles, several thousands of them, in shadowy columns, on foot, in stolen trucks and wagons, with the veterans of the Jewish Fighters' Organization circling around them, protecting them; and the band of brothers leading them.

They went with the pressure of the ocean of dead behind them and they moved like ants—indomitable.

Like ants. And every now and then, some of the ants strayed—briefly—from the path. Here and there, as they went, they passed Germans still wearing the black SS uniforms on their way under guard to the prisoner-of-war camps. Most often the guard was a single Russian peasant, his tommy gun slung on his back, a wisp of straw hanging from his lips. When this happened, there were always some five or six of the passing Jews who dropped out of line and drifted off when night came. And when the day broke, there would be the Russian guard, sleeping soundly and happily drunk. And there would be the SS men, dead at the roadside.

The Jews moved on. . . .

The village called Obernau nestles in the lush fields of Saxony just north of the Czechoslovak border. It is a pretty, peaceful place, and was so even in that grim winter of 1944. The war had passed by Obernau except, of course, that Stolhaus had been built there. Stolhaus was a slave-labor camp where captive Jews worked in Krupp von Bohlen und Halbach's munitions factory and slept in kennels the good baron's thrifty managers provided for them. The kennels were three feet high, nine feet long, six feet wide, and five Jews slept in each of them.[78] It was interesting to see and on occasional Sundays the villagers were allowed to tour the camp. On other occasions, the male population of Obernau would turn out for a kind of fox hunt, with the quarry being some Jew who had broken out of the camp and would invariably be flushed from cover in the golden wheat fields. Stolhaus provided other benefits to the good people of Obernau, the merchants and farmers grew prosperous selling food and amenities to the SS garrison, the SS men were virile and generous swains to the amiable village girls. For Obernau, it was a pleasant war.

Things changed a little, though, in mid-1944. Orders came from Berlin, the factory at Stolhaus was dismantled, the Jews were marched out, grass grew over the kennels. The jovial SS men went elsewhere, except for some few who sneaked back into the village, doffed their black uniforms, and married the solid farm girls they had been sleeping with. It was unfortunate, but it wasn't disastrous; the fields were still there and the crops were good and the village merely settled down to its normal quiet prosperity.

Until one frosty morning the village awoke to find the Jews back—the same old Jews or other Jews, it made no difference. There they were, like vermin in the fields, and where were the guards? Jews out of their kennels and no one hunting them? It was true, then, the war was lost. But lost war or no, there was no reason for the Jews to come to Obernau, let them fester in some other fields.

There were nearly three hundred Jews outside Obernau.

They were the column led by Malachi Wald and Avraham Becker, out of Lublin, across Poland, across German Silesia, across half of Saxony. They were poised to go through Czechoslovakia and Austria and down into Italy. At Bari, the Jewish underground army of Palestine—the Hagana—was gathering the rusty ships to run the DPs past the British blockade into Palestine. But the travelers were worn and cold and hungry, so Wald and Becker stopped them there, to rest in the fields at Obernau.

The Jews made their camp and sent ten men with a truck into the village to gather food and water. They had no money, who had money? They weren't intending to buy food, but to get it, to be given it by the Germans who had plenty and, as the Jews saw it, owed them some.

The villagers held a different view. What they saw was just another fox hunt brewing; bigger than the others and more exciting, but the same Jew foxes and the same end to the hunt.

The ten Jews were met by the village obermeister heading a solid, representative group—the two village policemen, some of the farmers, six or seven ex-soldiers, and the dozen or so former SS men, who had donned their black uniforms once again to lend tone to this familiar occasion. Six of the Jews were killed before they got the truck turned around and raced back to their camp.

An hour later, in the bright morning, Wald and Avraham Becker and twenty others came into Obernau in two battered trucks. They came with guns and grenades. They drove past the staring villagers to the town hall where the most substantial citizens had been called by the obermeister to a meeting to decide whether the Jews should now just be allowed to leave, or whether a few more should first be hanged as a warning to other locust swarms that might be following.

Wald and Becker and the others got off the trucks and stood at the windows and the doors and killed the Germans where they sat.

For three days, then, the Jews camped in the fields of Obernau and went into the village for food and water and fuel; and got them without trouble. Then they moved on. . . .

What happened at Obernau was not unique. The wandering Jews were killed and had to fight also at Annsberg, Glachau, Limbach, Einsfeld, Auerbach, Hildburghausen. By the time the Russians and the Allied armies finally cut the last flicker of life out of the Third Reich, a postscript—and not the last one—had been written to the long history of German hatred for the Jew. And even when the Reich was dead and the conquering armies spread out over Germany, the killing went on in the little villages beyond the control centers. The mass of Jewish survivors were being gathered by the Allies into DP camps, but outside those camps, wherever the wandering secret columns came on their way to Palestine, the Germans killed Jews when they could. Germany was beaten, and the Germans knew they had been demoted—übermenschen to mittelmenschen, as it were—but beneath them still were the ultimate untermenschen, lowest of the low, the damned Jews.

So it happened that in the closing weeks of the war the good German folk, shuffling among the ruins of their thousand-year Reich, found some small surcease of anguish in accomplishing the death of yet another few Jews. It was senseless, meaningless even in Nazi terms. But so it happened, and no one noticed. Among the crashing chords of the Götterdämmerung who could hear the cries of these last few dying Jews?

History is sometimes written thus, in the small type at the bottom of the page, the footnotes no one reads. These last killings were the footnotes that changed the history of some scores of Jews among those who fought to protect the columns of the wandering Jewish remnant in the German countryside.

They had come out of the forests and the camps. They had had enough of fighting and suffering and hate and pain. They were on their way to join the Jews of Palestine, but the British wouldn't let them through, and the Americans and the Russians and the French wouldn't

help them go, and the Germans killed them as they went.
They had come out of Treblinka and Sobibor and Auschwitz, out of Bergen-Belsen and Sachsenhausen and Buchenwald; and the Allied armies chased them and rounded
them up and shoved them once again into camps, behind
the fences of the DP camps at Feldafing and Bad Reichenhall and Foehrenwald. There they rotted in the thousands as they had rotted in those other camps for more
than six years, still locked in on German soil with the
stench of their millions of dead. And not one country
in all the world to say "Let them go! Let them come
to us!"

And the Germans, the guilty, guilty Germans, still
killing what Jews they safely could.

This is what the veteran fighters saw as they led their
Jewish remnant along the secret roads; and for some few
of them this did what all the armies guarding all the
borders of Europe could not do, it turned them back
from their way to Palestine.

*It was years later, in a kibbutz in Galilee, that Malachi
Wald said to me—and I quote him word for word: "I want
you to think of a man coming out of the camps or the
forests in 1945, and all he wants is to get out of Europe
where everyone he loved is dead, his whole people murdered, and they will not let him go. He comes out of the
camps and they put him back in camps; no country wants
him, only his people in Palestine want him, and they will
not let him go. Those who do this to him, who do it after
all his years of pain, are not the enemy who killed him,
but those others from whom he has the right to expect
kindness and mercy and justice.*

*"This man looks at the world, and what does he see?
The eyes that were closed to his suffering are closed still,
the hands that were not lifted to help him are not lifted
now. The Germans who killed the Jews are free and they
till their soil and have their jobs and their families, they
are the mayors and the policemen and the respected ones,
and the Jews are as homeless vermin. The Germans are*

*free and the Jews are back in the camps and no one
wants them.*

*"If you write it, Mike," said Malachi Wald, standing
there in the cold Galilee wind, "every word should be as
a knife cutting flesh. For what we learned in 1945—
what despite everything we had not, until then, really believed—what we learned cut our flesh then, cut deep and
brought a pain that never ends. We learned at last in
1945, that nobody in the world but the Jew cares about
the Jew. In all the world there is no justice for the Jew
except that justice which the Jew can take for himself.*

*"That's what we did. We stood at the crossroads then
and we turned our backs on Palestine and we started to
take our own justice—justice and vengeance!"*

So said Malachi Wald to me.

There is a Hebrew phrase, a fighting slogan going back
to biblical times: *Dahm Y'Israel Nokeam*—"The blood
of Israel will take vengeance." In the first months of
1945, in Germany, Wald and Becker, Judah Klein, Benno
the Messenger and Hannah Baum and fifty others left the
people they had till then led. They took this fighting slogan for their own and formed the secret organization
which came to be known, to those who knew of it at
all, by the first letter of each word; the Hebrew letters
daled, yod, nun; the letters that spell out another Hebrew
word: *DIN*, which means "judgment."

And from 1945 until this day they have taken vengeance, and imposed the judgment of the Jew, upon the
killers of the Jews.

Six

DIN—Judgment and Vengeance

The men who formed DIN in 1945 by that act separated themselves from the mainstream of what was at that time the Jewish reality in Europe.

When the Third German Reich crashed into ruin there were about half a million Jews left alive in the killing centers and the slave-labor camps which the Germans and their allies had built throughout eastern and central Europe. Perhaps another quarter million survived in the forests or in the rubble of the eastern ghettos. They all shared a common wish, a common urgent need—to get out, out of the camps, out of Europe. The land was accursed.

There had been Jewish communities in Europe for more than two thousand years, and of all those hundred Jewish generations not one had been allowed to live its time without paying tribute in blood to the non-Jewish majority. In all that time it had never mattered what temporal power ruled. Under king, emperor, parliament, revolutionary cabal, the Jews had been always less than equal in every country in Europe; often less than human; held in ghettos and hunted in the streets. Nor had it mattered ever what religious ethic prevailed at any time, in any place. Roman pantheist, Eastern Orthodox, Catholic, Calvinist. Lutheran—in the name of every god and of every way to god, they all taught contempt and hatred for the Jew; and out of their teachings through the centuries came always pogrom and murder. Finally had come the paladins of the Third Reich and the jackals who ran with them; and they had in time spread pain and death to all Europe—to Jew and Gentile—it is true, but first and worst to the Jew. And as long as it had been only the Jew enslaved, hounded and killed, no nation anywhere had opened a path for his escape, no armies had gathered, none gave the Jew arms for his defense. So that when it ended, the Jewish loss in proportion to population was six times greater than Russia's, eight times greater than Poland's, ninety times that suffered by the people of England, five hundred times that of the Americans.[79] In this last immolation, they had had this priority of pain; when the reckoning came would they be granted any commensurate priority of pity and relief?

In 1945 the armies of the United Nations liberated the starving Jews from the death camps and the slave-labor camps, gathered others in from the forests and the sewers of the ghettos. Liberated them and gathered them in and showed them the shape of the shining future prepared for them in the new free world—more camps, new camps; the barracks and the barbed wire and the empty sterility of Feldafing, Allach, Foehrenwald, Degendorf, Leipheim, Stuttgart, Bad Reichenhall. This was the future planned for them. Here no one killed them. Here they were fed and clothed and given medical care. They could marry and have children; and they could all, presumably, rot. It was perhaps to be hoped that they would do this quietly, for they were an irritant and an embarrassment to all the civilized world, which had no time for them, and had no shelter for them or plans for them beyond the camps.

The Anglo-American Commission of Inquiry put the matter bluntly in its report to the General Assembly of the United Nations:

> We know of no country to which the great majority [of the Jewish survivors in Europe] can go in the immediate future other than Palestine. Furthermore, that is where all of them want to go. There they are sure that they will receive a welcome denied them elsewhere.[80]

It was all true. No people anywhere would accept any significant number of the Jewish refugees into their country, save only the Jewish community of Palestine. And the European Jews had enough of living as Jews—and dying because they were Jews—among the uncaring and the criminal goyim. They wanted to live where they were welcome, among their brethren in the ancient homeland. But Britain held the mandate over Palestine and British policy excluded the Jews, and the British navy barred the way. That left the camps; only and endlessly—the camps. Full circle. Full stop. If there was to be any alternative, the Jews themselves would have to create it; and they would have to find somehow in their helpless misery the strength to force it upon the world. They began to do just that.

Dr. Zalman Grinberg, Wladislaw Friedheim, and Isaac Ratner sent runners out of Feldafing to all the camps of the survivors; and they came back with forty-one men and women, delegates of the trapped 1½ million Jews. They met in Feldafing and a man stood before them in the uniform of the Jewish Brigade, the Palestinians who fought in the British army through the campaigns of Italy and France. He was Major Zvi Caspi, bringing a message from the *Va'ad Leumi*—the national council of the Palestine Jewish community, and he said: "You are bone of our bone, flesh of our flesh. We in Palestine wait to welcome you with open arms, and it will be done. Be strong," he said, "united, be organized and disciplined."[81] That day in Feldafing, the delegates of the Jews in the camps formed the new Jewish resistance. They called it She'erit Hapleetah—"the Surviving Remnant"—and it grew into the loud troublesome organization that led the public struggle to force the gates of Palestine. For nearly three years She'erit Hapleetah published newspapers, sent delegations all over the world, organized 1½ million Jews in protest meetings and hunger strikes. And for nearly three years it served as cover for another organization that worked illegally and in secret across all Europe.

"You are bone of our bone," said Caspi, "flesh of our flesh," and even as he spoke the Jews of Palestine from whom he had come were giving meaning to his words. From Hagana, the Jewish underground army in Palestine, a hundred agents filtered into Europe. Yehuda Arazi went to Milan, Ehud Avriel to Belgrade, Shaul Avigur to Paris, Elkhanan Gafni to Bucharest, Moshe Bar-Gilad to Vienna, Hoter Yishai, Ephraim Deckel, Ruth Klieger, and others to Germany. They were the beginning of the group which came to be called Bricha (which is Hebrew for "escape"), the secret organization that operated under the cover of She'erit Hapleetah. They brought a plan. She'erit Hapleetah within the camps would mobilize the Jews who were willing at any risk to try for Palestine, and would filter them out of the camps to the Bricha agents. Bricha would take over from there; smuggle them across Europe to the Mediterranean ports and the fishing villages, put them on ships and run them—ship after ship after ship—to Palestine. They would send them against the British blockade, an endless flood of thousands of unarmed refugees in the leaking ships, men, women, and children by the thousands, month after month, until the British could hold them back no more. And so, indeed, it came to pass.[82]

The Palestinians brought the money to buy supplies, to pay for travel documents—real and forged, to buy trucks, to bribe consular officials, and police, and border guards, and port authorities. They bought and equipped and manned the ships. But more was needed. Men were needed who had the special skill and the experience to hide the refugees in the forests, to lead them at night across the borders, to guide them and guard them and bring them down to the waiting ships. For this, the Palestinians called in the commanders of the Jewish partisan brigades of eastern Europe, the ghetto fighters—Dr. Avraham Blumovicz from Byelorussia, Zvi Horowicz from Kovno, Abba Kovner and Abram Hornick from Vilna, Anton Zuckermann and Mordechai Rosman from Warsaw, they and others. And called in also those who had led the first columns of Jewish refugees out of the Lublin stockade—Malachi Wald, Avraham Becker, Mira

Lan, Benno the Messenger, Judah Klein, and "little sister," Hannah Baum.

For three days in Frankfurt the Hagana men who ran Bricha met with the former partisan leaders, speaking to them in small groups about specific assignments so that no one outside the Bricha executive would know the whole scope of the organization. The Palestinians spoke in terms of command, as they had a right to do, for they stood at the head of the new Jewish liberation movement in Europe. Bricha and She'erit Hapleetah were to come to include almost every adult Jew and many who would, in a world more innocent, be still considered children. Any Jew who stood outside cut himself off from the mainstream of the Jewish reality in Europe. At the end of the Frankfurt meetings, of the partisan leaders only Wald and those who had come with him stood outside. Those who joined the liberation movement were warmed by the vision of a new life as part of a renascent Jewish nation in Palestine; and between them and their vision stood only the practical barriers of the borders and the British. But the bitter few who went with Malachi Wald were barred by another mystique. They longed for the same fruitful life, and saw the same shimmering vision; but between this and them stood the martyred millions, and the killers alive in a world which had given no justice to the Jews and would likely give little in time to come. The thousands who were to travel in the rusting ships to the beaches of Palestine moved to the music of the Jewish national anthem: *Hatikva*—"The Hope." These few heard only the voices of memory: Mordechai Tennenbaum, dying with the fighters he commanded in the Bialystok ghetto—"In the name of the shed blood of our children, take vengeance!" Rachel Baum, torn and blinded at the gallows, calling down to the massed prisoners at Auschwitz—"Avenge me!"

The dead commanded them and they could not then acknowledge another allegiance. So they stood apart and went alone out of Frankfurt, and began the work of DIN.

They were all experienced at clandestine work and the

period needed for organization was a brief one. In the beginning they picked their people quickly; there were enough who shared their hate and had shared their past, and could be trusted. Later there were others, not from among those who had been with the Jewish Fighters' Organization of eastern Europe. These came individually, and were tested at peripheral tasks. Most important among these later recruits were those who worked within the Soviet or the Allied war crimes commissions and could open the files to DIN. There were two sergeants working in the transport pool attached to U.S. Army Headquarters at the I. G. Farben building in Frankfurt, and their equivalents in the French and British zones of occupation, whose ability to provide military transport was to prove useful. There was a young rabbi who had been a chaplain with the U.S. First Army, and whose concept of God and man was brought to a harsher reality by what he saw when Dachau was liberated.

Within weeks, DIN had a net spread across Germany and Austria—loosely meshed, inadequate to the task as it would always be, but ready to function. There were nearly three hundred people connected with the organization in mid-1945. Most of these were engaged in fringe activities. Some could obtain travel documents, or gasoline rations; some arranged the safehouses; many provided money—working the black markets, thieves among thieves in the concrete jungles of Germany and Austria. There were men in most of the major cities. There were contacts among the personnel who manned the stockades in which suspected war criminals were held for investigation. Each of these, everywhere, listened and watched and sent information to DIN. Each of them knew only what he had to know of the organization; and there were the cutouts between these many and the few who stood at the heart of DIN and did the killing. From the beginning, only Jews were taken into the organization at any level. Partly this was a security precaution, mostly it was a matter of principle. The men of DIN saw themselves always as agents of the Jewish people, taking vengeance alone—as Jews—for those who had been killed and tortured alone, as Jews.

The first major action came very soon, by happenstance; and it brought them the man called "Israel," who a year later would take Malachi Wald's place when he was betrayed into a British prison in Egypt.

In the last months of the war, the Nazi leaders had organized what they hoped would be an underground army. It was composed mainly of young men who had been educated in the years of the Nazi regime and knew nothing other than the bloody doctrine of "Rasse und Reich." This army was never intended to fight in the war, for the war was lost. It was intended to keep the ideology alive, to be a disciplined force available to the Nazi leaders who were going into hiding, and who would emerge at some anticipated opportune time of postwar chaos in Germany. The movement was called *die Werwölfe,* and the Reich Youth Leader "Golden Boy" Baldur von Schirach was appointed to command.

The Americans hunted von Schirach down in Alt-Aussee and in token of the menace that he represented he was next to the last prisoner to be released from the Fortress. When Schirach was taken, leadership of the fanatic horde fell to an unknown man whose deputy was Erwin Weinmann, once chief of the Nazi security police in Bohemia. In mid-1945, there were a hundred thousand Werewolves organized in units of company strength, drilling under the noses of the occupation forces in basements and forests and maintaining arms caches scattered throughout Germany.

One of these arms caches, twelve waterproof chests, was hidden under a boating pier in a small stream leading onto the main River near Ulm, in Bavaria. Two miles away, the Bricha had set up a marshaling area for illegal immigrants to Palestine who were being smuggled out of the Augsburg Jewish refugee camp. Camouflaging this marshaling area was a Zionist *hachshara* camp in which young Jews learned farming and commercial fishing techniques and such other useful pursuits, ostensibly against the day when the British might grant them legal immigration into Palestine.

Some of the boys from the camp, fishing in the river, hooked one of the twelve cases and went down into the water to see what had fouled their nets. The news of the underwater dump was brought to the Bricha area commander—the man called Israel—and he had one of the cases brought up and opened. It contained Schmeisser submachine guns and machine pistols, and ammunition. Israel had the case battened down again and replaced. Day and night thereafter, relays of boys from the *hachshara* camp sat in the trees with binoculars and watched the area, until the night the company of Werewolves came to care for the guns and to drill in the woods. Then Israel sent the news to Malachi Wald, and Wald sent him ten men of DIN.

It took another fortnight of watching until the Ulm company of the Werewolves came again, bringing with them—unexpected dividend—the deputy commander of the whole mad mob, Erwin Weinmann. They came, 140 of them, to unfurl the swastika flag and sit at a campfire with guns in their hands listening to a criminal sadist in his Death's Head uniform with the Knight's Cross on his chest tell them of the coming Fourth German Reich and the absolute, final end of the Jews. And to die, with their guns and their dreams, killed by eleven men with submachine guns and hand grenades who came out of the dark. A hundred and forty young fanatics, dreaming in their bootleg uniforms, lying dead in a wood— what for? . . .

Ask the question of someone else, not of the men who killed them, who had gone through the ghettos and the forests and had seen what young fanatics could do. Ask the question of someone who cannot remember these words:

> I cast my eyes back to the time when with *six* other unknown men I founded this association. . . .
> —Adolf Hitler, speaking at the Nazi
> party rally in Düsseldorf,
> January 27, 1932

There was trouble after the killings outside Ulm. It was hard for the disappearance of 140 young townsmen in a single night to pass unnoticed (though nearly five hundred Jews had similarly disappeared from that same community two years before without any noticeable ripples of curiosity). A search was initiated, the bodies were found, and an angry and sorrowing delegation of the burghers of Ulm went to the occupation authorities in Munich. The personnel of the Zionist camp nearby were the obvious suspects. No evidence was found in the camp, so the officials were hauled down to Munich for interrogation. Among them was Israel, not in his capacity as the Bricha commander—the investigators didn't know about that—but in his cover job as senior farming instructor.

To assure the Germans of the thoroughness of the investigation, the delegation from Ulm was allowed to be present and to have their lawyer put questions to the witnesses. The lawyer was from Munich, a public-spirited volunteer named Dr. Richard Lebküchner. Lebküchner's services were perhaps a bit inept; though the matter didn't come out at the time, he had been for years chief of the Munich Gestapo and he was used to a somewhat more rigorous interrogation technique. It presumably had been his sensitive empathy with the sorrowing Ulm citizenry that had impelled Lebküchner to contribute his services, but he seemed most concerned with the dead former security police chief, Erwin Weinmann. His questions seemed to center on the issue of whether any documents had been found in the SS uniform Weinmann had been wearing when he was killed, or in the civilian clothes he had worn to the Werewolves' rendezvous.

Israel had himself searched Weinmann's body immediately after the execution and had found nothing of interest save a collection of identification papers listing a choice selection of names and occupations for the dead man. Israel was intrigued by Lebküchner's performance and when the hearing adjourned, he followed him.

The good doctor led Israel to a café, and he watched while Lebküchner sat over a cup of ersatz coffee with a pudgy, middle-aged gentleman whose clothes were of a quality sufficient to constitute an indiscretion in poverty-stricken Munich. When the meeting ended, it was this second man who paid, signifying that he was the host and therefore the important one. When the two Germans parted, Israel followed the second man; and was, he noticed, himself followed by a burly soldierly type. That made the man he was tagging even more important. The little caravan trotted along briskly until Israel's quarry turned in at a respectable house and let himself in. He had a key, so he was probably at home and could be allowed to roost. For Israel, there was the problem of the man behind him.

Israel took this one for a long walk to the safehouse of DIN. He went in and sent out the two men who kept the house to persuade the man watching outside to share their hospitality, the invitation being emphatic. The burly man was a tough one and the questioning took several hours. Since one of the first things they discovered was the SS blood-group tattoo in the man's left armpit, they were not inclined to be gentle; and when he was battered and frightened enough, he talked.

He was, it turned out, SS Obersturmführer Hubert Schwartz, late of Auschwitz, and at the time in question bodyguard to Dr. Ernst Wetzel—the pudgy gentleman from the café. Wetzel's name was known to DIN, he was high on the international list of war criminals. At the very beginning of "the final solution," Wetzel had already been important, In 1941 he had been head of the Race Office of the NSDAP, and on October 25, 1941—as executive assistant to the Reich minister for the occupied eastern territories—he had written to Reichskommissar Heinrich Lohse in Poland instructing him to use the newly built gas chambers "to liquidate Jews who are unsuitable for work."[83] He had disappeared at the beginning of 1945 and was a fugitive. What was a man on the run doing with a bodyguard? Schwartz provided the answer. He had been assigned as Wetzel's bodyguard when Wetzel became commander of the Werewolves after Baldur von

Schirach had been arrested. This was big game, and the hunters moved quickly.

Schwartz had a key to Wetzel's house. Israel and the other two took that, and took Schwartz with them and left him with his throat cut in an alley on the way, and went to pay a call on Dr. Wetzel. They brought the commander of the Werewolves and a suitcase full of documents out of Munich that night. They questioned him for two days, and then they sank him in the Chiemsee near the Austrian border, with a load of iron wired to his feet, and went to ground in the Jewish refugee camp at Bad Reichenhall to await developments.

The Bricha agent in the Bad Reichenhall camp knew Israel of course, and when he questioned what Israel was doing outside his assigned territory and got no satisfactory answer, he turned to the executive of Bricha. They connected the events at Ulm with Israel's sudden appearance at Bad Reichenhall and called him in to a hearing. Bricha had a job to do in Europe and they could not allow it to be endangered by extracurricular activities however understandable or even laudable. Though Israel outranked them in Hagana (he was a lieutenant colonel in the Jewish underground army of Palestine), they were his superiors in Bricha; from then on he would do his assigned job and nothing else or get out of the organization.

For ten years in the Hagana and in the Jewish Night Squads which the British military messiah Orde Wingate had organized to protect the Jewish settlements in Palestine against Arab raiders, Israel had followed the orders of the Jewish community leaders in Palestine. Before that, in Germany in the early thirties, he had commanded the Young Zionist Guards—Hashomer Hatzair, the Jewish youth who had fought the Nazi storm troopers in the streets of Berlin. He had known no other life but that of disciplined obedience to the recognized Jewish authorities wherever he was. The Bricha leaders knew this, and knew therefore what choice he would make. He chose differently; he chose DIN.

There were no other developments in the matter of the

young men of Ulm, and of Wetzel and Weinmann. The name of Dr. Ernst Wetzel, whereabouts unknown, still appears on the wanted list of major war criminals. And the American Counterintelligence Corps never knew who sent them the suitcase of documents—the maps of the arms caches and the lists of the company commanders— that enabled them to break the Werewolves of the "Fourth German Reich." . . .

It was after Ulm that Victor Berger came to them, bearing gifts.

He showed up one day at the home of Fritz Grosz, who was the cutout between DIN and the people who raised money for the group by working the Münster black market, and offered his "considerable" services to the good work of killing Nazis.

It was a bad moment for Grosz. There was this bright-eyed blond, natty as a bridegroom in his French major's uniform, complete with the Free French Cross of Lorraine, the Croix de Guerre, and enough other gongs to decorate an entire front-line regiment. From the moment the caller opened his mouth, Grosz regarded him as though he were a well-dressed bomb. He couldn't just leave him there, ticking away on his doorstep, so he invited him in and they spent a time snuffling at each other while Grosz tried to decide whether his visitor was an agent provocateur, or a nut, or a man potentially useful to DIN.

Berger introduced himself as an intelligence officer with the French occupation staff. His work, he said, was hunting down war criminals for the impending trials. In the course of this, he'd come to suspect the existence of a group of ex-officio avengers, and the recent killings at Ulm had confirmed his suspicions. He had poked around and been led to Grosz. Now he wanted Grosz to put him in contact with the group so that he could join them. He was, he pointed out, in a position to be of help.

Grosz said he found this all very interesting, but he himself was only a merchant doing a little buying and selling, and much too old for such excitements. If Berger had been led to him it was because some mischief-maker was pulling his leg. Berger nodded pleasantly and agreed it must indeed be so; but perhaps Grosz would go along with the gag and take down a few particulars, and he would return in a fortnight just in case—well, just in case. Or would Grosz prefer to discuss it at a more formal interview, say at French headquarters? Grosz looked at his guest's icy smile, and shrugged. He would take the notes, he said, making it clear that he was merely humoring a lunatic.

Berger's papers, spread before Grosz, indicated that he was as he had said, a French officer hunting war criminals; that he'd had three years service in the French resistance as an agent of General de Gaulle's cloak-and-dagger Bureau Central de Renseignements et d'Action, working under Andre Dowavrin—the legendary "Colonel Passy." His papers described him as Jewish, and he offered to confirm this with some physical evidence. Grosz said he was prepared to take Berger's faith, on faith; and what was the point of it all?

The point was this: Berger had long been convinced that the coming war crimes trials would only skim the top political scum off the Nazi broth, and that many thousands of murderers would escape adequate punishment if such punishment were to be limited to legal procedures. For some time, therefore, he had been using his position and the information it brought him to accomplish a little private justice. Most recently, for example, he had killed Heinz Braune, who had been with SS Hauptsturmführer Theo Dannecker, who had been in charge of deporting the French Jews to Auschwitz during 1942. Now Berger was after SS Obersturmführer Konrad Schumann, who had come to Paris in 1943 as one of the agents in France of Adolf Eichmann's Gestapo Bureau 4 B IV. Among the 49,906 Jews Schumann had sent to the gas chambers had been Victor Berger's wife, his two children, his parents, his sister and her four children—all taken in a single raid, personally supervised by Schumann, on the Jewish quarter of the rue Cadet in Paris. Berger told Grosz he knew where Schumann was, but he would need help to

get him. If Grosz's friends would help, if they would give
him Schumann, he would give them the chance of killing
about two hundred SS officers at one time; and he would
work with them from then on.

Well, there it was. Victor Berger smiled and said good-
bye and left Grosz sitting there—a little fat man in his
fifties, with a problem. Grosz couldn't deal with it, of
course, so he turned it over to his cutout, Sergeant Meyer
Tugend in the American CIC in Frankfurt. Tugend
checked Berger out as far as he could and when there
seemed enough to indicate that all of the Frenchman's
story might be true, he passed it on to DIN.

The leaders of DIN decided to take a chance, and they
sent Judah Klein—the wigmaker of Treblinka—to negotiate with Berger. Berger told Klein that Konrad Schumann was among eight hundred SS men being held for
interrogation in the Münster barracks detention camp.
Schumann had false papers describing him as a noncom-
missioned officer of the relatively respectable SS battle unit
"Panzer Lehr," and Berger had kept to himself his
knowledge of who the man actually was. Also in the stockade were nearly two hundred men who were held together
in a single barracks building. They had been separated
from the others because they were known to have been
either officers at the death camps or members of the Einsatzgruppen, the SS mass-killing squads that had murdered about a million Jews throughout eastern Europe.
It was these two hundred murderers that Berger proposed
to give DIN in exchange for Schumann.

Berger was well known to the guards at the Münster
barracks, so he couldn't take Schumann himself without
running into difficulties afterward; but he had a plan.
He would provide Klein with credentials from the French
war crimes commission and a temporary transfer request
for Schumann. He would also give him an official command car, some French army uniforms, and a hundred
pounds of explosives. All these had been stolen some
weeks before and couldn't be traced; Berger had liberated
the loot from the previous thieves in an ex officio operation of his own. What Klein and his friends might choose

to do with these gifts was none of Berger's business;
at the moment all he wanted was Obersturmführer Schumann.

It was a deal. Four days later Judah Klein and five
other "French soldiers" drove up to the barracks compound with the proper papers and three cases of good
French wine in their command car. One of the cases
was opened in the messroom of the guard personnel while
Klein was having lunch with his hosts, and indeed contained wine. The contents of the other cases were distributed somewhat more surreptitiously by Klein's soldier
escort. They had just driven out of the gate again, with
Schumann handcuffed in the back of the car, when the
explosion nearly blew them off the road. (In those days
they were uncertain about the use of thermal fuses.)
Pieces of the occupants of barracks C rained down over
the entire camp. Nobody gave any thought to the de-
parted Frenchmen until the eighty dead SS men had been
counted and someone found time to wonder where the
hell the explosives had come from. By that time, Klein
and his friends were out of uniform again and far away—
six ordinary Jews sitting among their fellows in a DP
camp outside Düsseldorf.

Victor Berger took over Schumann, the command car,
and the unused half case of explosives, and drove cross-
country to Sondershausen.

Sondershausen is a pleasant little town whose inhabitants enjoyed a prosperous few years living off the concentration camps of Nordhausen Dora and Buchenwald
in the midst of which Sondershausen sat like a rose in
a cesspit. During the Nazi era it was a famous resort
town. One could rent a pleasant room for a very reasonable price which included meals and a sight-seeing
trip to the camps. The curio shops sold unusual sou-
venir photos and dolls with real hair and real teeth—
hobby work by some of the camp guards, most attractive.

Berger talked to Schumann all during the drive from
Münster, and by the time the car was parked in the town
square before dawn, the SS man was half out of his

mind for he'd been told in some detail just what was going to happen to him. Berger wrapped his gagged and handcuffed prisoner in a blanket and left him lying on the floor of the command car. Ten minutes later the car went up. The explosion shook the town and spewed flaming junk for hundreds of yards, and the resultant fires that spread through some of the charming gabled houses around the square lit the sky above the railroad station where Major Victor Berger was quietly waiting for his train.

There was an investigation, of course, but it was hampered by the need to conceal what had actually happened lest it disturb the restless citizens of Münster. It was publicly described as a terrible accident. There were references to the bursting of a faulty boiler which had in turn set off some stored military explosives. As the inquiry spread and the French military authorities were called in, Berger and his superiors made strenuous efforts to trace the men who had gone into the camp with, obviously, forged French papers and stolen uniforms. Alas, it all came to naught, and when Berger was mustered out of the army some months later, the investigation into the causes of the Münster tragedy had to be counted against him as a complete failure, a blot on his otherwise excellent record. . . .

Those who joined DIN at the time of its beginning sought a direct and personal vengeance. Each of them had a loved wife or husband, child or parent, brought pitilessly to degradation and brutal death; and each cherished the prayerful fantasy of a moment of terrible joy when the man or men directly responsible for this private agony would stand before him, to be killed by him. But every guilty man they sought had done murder many times over, and what each member of DIN had suffered at the hands of this man or that had been done also by this man and others to all the Jews of Europe. The avengers thus considered that the passionate vendetta each of them pursued was twin to the justice due the whole Jewish people. Therefore they would not limit their vengeance to those who had done them personal harm. They had indeed been taught, and had once believed, that guilt is only individual as between man and man. So they had been taught, but the years taught other truths and the blood of six million Jews bore sufficient witness to another reality. The German people themselves had expelled the concept of individual guilt, to drift in outer darkness with other wistful shades of the humanist tradition, awaiting a gentler time. Hundreds of thousands of Germans had taken a direct part in the destruction of the European Jews, and for this German guilt was massive and retribution could justly be matched to the dimensions of the evil done.

And so they killed men whose individual crimes were unspecified, as at the Münster barracks, knowing only that those they killed had brought murder and torture upon the Jewish people. There were enough of these anonymous guilty men—all the many thousands who had worn the Death's Head uniforms, the Totenkopf formations of the SS who had staffed the extermination camps, those who had manned the Einsatzgruppen that filled the mass graves from the Baltic to the Ukraine with a million Jewish dead, the men of the Gestapo. These they killed whenever they could and wherever they found them. But at the same time they sought always for individuals whose role in the *Endlösung,* in the "final solution of the Jewish problem," had been conspicuous. To assist them in this hunt, they called upon people outside their organization.

Help came first of all from the Jewish survivors. Every Jew who had been in a ghetto or a camp, who had worked as a slave for I. G. Farben or Krupp or Volkswagen, held forever engraved upon his memory the images of those who led in the torment he had known. Whenever it happened that such a man passed some familiar and hated face, however now concealed in innocent anonymity, he was eager to report to someone. Usually the survivors took such information to the headquarters of the She'erit Hapleetah, the Jewish DP organization. She'erit Hapleetah would send the report to the military authorities controlling the zone of occupation. That was official; unofficially, and often first, the reports went to one of DIN's contacts. There were dozens of Allied agencies dealing with war criminals, and in most of these were Jews who were ready to lend a hand to the shadowy group of avengers, to copy material from the files, to slip out the photo of a wanted man. In this fashion, for example, DIN got the personnel records and photographs of the officers who had commanded the Einsatzgruppen. They had been found by the Red Army among some captured Gestapo files and sent to Professors Tadeuz Cyprian and Jerzy Sawicki, who were to prosecute for Poland at the International War Crimes Tribunal. A Jewish lawyer working for Sawicki photographed this material and passed it along to DIN. Then there was another major source of information created for the group by those who carried out its judgments. Every man they took for execution was told he could ransom his life by leading them to any other wanted man considered more important than himself. The prisoner was warned that he would be held until what he told them was checked, and that if he had lied the manner of his own dying would then be very hard. In such circumstances many an übermensch forgot the vows he had sworn when he joined the SS or the Gestapo, and squealed on his blood brothers, and then was killed anyway. It wasn't cricket, but they weren't playing.

Very soon DIN had a priority list of *Ziele*—targets, names, photographs, records, and where these men had last been seen. After the Münster barracks raid they took this list and ushered in what is now remembered as "the first hunting season."

DIN's active members were divided into units and each such group was sent into one of the four military occupation zones that controlled Germany. Each unit leader was given a list of contacts in his zone of operation, people who—although not themselves in the organization—could be trusted to help. These contacts were asked to supply uniforms and at least a couple of I.D. cards for each unit. The identity cards most desirable were those of military intelligence or the military police. They also wanted military police armbands and insignia. Sometimes the contacts could get these from cooperative Jewish personnel. If necessary the required items were stolen. A soldier relaxing on a few hours liberty pass would find some pleasant civilian buying an extra drink for him and would wake up naked in an alley; or an MP would be held up at gunpoint on a dark street. In order to make the robberies seem nothing more than that, they took everything—money, watches, lighters, cigarettes, shoes— and the identification, insignia, and uniforms they were really after.

Military transport was a more difficult problem. Occasionally the contacts could find Jewish military personnel who had access to jeeps or command cars and could risk lending them for a time; otherwise these also were stolen. All of this was easiest in the British zone of occupation, for in this the Jewish Brigade could move. The battalions of the Jewish Brigade had their own transport and their own MPs. The cars were marked with the Star of David, but this could be covered, and the Jewish Brigade MP insignia was the standard British one. There was never an instance when a Palestinian soldier was approached for help that he refused it.

Once the men were thus uniformed and equipped there was in most cases a standard operating procedure. They would drive quite openly to a wanted man's home or to his place of work, or they would stop him in the street. The unit leader would show his identification and the man would be told he was wanted at headquarters for routine questioning. The traditional German respect for uniformed authority helped keep matters smooth. It did sometimes happen that a frightened man resisted, usually out of guilty panic. Then he was simply hit on the head and dragged to the waiting car. This open and unhurried violence was understood and respected by whatever Germans might be passing by, it was indigenous to their training and culture and therefore palpably legitimate. The prisoner was driven to a bombed-out and deserted area or to the fields and woods out of town. There for the first time he was called by his right name, told who his captors

were and what he was dying for—and then they killed
him. How he was killed depended on the circumstances;
most of the criminals were strangled. If the unit had
more work to do in the vicinity, they buried him or piled
rubble over him. It would take time then for the man's
relatives or friends to check through all the military occupation agencies that might legitimately have arrested
him. Sometimes, when they wanted no warning of violence to reach other criminals with whom the man might
be in contact, they took him quietly and without witnesses
and arranged a "suicide." There were enough Nazis hanging themselves at the time, and plenty who found it convenient to disappear. If none of these devices were necessary, they simply left the corpse where it lay; crimes
of violence were numerous enough to pass without com-
ment.

And so, among others in those days, the men of DIN
hunted down and killed:

SS Brigadier General Dr. Wilhelm Albert: chief of the
Security Police at Lodz; awarded the SS Ehrendegun
(Dagger of Honor) for his role in the final "liquidation"
of the Lodz ghetto, August-September 1944.

SS Major Dr. Wilhelm Altenloch: chief of the Security
Police at Bialystok; supervised the deportation of thirty
thousand Jews to Auschwitz, December 1942–January
1943.

SS Captain Hans Aumeier: commander of Auschwitz
Lager no. 1.

SS Major Hans Bothmann: commander of the "Bothmann Sonderkommando" which supervised the Chelmno
gas chambers 1942–44 (except for April 1943, when he
was transferred as an "expert" to the SS Prince Eugen
Division for the second Lodz ghetto massacre).

SS Colonel Dr. Hans Geschke: chief of the Security
Police in Hungary during the liquidation of 300,000
Jews in 1944. (Geschke's Ehrendegun award for this
"distinguished" service was accompanied by a letter

from Gestapo chief Himmler enjoining him to "keep your honour unsullied just as you must protect the honour of others and defend the defenseless. . . .")

Paul Giesler: gauleiter of Munich and lower Bavaria, 1943–45; supervised the functioning of the Dachau camp; drew up a plan to exterminate the Jews in the camp prior to its liberation.

SS Lieutenant General Odilo Globocnik: higher SS and police leader at Lublin; supervised the Einsatz Reinhardt massacres throughout Poland, 1942–43.

SS Lieutenant General Richard Gluecks: inspector general of all the concentration camps of the SS.

SS Brigadier General Dr. Ernst Grawitz: chief medical officer of the SS; directed the medical experimentation program carried out on the women of the Ravensbrück concentration camp.

SS Colonel Professor Albert Hohlfelder: awarded the Ehrendegun for this program of sterilizing Jews and other slave laborers by mass X-ray exposure.

SS Lieutenant General Dr. Friedrich Wilhelm Krueger: higher SS and police leader in the Generalgouvernement (area of Poland incorporated into the Third Reich); member of the planning staff supervising the liquidation of the Polish ghettos.

SS Lieutenant Kurt Mussfeld: "efficiency expert" of the Maidenek gas chambers; supervisor of Auschwitz crematorium no. 2, 1944.

SS Major Adalbert Neubauer: head of the "Neubauer Sonderkommando" during the Einsatz Reinhardt massacres in Poland, 1943.

SS Major Karl Puetz: chief of Security Police at Rovno; directed the second Rovno massacre, July 1943.

SS Major Christian Wirth: director of the death camps in Poland; organized the Einsatz Reinhardt massacres under Lieutenant General Globocnik, 1942–43.

In those two months of the "first hunting season" the small bands of Jewish avengers roaming through Germany tracked down and executed more than a hundred men who had for years committed or commanded mass murder. Then they gathered together again, called by the leaders of DIN to Alt-Aussee, in the Austrian Alps. . . .

The Alt-Aussee is a crescent of mountains that separates German Bavaria from the Austrian province of Salzburg. It is an area of barrier ice and sudden snowslide, wild and rugged and beautiful. In the 1920s, when Adolf Hitler was still only another loud-mouth ranting in the beerhalls of nearby Munich, the Alt-Aussee was already a Nazi stronghold. When Hitler became lord of the Reich it was in these Wagnerian surroundings that he built his "home," his eyrie at Berchtesgaden. In those triumphant years the Alt-Aussee became a playground of the Nazi elite, and the concentration camp at Ebensee was first established to provide slave labor to build their summer villas and mountain retreats.

In the closing months of the war, Allied intelligence agencies became aware of unusual activity in the Alt-Aussee. Long caravans of trucks guarded by SS units were reported traveling along the mountain tracks to the sleepy villages of Ebensee and Redl Zipf and to the German naval research station on the shores of Lake Toplitz.

In the Berne headquarters of the Office of Strategic Services, the head of the OSS in Europe, Allen Dulles, studied the vague reports coming from Alt-Aussee. Dulles had for some time been in contact with a curious clutch of turncoat Nazis to whom he had given his confidence under the chaste impression that they represented a "decent Germany" and that their SS uniforms, baggy from long wear and weighted with Hitler's medals, were a kind of camouflage under which beat hearts of purest gold. It was to these latter-day saints of the German anti-Nazi resistance that Dulles turned for information concerning Alt-Aussee. They warned America's "master spy" that the wildly mountainous area was being turned into an "Alpine redoubt" from which Germany would stage a massive final resistance. According to these informants, the 400,000 veterans of Field Marshal Albert Kesselring's

Army Group G were being pulled out of northern Italy
to man this fortress, and Hitler himself would take command from his nest at Berchtesgaden.

Dulles transmitted an alarming report to the Allied intelligence staff at Supreme Headquarters, and on March
11, 1945, the SHAEF intelligence summary sent to General Eisenhower put the warning into language that as-
cended to absolute ecstasies of anguish:

> Here [in the Alpine redoubt of Alt-Aussee], defended
> by nature and by the most efficient secret weapons yet
> invented, the powers that have hitherto guided Germany
> will survive to reorganize her resurrection. Here arma-
> ments will be manufactured in bombproof factories,
> food and equipment will be stored in vast underground
> caves, and a selected corps of young men will be trained
> in guerrilla warfare so that a whole underground army
> can be fitted and directed to liberate Germany from the
> occupying forces.[84]

Behind this frightening report of the Alpine redoubt
stood the prestigious Allen Dulles, and whispering at his
ear were SS Major General Prince Maximilian von Hohenlohe (who after the war was recommended by Dulles for
a top job in the West German intelligence service run by
Reinhard Gehlen and partly financed by America's CIA)
and Gestapo agent Hans Bernd Gisevius, a devious con-
niver who is now a consultant for the U.S. Department
of State. And behind the German informants, in this matter of the Alpine redoubt, stood SS Reichsführer Heinrich Himmler.

As far back as mid-1943, Himmler was convinced that
the war was lost and he set about planning to win, for
himself and for Germany, his own kind of peace. Under
the cover of Amt VI, RSHA (Department VI of the
Reich Main Security Office) Himmler established a top-
secret unit which included Prince von Hohenlohe, SS General Ernst Kaltenbrunner, and one of Himmler's famed
hatchet men—SS Major Alfred Helmut Naujocks. Prince
von Hohenlohe and the people who worked with him
were to establish clandestine contact with the western

Allies and endeavor to negotiate a "soft peace" instead
of the unconditional surrender of Germany upon which
the Allies and Russia were then mutually determined. As
part of this deal, Himmler's agents were empowered to
tell the Allies about the "impregnable fortress" of the
Alpine redoubt. In exchange for a separate peace that
would enable a strong Germany headed by Himmler to
continue the war against Russia, Himmler was prepared
to do three things: to arrange the assassination of Hitler;
to stop killing the Jews; and to deliver up the Alpine
redoubt without a fight.

According to Prince von Hohenlohe, whose reports to
Himmler on his negotiations with Dulles were found after
the war in the secret files of RSHA Amt VI, Dulles was
sympathetic to the project, at least to the extent of a
"soft peace" which would preserve Germany as dominant
in Europe, would enable Germany to hold part of its territorial gains, and would use this "greater Germany" to
establish "a cordon sanitaire against Bolshevism." Hohenlohe reported that Dulles "does not reject the basic ideas
and deeds of National Socialism" but he deplored its
excesses. The prince reported that "Dulles seemed quite
to recognize" greater Germany's right to hegemony in
Europe and Dulles is quoted as assuring Hohenlohe that
"there could be no question of Germany's partition or
the separation of Austria."[85]

So far, if Hohenlohe reported accurately and Dulles
was being candid, so good. But then things fell apart,
for Dulles was not making the policy of the western Allies and Churchill and Roosevelt, who were, refused to
countenance a separate peace that would desert the Soviet ally and unleash against her this greater Germany led
by Heinrich Himmler.

In the event, the major result of Himmler's conspiracy
was one the SS Reichsführer would not have welcomed. It
delivered Berlin up to the Red Army and gave Russia
a useful card to play in forcing the very partition of Germany that Himmler and his friends were trying to avoid.
On April 12 and 13, 1945, strong armored elements of
the U.S. First and Ninth Armies crossed the Elbe River

at Magdeburg. Berlin was only sixty miles away and by far the greater part of the German defending forces were holding an arc against the Red Army two hundred miles east of the city. But General Eisenhower held the Ninth Army along the Elbe and ordered the First Army *south*, crashing down the length of Germany against the Alpine redoubt in Alt-Aussee. As Eisenhower's chief of staff General Walter Bedell Smith was later to record, the SHAEF commander was obsessed with the fearsome prospect of a last-ditch German resistance in the Alpine redoubt, and he wanted to smash the fortifications before Kesselring could get his armies entrenched in the "vast underground caves" armed with all those "most efficient weapons yet invented." Eisenhower thus hoped to avoid having to fight, as General Smith put it, "a prolonged campaign in the Alpine area."[86]

On May 6, 1945, an armored spearhead of the U.S. First Army—the Ranger Battalions commanded by Major Arnold Pearson—hurtled into Alt-Aussee, and found it undefended. Kesselring's armies weren't there; neither were the secret weapons nor the armaments factories. The whole terrifying tale of the Alpine redoubt was an empty bluff used by Himmler's agents for bargaining purposes in their negotiations with Allen Dulles.[87] As an intelligence coup the estimate of the Alpine redoubt passed to SHAEF by Dulles was a blunder comparable to that achieved by the CIA in the debacle that took place some fifteen years later at Cuba's Bay of Pigs.

The Alt-Aussee was not a fortified zone and was never so planned. It was a bolt-hole, a way out for the big rats who were preparing to desert the sinking Nazi ship and did not intend to go naked into the wide world. For when Himmler sent Hohenlohe to Dulles, he also prepared an alternative plan in case the negotiations failed. This alternative was assigned to General Ernst Kaltenbrunner and Major Alfred Naujocks, and it was called Aktion Birkenbaum—Operation Birch Tree. The men involved in this had a number of objectives: to save themselves, their families, and their personal loot; to help other Nazi war criminals to escape justice; to prepare their return to power—if not political power, then at least financial. And if such plans, hatched by men who at that moment in time stood among the ashes of all their work, seem grandiose insanity, the cautionary truth is that they were successful to a surprising extent.

Aktion Birkenbaum grew from an earlier project called Aktion Bernhard which was the greatest counterfeiting effort in history. In 1942 the Gestapo had combed the concentration camps in Germany for skilled printers and engravers. These men were collected in the Oranienburg concentration camp and were set to work counterfeiting huge amounts of American and British currency. At first, the idea was to use this money to debase the financial structure of the Allies. This proved impracticable, the Reich couldn't get enough of the funny money into circulation to do the job. But a more limited objective was attained. The money was used to finance part of the German intelligence activities throughout the world. For example, £300,000 was to have been paid to "Cicero"— the valet of the British ambassador in Ankara who photographed and sold to the Germans the plans for the Allied invasion of Normandy. He was paid with Oranienburg counterfeits. (But then the Germans didn't credit the documents he sent them and made no use of this accurate information, so no one benefited from Cicero's fantastic achievement.) Twelve million fake American dollars went to German agents in South America. Two millions of these were paid to Argentine General Juan Bautista Molina to finance his fascist Alianza de la Juventud Nacionalista. Another four millions were distributed among various Argentine government and military personalities in payment for their successful effort to keep that country neutral and a base for German espionage in the Western Hemisphere for as long as was useful.[88]

In August-September 1944, the Oranienburg operation was closed down and the rest of this forged money was sent to Alt-Aussee, where $800 million worth was later found buried under the brewery at Redl Zipf.[89]

Most of the Oranienburg counterfeiters were returned to the camps from which they had come, but twenty of the best craftsmen were coopted into the new Aktion Birkenbaum and were brought to Alt-Aussee, where they were locked in special workshops and barracks in the Ebensee concentration camp. There they were set to forging identity papers, birth certificates, school records, marriage licenses. These were essential documents to be used by Nazi fugitives until such time as Major Naujocks and his associates could organize the escape routes that would take them beyond the reach of the war-crimes investigators.[90]

By the beginning of 1945, Aktion Birkenbaum was well underway. The Nazis who were to benefit from Himmler's foresight and had begun transporting their families and their loot, and in some cases themselves, to lower Bavaria and to Alt-Aussee—the regions that were to be the starting points of the escape routes. It was these caravans of privileged persons and privileged loot, both guarded by units of the elite SS–Das Reich Division, that Dulles's agents had spotted along the mountain roads of the Alt-Aussee.

No one knows just how much Nazi booty came into the area in those long caravans of guarded trucks. Enough was found by Allied investigators to render credible almost any estimate, however astronomical. Himmler's hoard, hauled out of the mountain caves above Ebensee, consisted of half a ton of gold ingots, fifty cases of jewelry and gold dust (each case weighing over eighty pounds), two million Swiss francs (real), and a $3 million collection of rare stamps. Hermann Göring's stolen art treasures, valued at $18 million, were discovered crated and carefully tucked away in the cool preserving air of the Alt-Aussee salt mines. The modest rewards that years of selfless patriotism had earned SS General Ernst Kaltenbrunner, miscellaneous cash and jewelry worth $2 million, were found in steel drums buried along the banks of the Traun River.[91] But a great deal was never recovered, or if recovered—never announced. Jewish investigators pressing claims for reparations against a most reluctant Austrian government have estimated that the Austrians collected and disposed of about $20 million worth of Nazi loot. Other millions are believed to have gone with escaped Nazi criminals and to have been invested by them in various businesses throughout the world. (Ex-Nazi fugitives hold controlling interests in 58 companies with Portuguese registration, 112 Spanish firms, 35 Turkish, 98 Argentinian, and 214 Swiss.) And a further indication of the extent of the Nazi hoards shipped into the Alt-Aussee is provided by the inventory found among the RSHA Amt VI files which contained receipts, totaling more than $30 million, signed by SS Oberführer Kurt Spacil ("Department Kaltenbrunner"); SS Oberführer Otto Vitzhen ("Cash Office—Albania"; SS Obersturmbannführer Paul Franz Gertsch ("Aktion Bernhard"); SS Sturmbannführer Wilhelm Hoettl ("Amt VI"); SS Sturmbannführer Gerhard Auner ("Cash Office —Rumania"); and finally, an amount of five million gold reichsmarks charged against "Cash Office—Skorzeny."[92] Also unaccounted for are the huge sums of ransom money paid by Hungarian Jews to SS General Kurt Becher. Becher claims he turned the money over to various German banks, on Himmler's orders, and that the great fortune he subsequently enjoyed in West Germany is only the proper recompense for his recently discovered business acumen.

In March 1945, the captive forgers of Aktion Birkenbaum were shot by order of Major Naujocks. Only three Jews of the group are known to have survived by slipping out of the special enclosed area and mingling with the prisoners in the Ebensee camp. One of these three brought the story to Malachi Wald. By then, Wald already knew a bit about Aktion Birkenbaum. Rumors of the escape plan had earlier seeped out to many hundreds of frightened Nazis who were not included in the original rescue lists drawn up by Kaltenbrunner and his associates. Like their more-privileged fellow murderers, these lesser paladins were also anxious to escape punishment and they poured into Alt-Aussee. By the time the Americans took over the region, the "civilian" population had boomed from the 18,000 listed in the 1943 census to more than 80,000 in June 1945.

After these fugitives came, at war's end, the Allied and Soviet war-crimes investigators; and after them came also the Jewish avengers of DIN.

The official investigators set up an internment camp just over the Austrian border at Salzburg, and another at Cham in lower Bavaria. Within two months the camps held more than three thousand suspected criminals. Some of these were held for trial; some few of these were actually brought before a judge; one—Kaltenbrunner—was finally hanged. Too many of the rest got out of the camps almost as soon as they were tossed in, their identities concealed by the forged documents of Aktion Birkenbaum. Adolf Eichmann and his colleagues—Hermann Krumey, Kurt Nowack, Hans and Kurt Guenther, Ernst Bruchler, Arno Meier, and Franz Beutel—were scooped up and thrown into the Salzburg camp; and got out again. Himmler's Adjutant General Karl Wolff was taken into Cham and had papers to prove he was some other innocent and was let go. The same thing happened to SS General Oskar Dirlewanger, who massacred the Polish partisans, and Herbert Cukurs, who led the Latvian fascists when the Riga ghetto was decimated; and Richard Baer, the last commandant of Auschwitz. In this or other ways, many slipped through the nets—Ludwig Hahn, once Gestapo boss in France; SS Brigadier General Fritz Katzman, who supervised the murder of half a million Jews in Galicia; Gustav Wilhaus, head of the Janow death camp; Dr. Josef Mengele, the "devil of Auschwitz"—others, many others.

None that DIN took got away again. They killed Bruchler and Meier and Beutel the day these men walked out of the Salzburg camp. They killed Colonel Fritz Suhren, who had been commander at Ravensbrück and had watched the Jewish women screaming as their ovaries were cut from their conscious bodies. They killed seven unit commanders of the Einsatzgruppen who had found their way to Alt-Aussee—Jager, Buchardt, Kroger, Seetzen, Muller, Persterer, Zapp; and twelve others who had done the same bloody work and had come with their commanders seeking escape.

Good enough, but little enough. This way was hopeless. They could do this killing all their lives, do no other thing than these acts of retribution—and what then? The guilty murdering men lived in the thousands and thousands among the nation of their sheltering fellows, and whatever a few dozen avengers might accomplish was as the casting of a stone into this endless sea of guilt and impenitent connivance.

There are levels of justice. On some levels, the Germans who had sown the wind had reaped the whirlwind. They had brought war upon the world and it had come home to Germany. Coventry had been destroyed, so then had Dresden; war for war, and war's dead for war's dead. But what beyond the clash of armies and the crash of bombs? What weighed in the scales of the blind goddess against the millions of Jews annihilated as Jews? The Germans had not left a Jewish family without its dead in all Europe, not one Jewish family whole. So be it then. What the Germans had done to the Jews as Jews, *these* Jews of DIN would do to the Germans—leaving not one German family whole.

Late in 1945, they quit the Alt-Aussee and began to work on Tochnit Aleph—Plan A; the plan to kill a million Germans. . . .

Seven / The Ways of Poison

No one in DIN can say who first thought of Tochnit Aleph. For it had begun, not as a plan but as a fierce great longing, in the bitter winter of 1944 when those few who were left of the band of brothers had come to the Lublin stockade out of the forest camps of the Jewish fighting resistance.

They had watched the Russian soldiers bringing into Lublin those Jews whom the Germans, in the plunging haste of their retreat, had left alive at the gates of the gas chambers at Sobibor and Maidenek and Treblinka and in the pens of the fifty-one slave-labor camps that encircled Lublin. They had watched the frayed lives of thousands unravel, at this very moment of rescue, into so many deaths—of disease and starvation, of bursting madness, of hopeless suicide born of loss and loneliness and unendurable memory. They had listened to men whom the Germans had dragged eastward in the long slave trains from Drancy in France to the *Judenreservat* at Lublin, and to others who had come a thousand miles westward out of the mass graves at Kiev. From the dreadful memories of these nightmare wanderers they had pieced together for the first time the full dimensions of the hell the Germans had brought upon the Jewish people of all Europe.

And so it had begun then, in the Lublin stockades—this wish, this dream, collective, shared, and spoken first in that time of searing catharsis; the seed planted then, to germinate during the next full year of bitter hate, nourished by the acid need to achieve a vengeance proportionate to the evil done. Until finally, in the winter of 1945, the bud burst and gave forth poison. They would poison the water supply of a million Germans, bringing death at the turn of a faucet; and that would be the end of DIN, this climactic act of retribution, the last honor to their urgent dead; and they who did it might then turn away in peace.

It was not a project for all the members of DIN. For even within such a group of avengers there could be only a few capable of bending their minds to so ruthless an objective. The leaders chose their men, no more than a handful, sifting them in their minds before approaching them. These enlisted, the other were told only that the time had come to cease the work of vengeance, to disband DIN. They had done their share and more, the leaders told them; the rest was for the judges and the prosecutors of the coming war-crimes trials. It was time for them all to turn their backs on the past, the future held a different duty. The Jewish nation was struggling to be born in Palestine and it would not be born without pain and violence. Men would be needed there who knew how to fight. And so, urged by their leaders, the avengers put down the knife and the garrote and the gun, and went along the secret roads to Palestine. Leaving only those few who had begun it all, the hardest of them.

So ended the first part of the history of DIN; and the few who remained in Europe set to work on Tochnit Aleph.

There were four problems to overcome: they had to find a poison that would be odorless, tasteless, colorless, and hygroscopic—capable of maintaining fatal virulence when mixed in almost any quantity of water. They had to select a city or cities, target areas free of Jews and of the personnel of the military occupation authorities. They had to place their people into positions enabling them to introduce the poison into the selected water systems. And they had to organize an escape route so that they could get away, if possible, at least as many of them as possible, from what would certainly be the greatest manhunt ever known.

There was a fifth problem, but it was not on the plane of practical planning and they didn't realize the weight it would have, so they didn't come to grips with it at the beginning; and it was to prove the most difficult of all.

They set up headquarters in Augsburg, with the man called Israel coordinating everything from there, and "the little sister"—Hannah Baum—as his lieutenant. Victor Berger was sent to Paris to prepare the retreat center. The escape, if they were to escape, would be as French Jews emigrating to Palestine through the Bricha organization at Marseilles. Berger was to acquire the French identity papers and arrange the safehouse that would shelter them while the hunt was high. They brought in two "technicians," civil engineers who had fled from Germany to Palestine in the early days of the Nazi Reich and had come to DIN as officers of the Jewish Brigade. It was these last two who chose the targets after careful study: Munich, Weimar, Nuremberg, Hamburg, and the Wannsee suburb of Berlin. There were no Jews in Weimar then, and no occupation personnel, and none of either in the residential district served with water by the Wannsee substation. The DP camps around Munich and Hamburg and the occupation personnel in those cities and in Nuremberg received water from mains that could be cut out of the central distribution systems when the time came.

The first selection made, the two engineers trained the men who were to try for jobs in the filtering plants of the target systems. These men were all German-speaking. They were given German identity papers and Nazi party cards, and discharge papers to show they had been invalided out of the Wehrmacht sanitation corps. All this took time, but when the time was over they had men working in the municipal water departments of Munich and Nuremberg. They failed to get their men properly placed in Berlin and Weimar and Hamburg, but they had done well enough. A total of 1,380,000 Germans used the water systems of Munich and Nuremberg, and with luck that would serve.

Wald and Avraham Becker and Judah Klein had been assigned to choose and obtain the poison, but it was Victor Berger who got the first leads, and that was by happenstance. In 1943, Berger had been a liaison officer between General de Gaulle's Bureau Central de Renseignements et d'Action in London and L'État Major de la Zone Occupée, the general staff in occupied France that ran the underground Armée Secrète. The chief medical officer of the BCRA was the noted French bacteriologist and chemical warfare expert Professor Pasteur Valéry-Radot. In the time they had both worked out of the London headquarters at 10 Duke Street, Berger and the professor had become friends, and when Berger went to Paris to organize the escape route for Tochnit Aleph he looked up Valéry-Radot and they arranged an evening reunion with other comrades-in-arms. Dinner done, and the liquor flowing, the talk turned to the state of the world and the sorry prospect for improving it. Since most of those present were or had been professional soldiers they came inevitably to discussions of the past war and to gloomy predictions about the next one—the hydrogen bomb, the cobalt bomb, the ultimate Doomsday weapon, and all the other great scientific achievements that seemed likely to send mankind reeling back into the caves. Valéry-Radot, riding his own hobbyhorse, told them that all these future weapons were as cumbersome tinker-toys compared to the horrors which could even then be brewed in a test tube by any reasonably competent bacteriologist or chemist. A couple of men, with a few not very heavy suitcases full of a variety of choice compounds and with access to the bakeries or dairies or bottling plants or the reservoirs of a city, could in theory at least leave the city a graveyard. The professor spelled it out for them, they could take their choice—this compound is an irritant poison unaffected by the heat of baking or cooking, that particular culture of a fairly common bacillus is hygroscopic and causes rapid paralysis of the respiratory system, or one can spread bubonic plague—the Black Death of the

Middle Ages—and there are spores that can be dusted over crops and cattle by low-flying airplanes. Well, all these were horror tales for some future mindless Armageddon, and they passed the brandy and went on to subjects more cheery. But Victor Berger remembered and went home and wrote it all down and sent it on to the Augsburg headquarters. So now the planners knew what it was they needed, the specific culture of the specific bacillus—odorless, tasteless, hygroscopic, and deadly. They were ready for the next move.

It was obvious that no one would have a sufficient quantity of such a bacillus conveniently on hand so that it might be begged or bought or stolen. It would have to be cultured to order, and whoever did this would want to know why. They would have to find somewhere a scientist able to do the work and willing to do it for the purpose intended. Clearly, they needed a Jew or several Jews uniquely skilled and motivated by the same boundless urge to retribution that drove them. If such were to be found anywhere, the chances seemed best in Palestine among the Jewish bacteriologists and microbiologists at the medical school of the Hebrew University in Jerusalem, or perhaps among the scientists who had gathered at the research institute in Rehovot around the Zionist leader Dr. Chaim Weizmann, who was himself one of the world's great biological chemists. There were scientists in Palestine who had escaped from Nazi Europe, but with their wives and children, brothers, sisters, parents trapped by the Germans, shot down by Germans and shoveled like carrion into the mass graves, tricked and beaten into the gas chambers by Germans to die the choking death, incinerated by Germans, their bones ground into meal and spread as fertilizer over the German earth to enrich the German crops that went to fill the German bellies. Oh, there would be men enough in Palestine to turn their hands and their skills to retribution, to give back to the Germans agony for agony!

Suddenly it all seemed possible, more than possible, real: this nightmare thing they had conjured up out of their need as centuries before the despairing Rabbi Judah

Low ben-Bezalel had brought to life the monster Golem
and sent him lurching through the streets of medieval
Prague to avenge his tormented people, and to teach the
goyim the lesson—oft-repeated, never learned—that the
blood of the Jew is spilled at risk. Suddenly, now, their
Golem seemed about to breathe, and they who had
created it stood before its looming reality and were ap-
palled. Through all the long months they had planned
this and lived for this, but believe in it, truly, in the
guarded depths of the mind, they had not ever. They
had been as men harried and helpless in the forest dark,
calling down upon their enemies the cataclysmic hammering fist of the Lord, and never expecting actually to
see it smashing down, awful and implacable; never themselves really believing in the living God of vengeance
whose aid they implored. They had decided upon Tochnit
Aleph in the full crescendo of their hate and it had
seemed to them just, and so it seemed still. But they were
not sure, or some of them were not. The destruction of a
million human beings as an act of retribution may shim-
mer in the long distance, radiant to the eye peering
through a veil of blood and pain; but to approach it,
to embrace it, must be for sane men a dreadful agony,
and no such men long engaged on such a project can
remain always capsulated in certainty, armored against
eroding doubt. So it was for them, and so—now—they
hesitated.

They had realized, of course, that what they planned
was different from the acts of vengeance for which DIN
had been formed. Different in kind as in degree, cutting
down the innocent and the guilty alike, as indeed the
Jews had been cut down, and in numbers—less. All they
had done until now and what they intended now to do,
had been done in the name of the Jewish people, and
they as its agents. But who had named them thus? The
weapon they had sought seemed almost at hand, but
who had authorized them to pick it up and cut so broad
and bloody a swath? There were those among them who
had answered such a question once before, when they had
raised the banners of revolt in the eastern ghettos and had

been asked, "Who set you as leaders among us?" The question then had been answered by the thousands who had followed them in the Jewish fighting resistance. But who would answer it now? And answer it, how? If in this dreadful project they were not the agents of the maimed Jewish people calling for retribution of such a size and such a kind, what, then, were they?

The answer lay where the weapon lay—in Palestine. This ancient homeland was once again the core of Jewish reality, and those who there led the struggle to build a new Jewish nation held in their hands the heart of the Jewish people. In all the world, Jews gave these Palestinians loyalty and saw them as "the leaders among us." They could answer. They could give the weapon, and the right to use it.

It was decided in Augsburg that Malachi Wald would go to Palestine. . . .

There was only one way for a Jew to get from Europe to Palestine in those days, with the blockade runners of Bricha. It wasn't quick and it wasn't safe; those who tried it could be caught at any border, or taken by the British destroyers that patrolled the Palestine coast; and if they were so taken they would be shoved into the detention camps the British maintained on Cyprus. This could happen to Wald and to whoever was sent after him, and there would be an end to all of it. Still, there was no alternative, so Wald contacted Bricha and asked to be included in the next group to be sent to Palestine. What happened then was what he expected to happen, considering who he was and the nature of his experience. Bricha gave him a group to lead.

The group assigned to Wald was made up of Jews who had been sneaked out of the DP camp near Graz, in Austria, and had been held by Bricha in the forests between Graz and Wildon until the column of two hundred was complete. Then Wald and the guides who worked with him led them down through the moutain passes to the area around Klagenfurt on the Austro-Yugoslav border. They slipped past the border guards at night, crossing above Jessenice, and filtered down through Slovenia to the Adriatic coast between Rijeka and Susak where Bricha had a ship waiting for them. A ship!—an ancient, rusting, sprung-plated fishing trawler, about as seaworthy as a barrel. For nine days they wallowed across the Adriatic and weaved among the Aegean Islands and crawled along the coast of Turkey, and then they broke into the Mediterranean.

Until then they had been in the shelter of Yugoslav or Greek or Turkish territorial waters and they had risked only drowning if the gasping pumps failed. Once they turned into the Mediterranean, they risked capture also. British destroyers patrolled the sea and British planes based on Cyprus flew reconnaissance sweeps overhead, and the British were paying little attention to international law when the beneficiaries were troublesome Jews. If the voyagers were identified as Jews, the chances were even that they would be boarded by force and dragged to the Cyprus detention camps; failing that, they would be dogged by the destroyers and taken as soon as they got into Palestine coastal waters. So from the time they left the shelter of the Turkish coast, the two hundred Jews lay packed and retching in the stinking fish holds, with the crew members sitting on the battened-down hatches repairing the nets that established them as legitimate fishermen. Most of the crew were Palestinians, Bricha volunteers from the Palestine fishing fleets; two were Croats and it was their task to answer the demands for identification bellowed through the loud-hailers of the British destroyers that raced alongside, and that roared away again when the wind brought back the shouted Serbo-Croat gutturals and wafted along the decades-old reek of fish that perfumed the trawler. Each new investigation, the sudden interrogation sounding from the loud-hailers and the pounding backwash of the destroyers as they sheered off, added to the burden of fear and misery of the Jews lying one upon the other, sweating and sick in the fetid holds.

Sick they were, and frightened, but no one died of it, and when Wald dropped down into the hold to tell them the Palestine coast was only twenty miles away, the two hundred "fish" considered that the worst was over. They were already then, each of them in his mind's bright eye, contemplating their new lives, sitting under their fig trees and gorging themselves on the milk and honey of the Promised Land. But Wald knew that the critical time was yet to come, at nightfall, when they would turn in the first dark before the rise of moon, and run for land. Five armed cutters, the *Loran,* the *Sea Lion,* the *Morta,* the *Sea Wolf,* the *Shark,* patrolled the sea approaches to Palestine. British military jeeps and half-tracks traveled the coastal roads. Arab auxiliary police prowled the beaches. Coast Guard observation points covered an arc from the heights above Ras Hanaqura on the Lebanese border, south to El Arish in the Sinai Peninsula. Somewhere, though, amid all this alert hostility, there would be friends to welcome them, the young men and the girls of the Hagana to bring them up off the beaches, and the members of the Jewish cooperative farm settlements to hide them. And if they could come within the grasp of these reaching hands, they would be safe; but only "if."

In the late afternoon the crew hauled up the nets and dumped the catch overboard again and turned out into the Mediterranean, standing away from the Palestine coast to avoid the attentions of the patrol boats. When darkness fell, they put about and angled through the coastal waters, going slowly and without lights and watching for the signals. They knew what to look for, and still it startled them—the sudden flare of flame bursting upward through the night as the Hagana dynamited the radio tower of the Sidna Ali coast guard station just north of Tel Aviv. The men watching from the trawler knew the raid was intended to pull the British land and sea patrols in to Sidna Ali to seal off the area under attack, and they swung their binoculars to focus on the dark beaches twenty miles north of Sidna Ali. A few minutes later the second signal came, the brief blinking of a truck's headlights pointing seaward from the fishing settlement called S'dot Yam—"the Fields of the Sea." That was their destination and they raced for shore, the creaky tub shuddering under the sudden erratic thrust of its straining engines.

All the boats of S'dot Yam were waiting offshore at the limit of the trawler's approach. Every man of the settlement who wasn't in the boats stood between the boats and the beach, hip deep in water. Beyond the beach, hidden among the scrub-lined dunes, a contingent of Hagana riflemen kept an ambush over the road that led inland from the settlement.

They worked with a lurching efficiency, a drill of rushing shadows splashing and stumbling in the dark. From the trawler down into the boats and toward the beach and out of the boats and into the water and helped or hauled by the men who stood there to the beach while the boats went back for another load. The women of the settlement were posted on the beach beside piles of the khaki clothing that in those days was a kind of civilian uniform for the Palestinian Jews. The refugees stripped and toweled and changed clothes. Then they were rushed to the trucks that would take them inland, scattering them among the Jews of the Galilee villages far from the coast. Behind them, settlers from S'dot Yam were already gathering together the discarded European garments and were dragging scrapers across the beach, smoothing the sand; the Hagana riflemen were drifting off into the night.

Twenty minutes, less perhaps, and the trawler was gone into the dark Mediterranean, the beach and the waters empty, the S'dot Yam boats bobbing gently at their moorings, the settlers in their beds. Another two hundred wanderers home from the ghettos and the forests and the camps, all fear gone, their long journey done. All safely home, except one man for whom the eternal return was this time only another way station on his unending and violent road.

The next morning Malachi Wald turned to the work that had brought him to Palestine.

For nearly a fortnight Wald, equipped now with identity papers describing him as a Palestinian-born building worker named Eleazar Ben-Chaim, traveled the underground circuit, speaking before select groups of Hagana officers, Bricha workers, the Jewish Agency and Zionist executives. These people knew who he was and only part of what he had done. They knew he had been one of the organizers of the Jewish resistance, that he had led the first columns of border runners out of the Lublin stockades. They knew, some of them, that he had once led a band of avengers who had hunted down and executed some scores of those who had murdered the Jews. And that was the extent of their knowledge. No one of those to whom Wald spoke knew anything of Tochnit Aleph. They honored him for his resistance record, sought his advice on the functioning of Bricha, welcomed him home; and they did not, any of them, understand him. The few who knew anything of DIN told him of a new Hagana group in Europe, Israel Carmi, Chaim Laskov (who would become chief of staff of the Israeli army), Marcel Tubias, Meier Zorea, Asher Ben-Natan, Moshe Karpowitz, and others. These would carry on the work of vengeance that DIN had laid down, Wald was told; he and those who had been with him in it could rest.

Wald couldn't rest. The Hagana was not organized for vengeance. Sooner or later, sooner than later, every man in Hagana would be called to the work for which it had been organized—to throw the British out of Palestine and to defend the new Jewish state that would then be created. In the time they would have for the task and with the resources which could for that time be spared them, the Hagana agents would hunt down a few guilty men; but they would not do what he and the ones he'd left behind in Germany were prepared to do, they would not kill a million Germans.

Wald kept his counsel. A fortnight passed, something more, and then he moved. He sought out Dr. Chaim Weizmann at his scientific research institute in Rehovot. For ten years Dr. Weizmann had been president of the World Zionist Organization and in that decade his had been the voice of moderation and reason, counseling the Jews to have faith in the decent integrity of the nations. Well, he'd been wrong, and the realization had broken him. By the time Wald met him, Weizmann had almost withdrawn from the world that had deceived and saddened him, and other men—harder, more cynical—had taken over the destiny of the Jewish people. But within three years the Jews of new Israel would call him forth from his biochemical laboratory to become the first president of the Jewish state, for he was the most prestigious Jewish statesman alive, universally honored, above all considerations of polity and expediency.

There is no record of their meeting, only what Wald remembers. It must have been a curious one—the old great man, sad and sick, half blind, with death already inside him, all fires banked; and the other, not half Weizmann's age, bitter and hard, a fighting man, host to a searing hate. Wald says that they sat together a whole afternoon and into evening. In that time he took Weizmann with him, all the bloody road he had himself traveled, from the Kovno ghetto and the mass graves and the torture chambers of the Ninth Fort, to the high and dirty business of the resistance; all of it, the starvation, the slaughter, the agony, the courage. He conjured up the martyrs to bear witness, the men and women whom Wald had known—Leo Ziman, caught by the Gestapo and tearing his veins open so that he might die before torture let the secrets out of him; Moshe Ilionski, blinded and made insane and locked in a box to starve to death, and keeping silent; Sara Menkes, nineteen years old, climbing up out of the mass graves at Ponar, driven by the need to warn the ghettos of forty thousand men and women and children and babies shot dead in a ditch, to call the Jews to resistance; Moshe Podhlebnik, shot in the head and set on fire, with the bones gleaming in the charred flesh, crawling through the night to bring word to the ghetto of the first gas chambers at Chelmno. Wald told it all, all he knew, and when he was done the old man sat before him, shuddering. And Wald asked him then: "They who did this to these, and to the thousands and the millions, they who did it, who applauded it or allowed it, shall they not now pay? That which they have sowed, shall they not now reap?"

There is no doubt that it was brutally done, and that the aging statesman was not equipped to bear it. He could not sit there in his pleasant home, with the honors heaped about him, and look into the fierce eyes of the man who sat before him, who had himself come out of this world of described horror. Wald told him then of Tochnit Aleph. Not all of it; just that he and those with him were prepared, and almost able, to spill equal agony upon the German people; and that they wanted Weizmann's help.

As Wald tells it, the old man seemed to shrink, the dimmed eyes clouded with pain. Then he said at last, "If I were you, having lived as you, I would do what you will do." And Weizmann gave Wald the name of a bacteriologist and signed a message for him.

Wald had taken a long step, one and a bit. The weapon was now surely within reach, and the authority to take it up almost so. A man honored as none other by the Jewish people had given moral backing to help answer the question that had unnerved them in Augsburg—"Who set you as leaders among us?" It was almost enough, for Wald and for those with him. Weizmann spoke with the voice of the Jews if any man did; but no one man did. It was almost enough, but not quite.

Wald took the next step, to Yitzhak Ben-Avi . . .

There weren't a thousand people in Palestine who had ever heard of Yitzhak Ben-Avi and probably not two hundred who knew what he did, but there were few men among the Palestinian Jews who were as important as he and none whose reputation Wald respected more. Ben-Avi was a member of the Hagana high command, in charge of all its activities in Europe; and he ran the Mossad, the center in Palestine that controlled Bricha.

There was another man with Ben-Avi when Wald walked into his office. This was Avshalom Mor, acting commander in chief of Hagana, and the third of the men Wald had come to see in Palestine. This meeting was different from the one with Weizmann, for they were all three of them warriors and leaders of fighting men, and they all knew well the same violent world. Ben-Avi and Mor knew who Wald was and most of what he had done. They had thrown a Hagana network over Europe from Constanta on the Black Sea to the tiny Port de Bouc at the tip of France's Mediterranean coast and there was little that a Jew could meaningfully do in all those thousands of miles that escaped their notice. But they had not known of Tochnit Aleph, and that one rocked them.

Wald told them most of it, holding back only three things: which were the target cities, where the poison was coming from, and that he had seen Weizmann. Ben-Avi asked about the poison and the targets but Wald shook his head and they didn't press him. No one could think that he was a man to be pressed. As Wald remembers it now, he had no specific reason for withholding information from these men. He thinks it was only habit, the automatic application of the doctrine of "the need to know" that keeps the compartments of a conspiracy separate, each participant told only what his task requires him to know. The important result was that Ben-Avi and Mor apparently assumed that the poison was already on hand and in Germany; and this assumption, it now seems clear, shaped what was to happen. The impression must have been strengthened when Ben-Avi and Mor asked what Wald wanted of them, for he did not ask for help in obtaining the poison. He said his comrades had sent him to seek moral approval for Tochnit Aleph. Not *consent*—they were not, in this, putting themselves under the orders of any other group—and not the approval of those Jewish leaders whose arena of struggle was bloodless, but the approval of those in Palestine who were, as were the leaders of DIN, the fighting men. And so he'd been sent to Hagana. There was more. He wanted authority to call upon the Hagana agents in Europe for help in the escape when the thing was done. And he wanted documents and a way back to Europe, for without Hagana assistance no one illegally in Palestine could hope to get aboard a ship, past the British guards.

The meeting ended there. They would keep in touch,

said Ben-Avi, it would take a week or so. And Wald
understood the Hagana commanders would discuss the
project.

It took more than a week, nearly a month; and though
Wald from time to time urged Ben-Avi to a decision, he
wasn't really impatient because the arrangements for the
poison also took time. Then Ben-Avi called him in again.
It had been decided. There was a British troop transport
leaving Haifa in a few days, carrying soldiers who had
done their stint in Palestine, and other odds and ends of
military and police personnel. Wald could go on this, as a
soldier in General Anders's Free Polish Corps who had
been wounded in the Western Desert and had been sent
to the Hadassah Hospital in Jerusalem for extensive treatment. It was a pretty good cover, it fit Wald's cadaverous
appearance and his heavily accented English, and he
could—if need be—speak Polish. It would also explain
why none of the soldiers aboard ship would know him.
Hagana would provide uniform, identity card, and military
travel documents. The ship was to lay over at Toulon.
The Hagana agent in Toulon would be alerted and he
would make arrangements. There would be other agents
available and waiting in Munich. Wald could take it from
there. Was there anything else?

There was nothing else. Wald was content. For him
and for those with him in Tochnit Aleph, Hagana was the
arm of the Jewish people and where it struck, the Jewish
people struck. It was the moral backing he sought. And
he had the poison. The road was clear.

In the uniform of the Free Polish Corps and with
papers to match, Wald went past the barrier at King's
Way in Haifa and through the checkpoint at the port
gates, and climbed aboard the troopship. Within the hour
he had hidden the knapsack with the curious netted can-
isters inside it, and he relaxed for the journey across
the Mediterranean. That night the ship touched at Alexandria in Egypt, and a squad of British MPs came aboard
and took Wald in handcuffs to the central prison. He
had been betrayed.

It was a shocking blow, and Wald was numbed. But he was given time to recover, months of it, first in the Alexandria prison and then later in the solitary cells in prisons in Jerusalem and in the fortress at Acre. Occasionally he was interrogated by men from the Special Branch CID, but the questions seemed random and routine, perfunctory explorations of how he had gotten his uniform and the false papers, and what he was going to Europe for. There was never a question that cut closer to the bone, and never any mention of the poison he had hidden aboard the ship—so he presumed this had not been found, or if found had not been connected to him. It seemed clear, then, that the British knew nothing about him as Malachi Wald, and nothing of his mission. But the manner of his arrest and the nature of his imprisonment, solitary confinement and being shunted from prison to prison without charges or trial, showed that they suspected he was somehow important, not just another Jew engaged in the run-of-the-mill underground activity that boiled then in Palestine. So it was also clear, since they knew so little and suspected more than they knew, that the British had not taken him as a result of their own intelligence work. Wald told them nothing and went back to one or another of the dank cells that constituted his world and chewed incessantly at two questions: Who had shopped him? And why?

In time he worked it out this way:

He had spoken at a number of clandestine meetings of high officials of the Jewish Agency, the Zionist Executive, the Hagana. Any of these meetings could conceivably have been penetrated, and the British might have thus been informed of his presence in Palestine and might have kept him under surveillance. But, with his experience and his caution, could he have been trailed all these weeks and not spotted a tail? Unlikely. And why would the British bother, having against him only that he was illegally in Palestine, as were thousands and that he'd been a leader of the Jewish resistance in Europe during the war? And if they had more than this, if they knew somehow of DIN and wanted to break it, would they not have followed him back to Europe? And would there not have been references during one or the other of the interrogations? All unlikely. Scrub it; and look further.

Well, then, it had to be concerned with Tochnit Aleph. That had to be the "why" of it, to stop Tochnit Aleph.

There were only four men who knew both who he was and why he had come to Palestine: Weizmann; the bacteriologist who had prepared the poison; and the Hagana commanders, Yitzhak Ben-Avi and Avshalom Mor. Take them in order: Weizmann. But Weizmann knew that Wald hadn't got the poison, and if he wanted to block Tochnit Aleph, he need only have denied Wald help. The same held true for the bacteriologist. Ben-Avi or Mor, then? Impossible though! Neither of these men would betray a Jew into a British prison . . . unless urgent policy left them only this odious alternative. But they did have other ways. They could have withheld the Hagana approval he had come to seek; and without the help of Hagana he could never get out of Palestine. Either way they could have ended it. But wait; *had* they these alternatives? As far as they knew? How had he put it to them? How had it been, actually? That he had been sent seeking "approval," not "consent"; that he and his associates were not in this matter putting themselves under Hagana orders. More. He had given them the impression, and deliberately, that the poison was already on hand, in Germany. So Ben-Avi and Mor and those they might have discussed the project with in Hagana *would* have thought that keeping Wald in Palestine, especially if he were to find a way to communicate with Augsburg, would not be enough to block Tochnit Aleph. If they were to block it, they had as far as they could know, only this unpalatable expedient: to cause Wald to disappear, in circumstances denying him communication and without exposing themselves; to send agents to Augsburg to tell the others that Hagana disapproved, that Wald had yielded and had sent the Hagana men to stop it. It might not work, but it offered a chance, and as far as Ben-Avi and Mor could know, the only chance. Thinking thus, seeing no alternative and determined to block Tochnit Aleph, they would force themselves to accept even a solution that would revolt them.

So he was left with Ben-Avi or Mor, one or both, acting for themselves or on behalf of the Hagana.

So he was left. Malachi Wald, betrayed into a British dungeon by those who, no less than he, were warriors for the Jews. Cast out like Cain.

He nearly went mad.

Thus it happened that Tochnit Aleph, the plan to kill a million Germans, foundered.

Two Hagana agents did come to the man called Israel in the safehouse at Augsburg, and told him what they had been sent to say. The Hagana, they said, opposed the project and Wald agreed. Wald joined Hagana in urging all of them to come to Palestine and enter the underground work there that he, himself, was now urgently engaged upon.

And if they did not agree? asked Israel, knowing that it was ended, that he and his comrades could not carry the awful weight of it without some Jewish authority to share the responsibility; knowing, as the Hagana men did not, that anyway they hadn't the poison; knowing all this but asking nonetheless, just to have it out and clear. If they did not agree?

Why, then, the two of them were instructed to say that Hagana denounced the project as dishonorable and dangerous to the Jewish people, an outlaw act which would have repercussions damaging to the Jews throughout the world. This being so, they said—playing the last card, a lie, but powerful—Hagana would stop it by any means. To help in this last eventuality, Wald had given all details, including the names and cover identities and work assignments of those men already placed in the target cities. If there were no other way, the Hagana would give this information to the Allied occupation authorities in Germany.

They told Israel they would give him two days to speak to the others and decide. Two days, they said, not more.

Avraham Becker and Hannah Baum were in Munich;

Israel went there, calling in Victor Berger from Paris and
Ben-Issachar Feld and Judah Klein from Nuremberg.
There was no debate. There couldn't be. They hadn't the
poison, and though they might still try to get it elsewhere,
they would not. It was not the Hagana's threat that held
them, they might have risked this, fled, and set the project
up in other places and in other ways. But for all of them,
as for Wald, the Hagana was the one Jewish authority
they recognized as supreme. It represented, as they themselves had once represented, the fighting Jews. Hagana
had decided at the highest level, and they—at this final
moment—would not go against it.

Tochnit Aleph was dead.

The next day Israel returned to Augsburg and reported
to the Hagana agents. The men who had been placed
in the water departments of Munich and Nuremberg
would be called back and advised to go the Bricha route
to Palestine. The six who had led them would go also.

But not just yet. For in Munich, when they had yielded
to the Hagana, they had also taken another decision. The
Jewish authority had set itself against Tochnit Aleph.
Wald, who had been one of them, their leader—if leader
there was—had deserted them, not even consulted with
them, had even informed against them. Well, this was
all bitter enough and against this combination they could
not persist. Clearly, it had been thus decided that the
Jews were not to do to the Germans what the Germans
had done to the Jews—unleashing death upon them, un-
limited without selection or pity. But DIN had been
formed originally to impose judgment and vengeance
upon specific killers of the Jews, and the Hagana did not
oppose this principle. So they would go to Palestine, in
time, but before they went they would do one final thing.
With acrid irony they called it Tochnit Beth—"Plan B."

It was Victor Berger who proposed Tochnit Beth. By
now he knew a lot about poison and had access to some.
Nothing as esoteric or as powerful as that for which Wald
had been sent to Palestine, but useful enough. There was,
for example, a chemical, heat-resistant, it could be baked

in bread. Enough of it, and a little was enough, would kill. And Berger could get it, quite a lot of it.

The discussion was brief, and concerned only the question of possible targets, and was quickly resolved. There was an interrogation center of the Joint Allied Control Council outside Nuremberg. It was something special; it held more than eight thousand SS men. They were a criminal elite, as had been the two hundred men in the Münster barracks that DIN had blown up when Victor Berger first joined them. All the men in the Nuremberg stockade were being held for trial on major war-crimes charges. Most of them had been death-camp personnel; or men of the Politische Abteilungen, the "Political Departments" that had been in charge of punishment by torture in all of the concentration camps; or veterans of the Einsatzgruppen, the traveling mass-murder battalions; or Gestapo interrogation specialists who had tortured resistance fighters in the German-occupied territories throughout Europe. There was also a contingent from the so-called "Blowtorch Battalion" of the First SS Panzer Regiment which had murdered 115 American prisoners of war at the Malmédy-Bagnez crossroads on December 17, 1944. Here was a target to which the Hagana could not object, a target comprising only guilty men.

It was decided. Berger went to Paris to arrange about the poison, and the others set about the reconnaissance.

They learned quickly that one German bakery supplied the bread for the camp, using flour allocated by the American army. The bakery was their first point of attack. Israel approached the German works supervisor at the bakery and offered him a story to tear at his tender heart, and a deal to seduce his grubby soul. The story was broached at a nearby bar, two good Nazi party members having a few friendly drinks. Israel told his new friend that he had a nephew, a poor orphan, a fine young lad who had, *natürlich,* been in the Hitler Jugend and whose entire family had been murdered in the American terror bombings in Düsseldorf. The boy had himself been hurt and still suffered terribly, and he was all alone. Saddest story ever head; the supervisor sniffled into the bottle of good bootleg beer that Israel had provided; and what was the deal? . . . Wait, there's more to the story: There was an uncle in Canada, one of the upstanding auslandsdeutsche, who owned a large bakery and was prepared to send for the boy to work in his bakery. It would be useful if the boy could get some experience before he went. The supervisor nodded; sure, for such a boy—all alone, he would do everything. Everything. And what was the deal? . . . The deal involved cartons of American cigarettes, worth quite a lot on the black market; half in advance and half when the boy had worked a month. . . . So? For such a story, and such a deal, why not? Settled. Send the boy.

And so Ben-Issachar Feld—Benno the Messenger, now named Franz Kruger and with papers to match—went to work as a baker's apprentice. He made a good impression, blond, blue-eyed, and a bear for work. He was willing to do anything, work all hours, run errands, take extra shifts. He was even happy to work permanently on the unpopular midnight shift. Quite a dependable lad, learned quickly. And also, of course, he kicked back part of his wages to the works supervisor.

Hannah Baum went to work, too, but her work was somewhat different. There was almost nothing that some hungry women wouldn't do in those days for a pleasant and generous American soldier who would give her affection—and coffee and tinned meat, and good bread. So in time Hannah had a boyfriend, an American sergeant who happened to run a mess-hall detail at the Nuremberg special stockade. This was important, they had to know what happened to the bread when it was delivered to the camp. Did the American guards eat any of it? Was it left about in a common kitchen? Who handled it within the camp?

Between them, Hannah and Benno got the information they needed. Ten thousand loaves of bread were delivered every day, nine thousand loaves of coarse brown bread and a thousand loaves of white bread. The American guards ate the white bread. Only the white bread? Yes, only the white; well, there were some crackpots—health addicts, you know?—who liked the regular bread, so a hundred loaves of that were set aside for the American personnel. . . . It was all handled this way: The bread was loaded on American army trucks at five o'clock every morning and taken from the bakery to the camp kitchens; separate kitchens for prisoners and guard personnel, separate mess halls, too. . . . The kitchens were at opposite ends of the camp, so one truck took all the bread for the guards directly from the bakery. . . . Inside the camp, the prisoners' mess details handled all food for the prisoners, under the supervision of American noncoms such as Hannah's boyfriend. Every now and then a guard team would go through the prisoners' kitchens, counting utensils, opening tins, fingering through sacks of flour and cereal and sugar, slicing open random loaves of bread. Standard security check.

The fact that the bread for the prisoners was handled separately from the bread for the guards made the project possible, the white bread would be unpoisoned and Benno, inside the bakery, could make sure that only untreated brown bread would be loaded on the truck for the guards' kitchen. But the problem of introducing the poison was complicated. Since some of the brown bread was eaten by Americans, they couldn't risk putting poison directly into the flour or the batter. And, besides, Benno told them that the workers at the bakery set aside bread for themselves and ate it while they worked. It wouldn't do to have the truck drivers coming for their bread in the early morning and finding a bakery full of dead men.

Benno brought out some loaves of bread and these were sent to Berger in Paris together with some questions for him to ask the chemist who was helping him. Would the poison be effective if it was dusted on the bread after baking? Would it spread through a loaf if it was somehow injected? . . . Back came the answers. Dusting was no good, not enough poison would remain through the normal handling for any guaranteed effectiveness. It could be injected, though, using any long-nozzled syringe, like an automobile grease gun or those rubber bulbs with long nozzles that were used in hospitals for enemas and douches and sprays. The chemist could get these in Paris. Some kind of a thin rod would have to be pushed into the bread first, to make a path so the nozzle of the syringe wouldn't be blocked going in. The syringe should be thrust in to maximum depth and then withdrawn slowly as pressure was applied to spread the poison through as much of the loaf as possible. There would be a small hole, and the bread would be a bit soggy for a while, but there was nothing to be done about that, and it wouldn't be too noticeable.

It could be done, then, but this way would not be an easy one to work out. As Benno Feld reported it, when the bread came out of the ovens the loaves were loaded on wheeled racks and brought into a large drying room which opened onto the outside loading platform. They could probably get into the room all right, but then what? How would they work? It would take several hours to inject the poison into the bread, handling each loaf separately; and though none of the bakery workers remained in the drying room, they were in and out all the time. And everything depended upon there being no suspicion that the bread had been tampered with, so they couldn't risk discovery at all.

They thought it over for a couple of days, and talked about it incessantly, and a plan took shape. The thing might be done under cover of a robbery. They could go into the bakery armed, hold up the workers and get them out of the way where they wouldn't see what was happening, and poison the bread. Then they would bring in a truck and load it up with flour, yeast, sugar, all valuable in the black market. It would look like a robbery, no one would examine the bread.

They went over it and over it. It would work well enough in theory; but the practice would obviously be tricky and the risks were multiple. They'd have to steal a truck and risk the alarm about that. A police patrol or some passing MPs might see the truck in the bakery courtyard or on the street; and a man would have to be immobilized on guard in the courtyard to warn the others if that did happen. After the job, they'd have to get the truck away and hide it, and in the early morning every moving vehicle was likely to be stopped for a check. Nor was that all. The job itself, inside the bakery, was very awkward. There was an armed watchman and his dog drifting about. There were more than twenty workers on the night shift, and they weren't always in one room. It wouldn't be easy to jump them all at once, and if one man got away, or if there was one man—hero or hysteric —who forced them to shoot him, the job would be blown.

Well, they could think of no other way. They'd have to minimize whatever risks they could and accept the ones that were inescapable. They decided not to steal a truck, thereby setting off an immediate alarm, but to have one of their contacts take it from the Jewish Brigade's transport pool on the basis of forged orders which might cover the soldier who got it for them. Then Benno Feld suggested they schedule the operation for a Saturday night. Work in the bakery, he told them, slackened off a bit before three in the morning. Usually the workers hung around, drinking up the free coffee, but Saturday night was a time for harder beverages and on most Saturdays about half the shift left and headed for the taverns when most of the work was done. That would make it easier. They could have a lookout signal when the men had left, then he could deal with the watchman and the dog. That was a tricky bit to handle quietly, but not impossible, these dogs were trained to kill silently, without raising an alarm. Once they were in the gate, Benno would unlock the door at the loading platform and they'd make the raid from there. They would only have a couple of hours at most until the trucks came from the camp, and they'd never be able to treat all the bread, but it was the best they could do. They'd mount it on the first moonless Saturday night, that would give some additional darkness to cover them and the truck; they'd pray for wet weather, too, it might hold the road patrols down.

When it came, they were ready. Victor Berger had arrived from Paris, in his French army uniform and with the poison and the syringes in the back of the military command car he had borrowed. They dumped the car and transferred the material to the truck, and Berger, Israel, and Avraham Becker drove in the truck to the end of the street that paralleled the bakery. Judah Klein waited in a dark doorway opposite the bakery entrance.

A little before three o'clock, on schedule, eleven workers left the bakery and headed for their weekly carouse. Minutes later, Hannah Baum teetered up to the gate with her whore's dress and the reek of beer testifying to her profession and her condition. She hung on the gate for a moment until the watchman and his dog appeared. There was a minute or so while she offered the man a real bargain in various delights, then the watchman hooked the dog's leash over his arm and fumbled the gate open and then he reached, to feel the merchandise as it were. Hannah leaned into him seductively and slid a knife under his ribs and Judah Klein came racing across the street to club down the dog slavering to get at Hannah but held by the leash still hooked around the dead man's arm. A moment more, and the corpses were hauled into the shadows of the wall, the truck there also, and Benno had opened the door to them and they were all inside, armed and ready.

The rest of it went like clockwork also: the workers surprised by the sudden onslaught and no wild men among them, submitting to the ropes and the taped gags, being herded into the office, tripped, their legs tied too, restraining nooses around their necks fastened to desks and radiators. . . . The "robbers" worked in sweating haste—they had only two hours before the trucks would come from the camps and they had to be well away by then. They loaded the truck first so that if there was an alarm and they had to run it would offer evidence of a planned robbery and nothing more. Then they worked with the poison, carefully, as fast as possible, but careful to leave no suspicious signs; going among the stacked loaves of bread, loaf after loaf, working to the absolute last dangerous limit of time until Israel called them off and they piled into the truck, all of them, and rolled away, leaving the gate locked behind them, the watchman dead behind them, the dog dead, one other man dead

—as they later learned—having strangled on a badly placed gag.

They separated minutes later, Israel taking the truck —and the risk of it—to hide it in Schwabach, thirty miles south, and lead the hunt that way; the others in Berger's French military car heading east to Sulzbach-Rosenberg where they had a car hidden with new sets of plates and identity papers and enough gasoline to get them two hundred miles to the Czechoslovak border, and the Bricha group at Plzen would help them on from there.

From Plzen they went to Prague, and waited there for Israel, and for news.

Israel came first, and without mishap. The news was delayed, but within a week they had it all, pieced together from the censored and garbled newspaper accounts and more reliably from the sources of Hagana and Bricha. It was not too bad. More than seven hundred SS men dead, nearly a thousand more dangerously ill, and with luck a fair number of these might die.

Well, they were done. Tochnit Beth finished, their work of vengeance done. Or so they thought, and waited a while for the hunt to slacken, and then filtered out of Europe to Palestine where the new battle loomed; where Avraham Becker was to be killed in the Negev desert and Judah Klein was to lose a leg when the riflemen went in against the armor of the Arab Legion of Jordan at Latrun. And where, in 1952, Malachi Wald would call them all together once more—to begin again the work of DIN.

Eight /

/ The World of
/ Malachi Wald

Each of the great wars has brought mankind ever closer to the ultimate abyss. Each has demonstrated anew, and ever more forcefully, how tenuous and fragile is the shifting balance between civilization's resilience and the leaping growth of its technical capacity to destroy itself. After each such conflict mankind staggers back from the awful brink resolved never again to go this suicidal way, resolved henceforth to abide by the fundamental and only rescuing commandments—to do justly and to give a sheltering compassion to the innocent and the needful. And then, the abyss being barely out of sight, only just around the corner of fleeting time, resolution fails. Men, remaining timid, heedless, unlearning, allow their aberrant leaders to take them again upon the same seductive path marked by unethical expedient and evaded issue. Until the guideposts provided by decent reason are passed and lost, and all that remains at the end of the road is the clash of ignorant armies, to be locked—this next time—in a struggle so skilled and so limitlessly savage that victor and vanquished alike must surely plunge into the unknowable pit from which will crawl some monstrous mutant generation, clutching in its paws the hideous and pitiful future of man.

Beginning in 1942, and throughout the war, the United Nations declared the punishment of those responsible for Nazi crimes to be among their paramount war aims. The pledges were unequivocal: "Not one crime will be left uninvestigated; not one criminal, whether directly or indirectly responsible, will escape punishment." . . . "Retribution must be swift, sure, and complete." . . . "There cannot be, there will not be, any pardon."[93]

The pledges were total; the action taken was considerably less. In November 1943, the Allied powers meeting in Moscow declared only that the *leaders* of the Third Reich would be punished. And at that time, the American and Soviet representatives favored summary executions of these criminal leaders, while the British argued for a trial observing "all legal forms."[94] During the following year, in the United States of America—at some considerable distance from the gas chambers and the mass graves—the voices of sweet reason began to be heard, counseling moderation. On June 15, 1944, the Federal Council of Churches of Christ announced its opposition to any large-scale trials and called for the punishment of only the "central" Nazi leaders, "those most responsible." Anticipating by more than twenty years Adolf Eichmann's argument in his own defense, the Council declared that Christian ethics forbade the punishment of those "who were implicated because they carried out orders."[95] The Protestant clergy in America thus followed their pliable brethren in the German churches who witnessed the agony of the Jews and nevertheless muted the voices they might have raised for justice. And within this curious concept of the Christian ethic it was thus argued for the first time that men ought to go guiltless before the law so long as the crimes they committed, however brutal, were done— as were Eichmann's—*im Auftrage* "by authority."

In such an atmosphere, it is hardly surprising that by April 1945 the American government had amended its original policy of summary execution of the Nazi leaders and adopted instead the British position of a properly legal trial; and it is only comic to record that by then the British had themselves progressed from moderation to total forgiveness, and were now opposed to any process at all against even the main architects of the extermination of the Jews.[96] But the British position seemed to be carrying tolerance too far, too soon. After all, there were millions and millions who had only recently been criminally brought to terrible deaths, and some small move toward justice would have to be made. What finally emerged from the London conference of pussyfooting diplomats seeking an acceptable evasion of the issue was perhaps the smallest such move possible. It was agreed to establish an international military tribunal before which would be brought those "major criminals" whose offenses had no particular geographic localization. And, indeed, before this International Military Tribunal at Nuremberg, twenty-four men did in time come to answer for the crimes of the Third German Reich. In the closing months of the war in Europe, the great pledge of the world community that "not one criminal, whether directly or indirectly responsible, will escape punishment" represented only so many words ringing emptily in the air.

It was within this immense and conscienceless vacuum that DIN had arisen in 1945.

Of the fifty men and women who had carried out the judgments of DIN, and of the three hundred who had helped, there were left in Europe at the end of 1946 only six—Avraham Becker, Judah Klein, the man called Israel, Benno the messenger, Hannah Baum, and Victor Berger. All the others had gone the Bricha route to Palestine. These six sat in the safehouse and considered the year of DIN.

In that first hunters' year, counting those who had just been killed in the attack by poison on the SS men in the Nuremberg stockade, a thousand murderers had fallen to their dark crusade in Germany and Austria. And in that time, except for the violent justice that they had administered, there had been no other. Because all who had joined DIN had been Jews, acting in hot hate for evil done to them and theirs, DIN's had been a justice flawed, the prosecutors, judges, and executioners identical and vengeful. There had been no alternative; either their kind of vigilante justice, or none.

But toward the middle of 1946, the picture began to

change. The horrors the Germans had wrought in all the lands to which they had come as conquerors stood at last inescapably revealed and the German people cowered beneath the bleak contempt of all the shuddering world. They were seen as barbarians, hardly human, human only within the chill definitions of science, a nation of murderers. Pushed by this surge of revulsion, and faced by the example of the Russians—who within six months of war's end had already executed more than four thousand Nazi criminals and sent ten times that many to prison—the leaders of the western powers began at last to give meaning to the pledges they had until then ignored. By the end of 1946, there were 480,000 Germans held in guarded stockades, awaiting trial for direct participation in mass murder and in other crimes against humanity. Another 3,445,100 were listed within the categories to be prosecuted for significant criminal complicity.[97]

It seemed clear that justice would be done at last, properly, in the light of day and in all majesty; and where there is such justice there need be none other. More than three million Germans in western Europe alone sweated in the shadow of the blind goddess; and a new world had arisen in which evil would not go unpunished. Thus did the six in Prague hope, as did the leaders of Hagana who now counseled and commanded the end of their work, and—hoping—so believed; and were, as they would learn in time, all of them mistaken. . . .

As, at the end of 1946, the full revelations of Nazi crimes had finally moved the world's peoples to demand justice for the Jews, so this same evidence—perhaps coupled with the awareness of their own contributory sins of callous omission—led the nations to seek some just and compassionate solution to the problem presented by the half a million Jewish survivors rotting in the DP camps in Europe. Neither the new justice, nor the new compassion, nor the new awareness, impelled the nations to open their own gates. Happily, though, there was a more comfortable alternative; one that the Jews themselves demanded, and themselves made possible. Day after day, the Jews in the camps clamored to go to Palestine; day by day, Bricha smuggled them in; and unceasingly, within Palestine, the Jewish underground resistance tore at the British garrisons and civilian administration. And the war-weary British people were growing unwilling to support by force a policy that had been morally indefensible since the terms of the Palestine Mandate included Britain's pledge to sponsor "the establishment in Palestine of a national home for the Jewish people."[98]

Thus pressed, physically and morally, on April 2, 1947, Great Britain submitted the problem of Palestine to the United Nations. On November 29, 1947, the General Assembly voted to partition the mandated territory into a Jewish and an Arab state. Many factors impelled the vote, but the record of the long debate offers sufficient evidence that the Assembly took its decision, in significant part at least, as an act of contrition.

The British government moved to sabotage the decision it had opposed, and its malice was directed against the Jews. Although Arab irregular forces were already attacking Jewish settlements and setting ambushes along the roads in the territory allotted to the Jewish state, the British forces disarmed the Hagana units wherever they found them and confiscated the tiny stores of weapons the settlements maintained for their defense. The regular armies of five Arab nations (including the British-trained and British-officered Arab Legion of Jordan) were mobilized on the borders of the Jewish territory, awaiting only the withdrawal of the British before launching the invasion which the Arab League had pledged would end with "the extermination of the Jews."[99] Nevertheless, the British refused to allow Hagana to take up defensive positions; and as the British forces withdrew to their ships in Haifa port, they turned over to the Arabs their garrison forts within the Jewish territory.

Great Britain thus became an active accessory to Arab aggression. The rest of the United Nations played a role considerably more passive but equally sordid. In the critical six months from the General Assembly's vote until the last British forces sailed from Palestine, the nations demonstrated that the vote had been only a ritual aimed at exorcising the ghosts of the Jewish dead and at appeasing the uneasy conscience of the world by incantations devoid of meaning or purpose.

For despite the clear storm warnings, the UN not only failed to provide troops to enforce its decision and to maintain the peace in Palestine, but the nations rummaged through the rubbish heap of recent history and brought forth again the reeking device of "nonintervention" with which they had dug the grave of the embattled Spanish republic in 1936. They embargoed the shipment of arms to either side in Palestine, thus equating the Jewish defenders with the Arab aggressors. They did this in full awareness that the Arab invasion armies were adequately supplied from national arms stocks and that Jewish Hagana had no such resources.

All this done, the members of the United Nations congratulated each other on their acts of enlightened statesmanship and hastened from the arena. Within that august assemblage constituting "the last great hope of mankind" there was none to remind the nations of the axiom in law and ethics that holds men responsible for the foreseeable consequences of their actions. None to point to the besmirched signposts of avoided issue and unethical expedient and to cry that these had been seen before and that they had always marked the road to ruin. The nations let war loose upon the Jews of Palestine; and in thus betraying the Jew, betrayed themselves.

On May 15, 1948, in Tel Aviv, the National Council of Palestinian Jews proclaimed the independent state of Israel. And on that same day, the armies of Egypt, Jordan, Syria, Iraq, and Lebanon crossed all the land frontiers of the new State. The Jews of Israel were left alone, as the Jews of Europe had been left alone not long before, to see whether they could survive this latest violent attempt at the final solution to the Jewish problem.

Well, not quite alone; and with important lessons learned. For between these two final solutions, the Jews had learned that no one rescues the defenseless; had learned that a small and threatened people which looks for its survival to the conscience of the world is soon dead, and in no position to take comfort from the subsequent anguish of repentant mourners arriving, alas, late upon the scene. So when war came to the new Israel, the Jews were outgunned and outnumbered, but not precisely defenseless and not entirely unprepared.

The five invading Arab nations sent 30,000 men into battle. A fourth of these were the irregulars of the "Arab Liberation Army." The rest were regular soldiers, well trained, well equipped. They had tanks, armored cars, field artillery, air forces; and they had the initial advantages of the aggressor, able to choose the times and places of their attacks.

At the beginning of the war, Hagana could deploy 18,000 fighters. A third of these were women, and boys and girls under eighteen. Most of the 12,000 men who formed the backbone of the Jewish forces had been trained only in the tactics of an underground resistance, rarely operating in more than platoon strength. Most of the officers, and about 2000 men, were better trained, having served in the Jewish Brigade with the British armies in Europe. Hagana was ill equipped for a regular war, having only the weapons that are usual for an underground movement, and not enough of these. Even ammunition was scarce; it worked out at 50 rounds per rifle and 700 rounds for each machine gun. There was no armored transport (except such as was improvised by hanging metal plating on civilian busses and trucks), no field artillery, no heavy mortars, and the only planes available were eight light civilian aircraft of the Piper Cub class—sitting ducks for the Egyptian and Iraqi fighters.[100]

Weighing against all this, Hagana had the advantages of superior commanders, exceptional knowledge of the terrain on which the battles were fought, and the morale that comes when both soldiers and civilians are disciplined and aware that there is no bearable alternative to victory. The Jews of Israel knew that what the Arabs promised them was "annihilation." And there was one additional factor. The Jewish communities throughout the world were this time determined that nothing whatever, neither the laws of their own countries nor the easy counsels of their governments, would keep them once again impotent witnesses of their brothers' agony. From mid-1947, when it seemed clear that a Jewish state would be established in Palestine and that the Arabs would fight to destroy it, the commanders of Hagana had been secretly mobilizing support among the Jewish communities in the western world. In the first phase of the war, Hagana's forces were committed to a fluid defensive strategy aimed at blunting the Arab attacks until help could come from the Jews abroad. Time was the essential need, and the Israelis bought it with their lives. Everything that was vital to the existence of the Jewish state was held against all odds for a terrible month until the exhausted and stalemated Arabs accepted the first truce on June 11, 1948.

It was not the Arabs alone who were exhausted. Hagana's commander on the northern front, Brigadier Moshe Carmel, spoke for all his comrades when he welcomed the truce as "dew from heaven." There is no doubt that the tenacity of the defense in that first month, and the clandestine activities during the month-long truce that followed, brought the survival of Israel. For in those two months the Jewish people everywhere began to move, and what they did began to be effective. So that when the fighting resumed on July 8, the scales were more nearly in balance and Hagana could move to the offensive. From then on, the Arabs were beaten. In those two months the Hagana agents abroad and the Jewish communities they worked with completed the organization of the greatest volunteer operation of military recruitment and arms smuggling since the International Brigades marched to the defense of Republican Spain.

Early in 1948 a chubby and convivial Palestinian named Teddy Kolleck settled down in Hotel Fourteen in New York City. He had some kind of vaguely defined job with the Jewish Agency for Palestine; and within the New York Jewish community he soon won a considerable reputation as a trencherman and general bon vivant.

He was Hagana's chief agent in America and it was his task to organize, and find the money for, an arms procurement program.

Soon after, another Palestinian showed up in New York. This one was the antithesis of Kolleck, an austere, stiff-backed ex-major in the Jewish Brigade, with the Cantabrigian stutter prominent in his voice and references to his years at Cambridge excessively frequent in his conversation. He was named Wellesley Aron, and his job was to recruit military specialists for the war all knew was coming in Palestine.

Kolleck and Aron set up parallel networks that soon covered the United States. The Jewish Agency had long sponsored a somnolent organization called "Land and Labor for Palestine" whose object was to enroll American Zionist youth for a year's voluntary service as farm workers in the Jewish collective farm settlements in Palestine. Aron took over Land and Labor and infused new life into it. He set up regional offices in all the major Jewish communities from New York to California. In San Francisco, Arnie Berg—under cover of his work as a trade-union consultant—took the area north to the Canadian border and east through Idaho. From San Francisco south to Mexico and over to Texas, the work was handled by a Hollywood publicist named Irving Hamlin. Very soon, there were several hundred young men suddenly eager to work the sacred soil of Palestine. They came from the universities, shops, and offices; they had three things in common—they were all Jews, they were all veterans of World War II, they were all eager to fight for the Jewish cause. In each area, volunteer screening committees (themselves carefully selected by the regional directors from active Zionist workers) ran security checks on the applicants, had them medically examined, reviewed their military service records, listed them according to a priority of military skills, and helped them get their passports. Then they waited. When Israel was declared independent, and the British blockade had been removed, and the war had begun, Land and Labor moved them in a steady stream to New York. There Jewish travel agents organized them into "youth-group tours" and sent them to Paris. In Paris they were met by Hagana agents and escorted to Marseilles. Just outside the port city, the Jewish Agency had been gathering thousands of European DPs into the Grand Arenas camp pending the day when the withdrawal of the British blockade would open the gates to Palestine.

From the time of the first truce in the Palestine war, on June 11, these fighting volunteers mingled with the Jewish survivors of the concentration camps who came in the immigrant ships to Haifa. Under the terms of the truce, the import of fighting personnel into the area was forbidden, and observers of the UN Truce Supervision Organization met every ship to enforce the embargo. The observers may have noted that some of the immigrants were bright-eyed and sturdy beyond the usual run of European DPs, but they all carried documents issued by the Red Cross or the United Nations Relief and Rehabilitation Administration describing them as refugees, or stateless persons; and who was to know which documents were real and which were forged?

Volunteer "farmers" came also from the Jewish communities in Manchester and in London's Golders Green, from the gilded ghettos of Johannesburg and Cape Town; some from France, Holland, Switzerland.

In Israel, Hagana organized them into Mahal: *Mitnaddeve hutz la-Aretz*—"the overseas volunteers." By September 1948, the Mahal units numbered nearly four thousand; and their effectiveness could not be measured by numbers alone. The Mahal men were all tough combat veterans. Nearly all of the air crews in the new Israeli air force were Mahal; as were half the officers and ratings in the new "junk-boat" navy of armed fishing trawlers and war-surplus cutters. A third of the men in Hagana's new armored and artillery formations were volunteers from abroad. In the new officers' training courses, half the instructors were Mahal.

At war's end, one out of every five of these volunteers had either been wounded or was among the six thousand Jewish dead.

While Wellesley Aron was organizing Land and Labor in the United States, Teddy Kolleck was busy gathering about him a talented group of amateur arms smugglers. In the sleepy southern California town of Sunland, an American World War II bombing pilot named Leo Gardner set up a "flying school" that didn't seem to have many customers. What it did have was a dedicated band of ex-U.S. air force mechanics who refitted the obsolete planes that Al Schwimmer and Hank Greenspan were buying out of the war-surplus dumps the air force maintained in Texas and Arizona. These were transferred to dummy civil aviation companies in Mexico and Panama and flown by easy stages to Europe. In San Francisco, Arnie Berg branched out from personnel recruitment, and began buying old tanks and half-tracks and shipping these out as "scrap metal." Danny Agronsky, who came from Jerusalem as one of Kolleck's aides, went all the way to Hawaii to pick over the mountains of bazookas and mortars and field artillery which had piled up during the war in the Pacific and were on sale as junk.

Under Teddy Kolleck's stimulus, within the Jewish communities along the eastern seaboard—in Newark, in New York, in Miami—a corps of ferociously active women were organized by Bee Jaffe into "Materials for Palestine." They concentrated on medical supplies and ambulances, and later on recruited volunteer medical teams to go to Israel. All these people and all this equipment traveled via Jewish-owned shipping lines, at first to Marseilles and toward the end directly to Haifa. Before the cargoes were loaded aboard the ships, Kolleck and his associates nestled grenades and ammunition and an occasional machine gun among the bandages and the stretchers; and some of the jeep-powered ambulances served in Israel as gun carriers and armored transport.

In October 1948, the FBI broke the Hagana network and eleven of its leaders were subsequently indicted for violation of American laws governing arms exports and the activities of foreign agents. Soon afterward, the recruitment of military personnel was closed down also in South Africa and in England. But by then a lot had been accomplished. And nothing stopped the flow of money that the Jews of these countries poured into Hagana's European bank accounts. In a single year, these contributions amounted to more than $500 million. Most of this money was used to finance Rechesh—Hagana's arms procurement program in Europe.

Rechesh had begun early in 1947 when the Hagana high command ordered Yehuda Arazi, in Italy, to take the job on in addition to his duties as head of Bricha (the organization that was running Jews from Europe past the British blockade of Palestine). From then until early 1948, Hagana agents bought small quantities of arms in the black markets that burgeoned within the anarchy of postwar Europe and filtered them down into Milan. In Milan they were packed into dummy generators and cement mixers and construction equipment, and thus ultimately landed at Haifa port. There they were cleared through British customs as equipment ordered by Solel Boneh, the Jewish-owned construction cooperative which had for years built roads, factories, and British military bases throughout the Middle East. In the first five months of its existence, Rechesh thus delivered to Hagana 200 Bren guns and spare parts; 1000 British army rifles; 200 German army rifles; 400 submachine guns; 500 pistols; 3000 hand grenades; 1.5 million rounds of miscellaneous ammunition.[101]

In September 1947, the Jewish authorities in Palestine were certain that the UN would vote to establish some form of Jewish state. They were certain, also, that the Arab countries would force a war upon them; and they felt they could count upon no nation to give them, officially, the arms they would need. They decided to try to raise Rechesh to the nth power; to obtain some kind of status for it somewhere in Europe that would enable them to expand arms procurement beyond the level of a small-scale smuggling operation. The move was made in Czechoslovakia.

Hagana sent Ehud Avriel and Uriel Doron to Prague to negotiate with the Communist-dominated Czech government. This was no ordinary cloak-and-dagger mission, and these two were no ordinary emissaries. They were artful and ruthless manipulators, well qualified to find their way in the Borgia court that Prague resembled in those conspiratorial days preceding the Communist take-over of February 1948.

It was the task of Avriel and Doron to convince the Czech Communists of the financial and political advantages that would ensue if Czechoslovakia were to help the Palestine Jews in the coming war. The financial aspects were clear. The bright image of political advantage the Hagana men sketched in Prague went something like this: The Arab countries were reactionary regimes under British-French-American hegemony. The Jewish state, however, would be born a virgin, unsullied by such alliances. The Jewish community in Palestine was a workers' society with a dominant labor-Socialist orientation. If the Jews were to triumph, and particularly if they had been helped to their victory by Communist aid, might not such a new state gravitate to the eastern socialisms and serve thereby as a wedge to crack western influence within the corrupt feudalisms of the Middle East? Nor did Avriel and Doron ask for exclusivity. Czechoslovakia was already selling weapons in substantial quantities to the official Arab purchasing missions. The Jews offered no objection. (In fact, they did object, and Hagana was even then organizing units to sabotage the flow of Czech arms to the Arab states; but there was no need to allow an excess of candor to complicate the delicate business of buying a true friend.)

As had been hoped, all this weight of real financial—and apparent political—advantage proved enticing. The Czechs recognized the unique opportunity of acting publicly and profitably as friends of the Arabs, while acting secretly—and profitably—as friends of the Jews. Betting thus on both contending sides in the coming struggle, how could they lose? In April 1948, the Czechs and the Hagana emissaries concluded a secret agreement which provided that an initial payment of $100 million in hard currencies would be paid into Swiss banks to the order of the Czech government. In return, Czechoslovakia would allow Hagana to use two small army airfields as transfer points for airlifts and as refitting bases. In addition, Czechoslovakia would sell to Hagana eleven Messerschmitt fighter planes that had been left behind when the Germans evacuated the country. The whole deal would go into effect once the Jewish state had been officially established.

On May 20, 1948, five days after the Jewish authorities in Palestine proclaimed the state of Israel, the Rechesh teams in Czechoslovakia sent the Mahal aircrews on the flight that initiated Operation Balak—the airlift to Israel. The first of the third-hand Messerschmitts, with its wings and propellers demounted, was loaded aboard a DC-4 and flown to the improvised Ekron airstrip in Israel. Using the ten war-surplus cargo planes that Hagana agents had acquired in the United States and in South Africa, Operation Balak within two months had delivered nearly 250 tons of arms, equipment, and aviation fuel, plus the eleven Messerschmitts. (Five of these proved inoperable under combat conditions, but they were cannibalized to keep the others in the air.)

A few months later, Yitzhak Ben-Avi signed a similar deal with Yugoslavia. After that, the old Spitfires and Beaufighters that Hagana acquired were fitted with wing tanks and flown under their own power on the shorter route from Yugoslavia to Israel. From then until the end of the war, these two European bases were the main funnels through which poured the equipment that Hagana bought secretly throughout the world.

It comes down to this: It was Rechesh, and the other arms procurement operations, that gave Hagana the weapons of victory. It was the Jewish communities that supplied the money to buy these weapons, and to pay for the Czech and Yugoslav bases that made their delivery possible. It cost nearly $500 million, and the money came only—and freely—from the Jews. In America, in England, in South Africa, in France, thousands of individual Jews risked their liberty by violating their countries' laws and engaging in illegal arms smuggling on behalf of the new Israel; or risked their lives by coming to

fight for it. No nation, as a nation, was moved by conscience, or goodwill, or by public outcry, to save from
destruction the state to which these nations had themselves given legal birth. Only the Jews saved the Jewish
state. And, as a result, that state survives, holding to
the harsh philosophy shared by all other nations without
exception: that in our squalid world force is still the final
arbiter, all else is a distant dream. No other people
adheres to this grim concept with more historic right,
for within a single decade the Jews of Europe and the
Jews of Israel were both nearly destroyed, and in the wide
uncaring world none gave help.

This recent history, piled on the centuries of prejudice
and persecution and pogrom, has planted deep in every
Jew a kernel of knowledge—instinctive, unwelcome, bitter as gall. And within the root issues of justice and of
survival, the Jew will not trust the Gentile; for the Gentile world has done little—and that little, late—to soften
the bitter heritage of oppression that the Jew is born to.
The people of the Book will henceforth await evidence
more firm than now exists before they will again embrace
the costly and uncertain hypothesis that the ethical teachings of the Bible which the Jews gave to mankind are
more effective safeguards than is the sword.

During the time of the British Mandate, the maximum-
security prison in Palestine was housed with a citadel
which had been built in Acre by the Knights Hospitalers
(the Knights of St. John of Acre) at the beginning of the
third crusade, and had been the headquarters of the order
for a hundred years until it fell to the Saracens in 1291,
bringing down with it the ninth crusade and ending the
Latin kingdom of Jerusalem.

In the centuries since then, the citadel had been many
times ruined and restored; and when Malachi Wald was
brought there in mid-1947, having come by way of the
prisons in Alexandria and in Jerusalem, the Acre citadel
was as a tourist attraction marvelously glamorous, and it
was cold hell to live in. Most of the prisoners were held
in the upper parts of the central keep, which the Turks

had rebuilt in the eighteenth century and which was merely uncomfortable and insanitary. But those, like Wald, condemned to solitary confinement, were housed—if that is the word—in the cellars of the keep under conditions truly medieval. In these ancient dungeons, the newly installed electric lights burned constantly, what little daylight filtered in wandered like some lost sprite through the slotted archery embrasures cut, eight hundred years before, in the twelve-foot-thick stone walls; and although the surrounding moat was now only a dry channel choked with weeds and rubble, the centuries of damp had permeated the place and the cellars were chilly in summer and freezing in winter, and in all seasons they stank. What exercise these special prisoners got, they took one at a time in a corner of the noisome moat where they could compete for lebensraum with the other dangerous wildlife—snakes, scorpions, and starving rats.

It was not a regimen calculated to render any man fat and sassy. It was particularly rigorous for Wald, who had been tubercular as a youth. Within a month, he had a constant cough and a persistent low-grade fever, both of which he exploited with piteous effect so that he was transferred to the security ward of the prison hospital which offered, to a man of his experience, enticing opportunities for escape. These possibilities were never to be exploited because, a week later, Wald was allowed to receive his first visitor since he had been arrested at the Alexandria docks. It was the man called Israel.

Together with the other members of DIN's leadership who had been involved in Tochnit Beth (the attack by poison on the SS men in the Nuremberg stockade), Israel and Avraham Becker had arrived in Palestine a month before and had set to work tracing Wald. They had established Wald's identity under the cover of a Palestinian-born building worker named Eleazar Ben-Chaim, but the disappearance of "Ben-Chaim" had brought them to a dead end until Yitzhak Ben-Avi, of the Hagana high command, told Israel the truth. Israel had been a general-staff officer in Hagana before he'd gone to Europe for Bricha, and he was now slated to command a brigade

in the war everyone knew was coming. Ben-Avi trusted
him, and trusted him also to comprehend the pressing
reasons of policy that had led Hagana to the desperate and
distressing measures they had taken against Wald and
against his Tochnit Aleph—the plan to poison a million
Germans. Israel had listened, and had indeed understood;
but he pointed out that Tochnit Aleph was dead, that
DIN was disbanded and most of its members were in
Palestine. There was no reason any longer for Wald to
suffer. And Israel undertook to guarantee that he would
bring Wald to a similar understanding, and that Wald
would not use the story against the Hagana high command.

Hagana's intelligence apparatus—Shai—was put to
work and quickly traced Wald's journey through the prisons at Alexandria and Jerusalem to Acre. A Hagana
lawyer drew up a petition for a writ of *habeas corpus*
demanding that the superintendent of Acre prison, Major
Clow, deliver up one Eleazar Ben-Chaim, illegally in-
carcerated without trial or due process of law. Facing the
scandal of illegal arrest and imprisonment, and having
nothing against "Ben-Chaim" but the vaguest—if darkest
—suspicions, the British decided to release him; and it
was this news that Israel brought to Wald in the prison
hospital at Acre.

So Wald was out. And it was up to Israel to fulfill
his part of the quid pro quo that he had promised to
Yitzhak Ben-Avi. To do this job, Israel called in Avraham Becker.

Of all the band of brothers who had gone together
the long way from the Ninth Fort at Kovno to DIN's
dark crusade for retribution, Avraham Becker and Malachi Wald had been the closest. Becker knew immediately
what the imprisonment, the imprisonment itself and the
manner of it, had done to Wald. The man who faced
Becker in the Tel Aviv hotel room was as he had been
always—lean, tough, enduring; but he was also now cold-
eyed and bleak, a stranger to the world. Becker, seeking
his friend, saw the stranger, and did out of love the
single right thing. He made no reference to what had

been done to Wald. He offered no apologia to Wald's cold logic. He said only that he had a job for a Jew. And thus, by that thin only thread—mystic and inexplicable, stretching over the ages of time and the oceans of space to bind stranger to stranger—Becker pulled this stranger to him; and pulled Wald also, as the years would prove, back to life.

For nearly a year Wald had been as a man entombed, and he knew of that year's developments only what one or another of the prison guards had casually told him. He knew of the UN decision to partition Palestine, and that the Arab states intended to frustrate the decision by force. In the Tel Aviv hotel room that day, Becker outlined to Wald what Hagana was doing throughout the world to prepare for the coming war.

And then Becker came to the work he had for Wald.

Yehuda Arazi, heading Rechesh in Europe, had been reporting from Rome on the constantly increasing activities of the Arab arms procurement missions. Arazi argued that only by organized interference could the Jews offset the advantages the Arab arms buyers had in money and by virtue of their official status as agents of existing sovereign governments. Arazi had already mounted occasional sabotage actions; but these had been sporadic, and the use of Rechesh agents for such work was a security risk which violated the primary rule dictating a separation of function in any clandestine network. So Hagana decided to organize a sabotage group independent of the rest of the European apparatus. Becker was to command this, and he wanted Wald.

Becker put it thus simply and without urging; the urging was contained within the need and was emphasized by the obvious fact that not every Jew willing to risk his life under Hagana orders was equipped to do this usefully as a saboteur in Europe. There was no more discussion, and Wald agreed.

Becker took Wald to Rishon-le-Zion, the vineyard town established sixty years before by Baron Edmond de Rothschild where Victor Berger was running a refresher course for saboteurs within the labyrinthine wine cellars that honeycombed the town. It was like the reunion of a college fraternity. Berger had brought along two of his roughneck friends from the French maquis to serve as instructors; all the others selected by Becker had come out of DIN. Ben-Issachar Feld was there, Benno the Messenger; Mira Lan, who had been with Wald from the partisan days in the Rudniki forest; and Judah Klein, the wigmaker. Hannah Baum was there, too, strangely and happily matched to the slow-moving Palestinian vintner she had married six months before. From time to time Berger laughingly tried to persuade her that the best possible cover for a saboteur was to be, as she was, obviously pregnant. Hannah ran the house in which the unit was quartered, and when Wald arrived she became a sort of Yiddishe mamma, coaxing him to eat the heavy Polish dishes she prepared, fattening him up, and warming the chill out of his eyes during the long evening strolls she and her husband took him on.

There were fourteen of them, and they stayed at Rishon-le-Zion for two weeks. During that time, Hagana sent them a large case marked "Spare Parts—Agricultural" that Arnie Berg had forwarded from San Francisco via Teddy Kolleck in New York and the "Magenta" smuggling net. It contained a choice collection of dirty tricks originally developed for America's wartime Office of Strategic Services. Berg had liberated them when he'd been detached from the OSS and sent them along when he began his new career as a Hagana arms buyer. Berger and his two French pals gurgled over them like three kids finding their long-lost favorite toys. The most useful of these were a number of "cigarette cases" made of an opaque celluloid and containing napalm jelly and a preset time fuse. When the fuse went off, the thing spattered liquid flame over a sizable area. There were also the "fireflies," little plastic cylinders of explosive sealed by a rubber ring. You dropped a firefly into the gasoline tank of a truck. The gasoline would erode and loosen the rubber retaining ring allowing the gasoline to mix with the explosive. The chemical action would set off the firefly, shattering the tank. If the truck happened to be carrying

shells or explosives, the result would be an exciting fire-
works display hurtling down the road, and—probably—
a widely distributed driver. Arnie Berg's gift package
even included three torpex limpet mines. Heavily mag-
netized, these could be fixed to a ship's hull below the
waterline and the fuses set to blow when the frogmen
were well away. There was some debate whether to take
the torpex mines along; they were heavy and too bulky
for a man traveling light. Finally Berger decided to have
them sent separately to Yehuda Arazi in Rome; one
never knew when the opportunity might knock. (Opportunity did, in fact, subsequently knock, at Bari harbor
in Italy; and the mines were used to scuttle the *Lino*
with its cargo of miscellaneous hardware including ten
thousand rifles which the Syrian arms buyer Major Fuad
Mardam had bought from the Czech government.)[102]

When Becker judged his group sufficiently trained, Hagana fitted them out with a fancy assortment of identity
papers in various languages, and smuggled them and their
equipment over to Europe to raise hell.

By Hagana orders, Czechoslovakia was excluded from
their operational area even though it was a major Arab
arms procurement center. Hagana was unwilling to endanger the new deal for Czech cooperation with Rechesh
by turning the saboteurs loose in that country. In all
the rest of Europe, the Arab arms channels ran through
the black markets where there were men whose only
heritage from the most terrible of wars was a violent disregard for anyone's misery but their own; who were prepared to deal in arms as they were prepared to deal in
food, or blood plasma, or antibiotics. And since such
black markets flourish best where anarchy rules the city-
jungles, the greatest of these were in Germany—in Hamburg and Frankfurt; and here the Arab way was easy—
was not the enemy the same damned Jew? Well, then,
here are the arms to kill the Jew; for money, surely;
but also for the cause!

And so it was that though Becker's men worked wherever their information led them, the concentration came
to be among the hated and familiar German people. They

fought the kind of war they had known before, a dirty war, as are all underground wars. Arab arms buyers were kidnapped and beaten, and sometimes killed. Those who sold to them were handled similarly; their trucks were hijacked or blown up; their depots burglarized and burned. And German arms dealers who when taken were found to have in their armpits the SS tattoo were always killed.

For six months, Becker's group raided the black-market arms channels, until within the European underworld the rumor spread that the Jewish partisan brigades of eastern Europe had joined into a single secret army to do this work. But by then, also, every security service in Europe was alert to this specialized crime wave and was searching for its perpetrators. The Jewish authorities in Palestine decided that the risks of capture, and the attendant political complications, had grown too great. Hagana ordered them home; and Becker and his men were put into uniform to do the rest of their fighting in the open, as soldiers of the Jewish state, most of them in the Givati Brigade that fought in the Negev and at Latrun.

Those who had come to DIN from the Jewish Fighters' Organization of eastern Europe and had gone on to join in Israel's war of independence had been engaged in one kind of war or another for nearly seven years. It is a long time to hold back death.

By 1949, when that first Israeli-Arab war ended, half of those who had worked with DIN were dead. Of the command group Becker was dead, and Mira Lan, and the man called Israel. And all of those who survived—save only the "little sister," Hannah Baum—bore the scars of shrapnel, or bullet, or bayonet. They were all of them tired, and none of them whole. They wanted to come forth at last from the violent dark; to warm themselves, like other men, in the bright dawn of the new world.

Malachi Wald remembered the skills of the lathe and the plow that his uncle had taught him in the innocent years before the Germans came to the Ninth Fort at Kovno. He went up to the green hills of Galilee to join one of the new kibbutzim along the Lebanese border.

Ben-Issachar Feld, Benno the Messenger, realized with some surprise that he was still young enough to begin at the beginning. He enrolled at the Hebrew University in Jerusalem to study—what else?—Hebrew literature.

Judah Klein came clumping out of Tel Hashomer hospital on the wood and aluminum leg they had given him to replace the one he had lost in the third attack at Latrun. Hannah Baum and her husband were waiting for him. They took him to their home in Rishon-le-Zion, and there they went to work on him. Shlomo led him on easy walks through the pleasant town, and explained the fascinations of the wine industry as he guided him through the labyrinths of the winery he managed. Hannah stuffed him with good Polish cooking. The baby Avraham cooed and clutched at him and called him *Dod Yehuda*—"Uncle Judah." What lonely man could resist such a seduction? Judah Klein, the wigmaker of Treblinka, began the slow thaw that was to turn him into the winemaker of Rishon-le-Zion.

That left of DIN's command group only the *guerrier* Victor Berger. Even he, who alone among them had been a warrior by chosen profession, had now had enough of arms and armies. He decided against a proffered commission in the training command of Israel's new regular army. He went to work for Solel Boneh, the construction company owned by Histadrut, Israel's General Federation of Labor.

And then—there was the American, Arnie Berg.

Fleeing the FBI arrests that broke Hagana's network in America, Berg came to Israel in October 1948. He enlisted in the Seventh Palmach Brigade in time to fight in Operation Hiram, the sixty-hour campaign that hurled el-Kaukji's Liberation Army out of Galilee. At the end of December, the Seventh Palmach was one of the five brigades mobilized for Operation Horev that brought the surrender of the Egyptian forces in the Negev, ending the fighting war. By that time, Berg was a company commander and entitled to share the privileges of rank, which in the Israeli forces included a casualty rate nearly three

times that of the enlisted men. On December 26, Arnie
Berg came out of the attack on the Egyptian entrench-
ments at Auja with bullet holes in his side and thigh.
Like most of the others, he was taken to Tel Hashomer;
and when his turn came for physiotherapy, the man
complaining under the hands of the implacable therapist
at the next bench was an old acquaintance—Judah Klein.
They went through the usual where-and-when routine
until they remembered the first hunting season in Alt-
Aussee, when Arnie Berg of the U.S. army's War Crimes
Branch and the men of DIN were hunting the same
quarry in their different ways.

Klein left the hospital for the wine cellars of Rishon-
le-Zion; and Berg for a job with the Jewish Agency, which
would, in time, send him to help organize the mass immigration to Israel of the Jews of Yemen and of Iraq.
But by the time they left the hospital, the two of them
were friends and Arnie had met the others of DIN's command as they came to visit Judah. So when, in 1953,
a man with a valid American passport was needed to help
in the killing of Hans Groetner, they thought of Arnie
Berg, and he was willing.

But that was later. In between came the time of quiet
. . . and of justice denied.

In 1946, when DIN had disbanded, each of the big
powers—the United States, the Soviet Union, Great Britain, France—controlled one of the four zones of occupation into which Germany and Austria had been divided.
The occupying powers were bound by their collective
pledge, endorsed also by the entire membership of the
United Nations, to hunt down and prosecute those "responsible for, or participating in" the crimes of the Third
Reich.

Investigators of the United Nations War Crimes Commission and of each of the four powers fanned out over
Europe, seeking first of all the 36,529 individuals named
as "major war criminals" in the eighty lists issued by the
UN commission. These were to be tried on capital charges
of mass murder.[103]

Members of the following ten groupings were declared subject to automatic arrest wherever they were to be found:

1. Nazi party officials down to ortsgruppenleiter (members of the party's local district branches)
2. Gestapo and SD (Sicherheitsdienst—"Security Service")
3. Waffen SS (the armed SS) down to the lowest non-commissioned rank
4. General Staff officers
5. Police officers down to lieutenant
6. Sturmabteilung (the storm troopers of the Nazi party)
7. Ministers and leading civil servants down to local mayors, and the civil and military town commanders in the former German-occupied territories
8. Nazi party members in commerce and industry
9. Judges and prosecutors of the so-called "People's Courts"
10. Allied traitors

Within the American zone of occupation alone, these proscribed categories were ultimately found to include 13,199,800 persons.[104]

The International War Crimes Tribunal at Nuremberg judged three major Nazi organizations as "criminal," subjecting all persons who were members on or after September 1, 1939, to automatic arrest and imprisonment: the Nazi party leadership (all members); the Gestapo and Security Police (all echelons except clerks, stenographers, janitors); all members of the SS without exception. "Voluntary and knowledgeable" membership in these organizations was sufficient for automatic imprisonment for terms ranging from five to ten years, plus additional punishment for other crimes, individually proven. These organizations were defined by the tribunal as having served "the dominant functions of the Nazi terror."[105]

All this, from the viewpoint of those who sought justice and retribution, was promising. Cynical observers, particularly if they were Jewish, could and did point out that in all the grim detailing of Nazi crimes on the charge

sheets, the indictments—and even, subsequently, within
the judgments themselves—there was never, not once,
any mention of the mass murder of the Jews. Beginning
with the Declaration on the Punishment of War Crimes
signed in Moscow by Roosevelt, Stalin, and Churchill and
published on November 1, 1943—and thereafter endorsed by the United Nations—the millions of Jewish
victims were moved, as it were, from anonymity to ob-
livion.

The Nazis had created their unique apparatus of murder for the avowed primary purpose of killing the European Jews—*as Jews, and because they were Jews.* The
Jews were both proportionately and in absolute terms by
far the largest number of victims of the crimes for which
the Germans and those who ran with them now stood indicted. Nevertheless, the Jews as such were unmentioned
in the call of the nations for justice. The French victims
were mentioned, the Dutch, the Belgians, the Poles, the
Norwegians; the Cretan peasants were not forgotten . . .
only the Jews, special victims, were specially omitted.

As a leading historian of the holocaust, Professor Raul
Hilberg, puts it:

> What happened to the Jews . . . ? The Jews are among
> the "French hostages"; they are a component of the
> "people of Poland"; they are lost in the "territories
> of the Soviet Union." The Western and Soviet govern-
> ments alike were able to take from the Jews their
> special identity by the simple device of switching clas-
> sifications. Thus the Jews of German nationality became
> Germans, the Jews of Polish nationality were converted
> into Poles, the Jews of Hungarian nationality into Hun-
> garians, and so on. . . . The repressive pattern mani-
> fested itself primarily in a refusal to recognize either the
> special character of the German action or the special
> identity of the Jewish victims.[106]

This did not arise as thoughtless happenstance within
the urgent confusions of war and victory; it was the result of reasoned policy aimed at denying the existence of
a Jewish people in order to abort the birth of that peo-

ple's claim to a *national* identity—an identity which would complicate the Soviet plans for the postwar reorganization of eastern Europe, and would embarrass—as it did subsequently embarrass—the British mandatory power in Palestine. It was in pursuit of this policy that the Red Army Partisan High Command in May 1944 had demanded the dissolution of the Jewish Fighters' Organization, and had moved to enforce this dissolution by killing Jewish partisans who refused to obey.[107] And this same policy guided the British government when, in England, and later in Belgium, they ordered that German Jews who had fled seeking sanctuary from the Nazi terror be interned as "enemy aliens."[108]

Achieving the disappearance of, as it were, the Jews as victims, as Jews, was important to the Russian and the British delegations at the Moscow Conference which drew up the tripower declaration on war crimes. For the Americans it was, then, only a convenience in stilling what qualms of conscience might very occasionally surface in Washington to remind the American government that it, too, had failed—had refused—to help the Jews of Europe when rescue had been still possible. So the Americans just went along with the others; and the wisdom of this accommodation was soon proven for them all when, for each of them, it became politic to restore the Germans to international repute and respectability in order for the three powers to hasten their selected Germanies into alliance—one with the east, one with the west. Thus, when the time came, the Soviet Union and Poland forgave their East Germans for what had been done to Russians and Poles; and America and Britain forgave their West Germans for what had not been done to Americans and Englishmen. And no one needed to consult the still stiff-necked and unforgiving Jewish people who—by the elision of the Word, which alone has diplomatic reality—had been caused to disappear from the lexicon of German crimes, and had no place in court.

But all this was to come clear only later. The beginning was brighter. . . .

On October 1, 1946 the four-power International War Crimes Tribunal at Nuremberg delivered its judgments on twenty-one top officials of the Third Reich who had been defendants during the year-long trial. Three were acquitted, one was sentenced to ten years' imprisonment, another to fifteen years, two to twenty years, three to prison for life. The other eleven—Göring, Streicher, Frick, Ribbentrop, Kaltenbrunner, Sauckel, Keitel, Jodl, Frank, Rosenberg, Seyss-Inquart—were sentenced to death; and, except for Göring, who committed suicide in his cell on October 16, they were hanged.

It augured well. But it did not happen again.

The International Tribunal never again convened. Immediately after the first—and last—international trial, the four-power Control Council for Germany authorized each of the powers to hold subsequent trials on its own, in its own zone of occupation. In actual effect, this passed the torch to the Americans; and it is they who allowed it to flicker and who—finally—put it out.

During the last weeks of the war, several million Germans fled westward, hurtling out of the path of the dreaded Red Army and into the far less terrifying embrace of the Americans. None fled faster than those Germans and Lithuanians, Ukrainians, volksdeutsche whose activities had been such as to give them cause to believe that the advancing Russians would—as they did to thousands who didn't go far enough or fast enough—shoot them on sight. Thus, there was a mass immigration of war criminals into what became the American zone of occupation. Henceforth, it is America and American policy that dominates the history of the war crimes prosecutions.

Within the American zone, the Subsequent Proceedings Division headed by General Telford Taylor had prepared a trial list of nearly five thousand persons who had, in leadership positions, "served the dominant functions of the Nazi terror" and would be—upon conviction—likely candidates for the noose.[109]

Then the rot set in.

Because of "lack of time, staff, and money," this list was cut down until only 185 men remained to be arraigned in the twelve American Subsequent Proceedings at Nuremberg. The rest were arbitrarily "downgraded" and their names were added to the list of more than 13 million suspects who were to be brought before the lesser "denazification courts."[110]

Thirty-five of the 185 top officials were acquitted. Most of the rest were sentenced to prison terms ranging from time already served in pretrial detention (and so they were immediately set free) to twenty-five years. Twenty-six of the defendants were found to have been "knowingly and significantly responsible"—as one judge put it —"for criminal acts and policies on a scale unmatched in history." The twenty-six men were sentenced to be hanged in the Landsberg prison. It is instructive to examine what happened to them.

The 185 accused in the twelve Nuremberg trials had been represented by 206 German lawyers. Of these distinguished members of the German Bar Association, 136 had been members of the Nazi party, ten had been officers in the SS and were themselves protected only by their position as counsel to the defendants from prosecution for membership in an organization the International Military Tribunals had declared "criminal." The empathy between counsel and accused was thus understandably ardent; and the defense was tenacious and extraordinarily long-winded. Delay after delay was demanded, and granted, and it took over two years for the trials to reach judgment day.

Meanwhile, the international climate had been changing and by the time the twelve trials ended in April 1949, the effects of the cold war could be felt even within the thick-walled isolation of the medieval fortress at Nuremberg. "We have the Russians to worry about," Judge James Morris said to prosecutor Josiah DuBois, "it wouldn't surprise me if they over-ran the courtroom before we get through."[111] Judge Morris was, at the time, presiding over the trial of the directors of I. G. Farben. The giant chemical combine had bought 35,000 Jewish slave laborers from the SS and had worked 25,000 of them to death in the company's Buna plant at Auschwitz, and the trial was of sufficient weight to crush a lesser man beneath the responsibility of judgment, but—clearly —Judge Morris could carry an unusual burden of worry. He was not alone. In Washington, too, concern about the Soviet Union was paramount, and there was talk about the necessity of building up West Germany as a buffer against the chill winds blowing from the steppes. The talk soon became policy, which—being like peace, indivisible, was quickly reflected in American attitudes toward Germany and Germans. As the American Chief Prosecutor, General Telford Taylor, noted, "the sentences became lighter as time went on."[112]

Not only the sentences, the entire American policy toward Germany became lighter—as did the British and French policies. The three western powers moved quickly toward restoring sovereignty to the German people under their control. On August 14, 1949 (four months after the last verdicts in the twelve trials), the people in the three western zones went to the polls with the benediction of the tripartite Allied High Commission for Germany. On September 15, the newly elected Bundestag chose Konrad Adenauer as chancellor by a majority of one vote —his own.

Six days later, the Allied High Commission officially recognized the new Federal Republic of Germany; and thus, so quickly, the German people began listening for glad tidings wafting in on the sudden winds of change.

The new chancellor told them what they wanted to hear. The nation had never surrendered to the Allies. The German military leaders, said Adenauer, "had no mandate from the German people to submit to the terms of unconditional surrender." Balm to the shattered national ego, this was only a new lyric to the old song of "betrayal" that had sounded in Germany after World War I. (*That* time it had been the invincible German army that had been betrayed by the home-front civilians led astray by—who else?—the Jews.) Adenauer sounded the pitch, and his people took up the song, every German heart beating to its inspiring message—that if the people had not surrendered, they could not be bound by the terms of that surrender. Iron logic for the iron German soul. And they had an Iron Chancellor again, to spell it out for the dullards among them: "A nation like Germany," Adenauer thundered, "with one of the front seats in mankind's history, has a right to think along nationalistic lines. . . ."[113]

Here was a father figure once again to lead them to their destiny; to bring them lurching up off their knees and back at once to arrogant pride, confirming again the evidence of history that argues that only these two postures are comfortable for the Germans—either taking orders, or giving them; the Germans, as the bitter quip has it, "are either on their knees, or on your neck."

"The foreigners must understand," said Adenauer, "that the period of collapse and of unrestricted domination by the Allies is over."[114]

The foreigners understood and looked about for ways to express this understanding, and were helped in their search by the voice of German public opinion, bellowing in outrage—"Here!"

The "here" being the inhuman plight of the condemned murderers in Landsberg prison, and of all their comrades sentenced or awaiting trial . . . the whole vengeful affront of calling Germans to account for what Germans had done. . . . Germans, their fathers, their brothers—them!

The new Bundestag passed a unanimous resolution calling upon the American high commissioner, John J. McCloy, not to carry out the death sentences upon the Landsberg prisoners.

Although, by the ordinance of October 18, 1946, which established the American Subsequent Proceedings Tribunals, the judgments were final, McCloy began to review the cases with the help of an advisory board on clemency. The board was directed "to consider anything that might warrant mitigation of sentences."[115]

But this did not satisfy the Germans. They wanted guarantees that the death sentences would be remitted. To bolster its original unanimous resolution demanding amnesty for the Landsberg men, the Bundestag included the abolition of the death penalty within the new German federal constitution, and then sent a parliamentary delegation to McCloy to argue that carrying out the death sentences would show lack of respect for the German constitution, "with far-reaching consequences for American-German relations."[116]

There was never any question, of course, as to the guilt of the condemned men. And McCloy cited examples from the Medical Case in which the defendants now awaiting execution had been convicted of killing concentration camp inmates, men, women, children, even babies, in the course of medical experiments—exploding them in high-altitude tests, freezing them to death, drowning them, infecting them with typhus and malaria, performing major operations without anesthesia. He called the attention of the Bundestag delegation to the Army High Command Case in which military commanders were found guilty of carrying out the so-called "Führer Order"—the mass murder of "undesirable elements whose existence was offensive to the Germans [because] of racial impurity." Among the condemned men was Otto Ohlendorf, who, by his own admission, was responsible for the murder of sixty thousand Jews and gypsies; and Paul Blobel, who admitted responsibility for the massacre of thirty thousand Jews in Kiev and had told the court that he was "sorry . . . sorry there were no more of them to be killed."

"I cannot understand," said McCloy, "how human beings can commit such crimes."[117]

The Bundestag delegation were unconcerned. They were not contending that the condemned men were innocent or even that there were any circumstances mitigating their guilt. Dr. Herman Ehlers, who as president of the Bundestag headed the delegation to McCloy, put their position baldly. The Germans demanded modification of the death sentences "on the grounds of political and psychological factors." And, in case his meaning was obscure, Dr. Ehlers reminded the American high commissioner that this was a time "when West Germany is being called upon to make a military contribution to Western defense."[118]

McCloy and his clemency board agonized between

justice and political expediency and finally arrived at a compromise which—inevitably—was neither just, nor sufficiently expedient. Seven of the death sentences were confirmed; nineteen were commuted to time already served. On February 1, 1951, the federal minister of justice, Thomas Dehler, indignantly served notice of appeal to the U.S. Supreme Court and the executions were delayed to await the outcome. The Court refused jurisdiction; and, beginning at one minute after midnight, on June 7, 1951, the seven men were finally hanged.

And of the others at Landsberg prison?

Among them were the heads of I. G. Farben—convicted in the deaths at Farben's Buna factory in Auschwitz of 25,000 slave laborers. One of these businessmen was Fritz Ter Meer, who spoke for all of his comrades when they walked out of Landsberg in August 1950. "Now that they have Korea on their hands," said Ter Meer, "the Americans are a lot more friendly."[119] In due—and brief—course, all the remaining Landsberg prisoners benefited from this new era of gemütlichkeit. By 1951, they were all free.

The Landsberg farce was staged on a gigantic scale throughout West Germany.

From 1945 on, 13,199,800 persons had been registered for trial because of their membership in proscribed and criminal organizations whch automatically rendered them subject to punishment. The extent of this punishment was to be fixed by the denazification tribunals which were run by the Allied Control Commission until May 1948, and were thereafter handled by the German Länder (provincial) courts under the general supervision of the commission.

Of the 13 million registrants, 3,441,800 were—after further investigation—found to be "chargeable," and by the end of May 1949, 3,432,500 of these were listed as "chargeable cases completed." How were they completed? The great majority of them—2,477,300, more than 72 percent—were simply "amnestied without trial." Of the remaining 955,200 who were brought to trial, a further

314,600 were amnestied in the course of the trials, and 18,300 were "exonerated."

That left, of the original 13 million, 622,300 guilty men to be sentenced.

Of these, 75 percent (462,700) were fined, and/or made "ineligible to hold public office" or subjected to other "employment restrictions"; 30,500 were sentenced to "special labor without imprisonment," which meant —for those physically capable—reconstruction work in the West German cities while living at their homes; 9600 were "assigned to labor camps" for varying terms of up to five years; 25,900 had parts of their property—defined as "illegally acquired"—confiscated and suffered no other penalties.

This left 93,600 "major offenders" who were sentenced to terms in prison or in labor camps for up to ten years. By the end of 1949, less than 300 of these were still serving their sentences.[120]

So much for the 13,199,800 men who had been registered in the American zone for having formed the mass base of the whole structure of Nazi criminality.

There are no comprehensive official statistics for the British zone, but the available evidence indicates that the British followed the American example. Between war's end and mid-1947, British military judges had caused eleven officers of the SS to be hanged. Dr. Bruno Tesch, who had invented and supplied the Zyklon B gas to the death camps, was hanged. Nine of the top officers of the Oberkommand Wehrmacht were sentenced to life imprisonment. But, from 1947 on, for the British as for the Americans, the infection of political expediency drained the vigor from the judicial process. No more death penalties were carried out, no more life sentences were imposed; and by 1955, all but seven of the criminals imprisoned by the British were free.[121]

Overall statistics are lacking for the French zone also. What is available shows this pattern: 2,345 were tried; 1,160 of these were sentenced to various terms of imprisonment; 808 were condemned to death, but 703 of

these were tried in absentia and never brought to justice.
Of the remaining 105 men condemned to death, 54 were
executed. By 1955, all but fourteen of the criminals imprisoned by the French were free.[122]

The Soviet Union has released no statistics. Authorities
on the subject estimate that between 100,000 and
250,000 Germans were shot or imprisoned in the closing
months of the war and during the first two years thereafter. The only official guide, however, is the announce-
ment of the Presidium of the Supreme Soviet when—in
1955—the Russians partly complied with Chancellor
Adenauer's plea for the return of German prisoners:
8,877 were released before the expiration of their prison
terms; and 749 were—as the Presidium phrased it—
"transferred" to the Federal Republic of Germany and to
the German Democratic Republic.[123]

The past was dead, and the dead were dead; and both
were an embarrassment to the plans of the living and
therefore best forgotten.

Before the bloody decade of the forties had ended,
America and the Soviet Union—snuffling with impatient
lust for strategic advantage in the cold war—were hasten-
ing their chosen Germanies to the altar of alliance; each
bull-necked Brunhild stripped of her butcher's apron, and
garbed instead in the sudden purity of innocence, miraculously renewed.

By 1950, the western powers had their new Federal
Republic of Germany; and the new German Democratic
Republic was in the Soviet bloc. By 1952, Pankow was a
military partner in the Warsaw Pact alliance; and Bonn in
NATO. For the Germans of east and west—particularly
for the Germans—the cadenced crash of German boots
and the rumble of German tanks sounded their return
to full sovereignty and equality within the divided family
of nations.

And both armies were from the new beginning led by
those who had led the Nazi Wehrmacht; who had sworn
their oaths of fealty to Hitler, and proudly accepted their
medals from him; who had connived at mass murder, or

acquiesced in it; who had devastated all Europe in a war of such deliberate schrecklichkeit that no depths of horror remained unplumbed in the areas they controlled; who had renounced no evil done in the name of the Third German Reich they served until their criminal state had come crashing down about them, leaving them still unashamed, but at last naked and afraid.

East and west of the dividing line, 90 percent of all officers of staff rank in both armies had been officers of the Nazi Wehrmacht. Of course. Who else was there who knew the job? As the *New York Times* reported from Bonn, the Federal government found it "impossible to recruit desirable officers for the West German military contingents unless a substantial number of war criminals are released from allied jails." So they were released.

But only with regard to the professional armies is the ex-Nazi's place in the two Germanies similar. In East Germany, the guilty men did not regain positions of public status as they did in West Germany. So that even as late as 1965, and with—one may reasonably assume— the worst will in the world, the West German authorities could find and publicize only 235 men who had been at all prominent in the Third Reich and were again in such positions in East Germany.[124] In West Germany, there were—and are—thousands.

This difference was not a virtue of East German policy. It was a by-product of communism and of the first burst of vengeance the Russians wreaked upon the Germans within their sphere at the end of the war and for two years after. In those final weeks of the war, Russian soldiers killed thousands of SS men and others who had carried out the brutal Nazi policies in the eastern areas. And until 1948, the military courts in the Soviet orbit— especially in Poland and Lithuania—dealt more harshly with the Germans and their collaborators than did the courts in the western zones of occupation. But then in the east, also, hot justice yielded to the expediencies of the cold war. By then, though, most Germans who had been implicated in criminal actions and could get away from East Germany had done so. Thousands more went later, with the 11 million people who found communism un-palatable and flooded into West Germany. This was par-ticularly true for the political and industrial and com-mercial elite of the Third Reich, who could see no future for them—and little profit—in a Communist society.

In a little time, there was plenty of profit to be made in West Germany. By the early fifties, West Germany was already dominating the European economy. It was a *Wirtschaftswunder*—an "economic miracle." But there was more to the miracle than the miraculous; more to it, even, than the undoubted capacities and the ferocious energies of this devil-haunted people. There was a roar-ing flood of American money.

From the end of the war until 1949, GARIOA (the American organization for Government and Relief in Oc-cupied Areas) spent $580 million a year to keep the West Germans from starving, to supply essential public services. At the end of 1949, Marshall Plan aid began to pour in, to be used for rebuilding the German industrial infra-structure. By mid-1953, this aid had already totaled over $3.5 billion.[125] And beginning in 1950, American busi-nessmen lent their financial muscle to Washington's pump priming. In that year, private American business invest-ment in West Germany amounted to $204 million. Within four years, this had grown to $332 million. (By 1965, the American businessman's share in the West German economy totaled $2.5 billion—38 percent of all American private investment in Europe.)[126]

West Germany thus received a greater share of Ameri-can aid, proportionate to population, than did any other European country. By the quaint logic of the cold war, America thought it more important to woo—or bribe—the erstwhile enemy than to ease the agonies of her war-time allies.

Thus, the *Wirtschaftswunder*. And the men whom this miracle profited most were those same German industrial-ists who had financed Hitler in his reach for power, who had reaped a rich harvest from the Nazi rape of Europe, and had—for this purpose—knowingly collaborated in the criminal acts of the Third Reich, including mass murder and enslavement, and are now—in West Germany today—once again prosperous and powerful.

Examples abound. Among them:

I. G. FARBEN: contributed 40 million marks to Hitler and the Nazi party from 1933 to 1944 (*Nuremberg Trials,* VIII, 1245, 1249); provided technical assistance to the Gestapo and sent Dr. Karl W. F. Tauboeck—chief chemist at Farben's Ludwigshaven laboratory—to guide the sterilization experiments carried out on gypsies imprisoned in the Lackenbach concentration camp;[127] "bought" 40,000 slave laborers from the SS to man the Farben factories at the Auschwitz and Manowice concentration camps and at the Silesian Fuerstengrube coal mines; 25,000 of these slave laborers were "literally worked to death" or sent by the Farben managers to the gas chambers when they could no longer work. (*Nuremberg Trials,* VII, 58).

For these and other crimes, the principal directors of I. G. Farben were convicted and sentenced by the U.S. Military Tribunal at Nuremberg. Here is what happened to them:

Fritz Ter-Meer: sentenced in 1949 to imprisonment for eight years; released in 1950; by 1955 was deputy chairman, T. G. Goldschmidt AG; director, Bankverein Westdeutschland AG; director, Düsseldorfer Waggonfabrik.

Otto Ambros: sentenced in 1949 to imprisonment for eight years; released in 1950; by 1955 was director, Scholven-Chemie AG; director, Telefunken GmbH; director, Gelsenkirchen Buer; director, Feldmuehle Papier und Zellstoffwerke AG.

Heinrich Butefisch: sentenced in 1949 to imprisonment for six years; released in 1950; by 1955 was director, Feldmuehle Papier und Zellstoffwerke AG; director, Ruhrchemie AG; director, Deutsche Gasolin AG; director, Technical Committee of Experts, International Convention of Nitrogen Industry.

FRIEDRICH FLICK KOMMANDITGESELL-SCHAFT: from 1933 to 1944 contributed 100,000 marks annually to Gestapo head Heinrich Himmler for "special purposes"; contributed 7 million marks to Hitler and the Nazi party from 1933 to 1944; by 1944 was the second-largest steel producer in Germany; bought and used 48,000 slave-laborers, 80 percent of whom died. (*Nuremberg Trials*, VI, 26, 55, 787–788).

For these and other crimes, Friedrich Flick was sentenced by the U.S. Military Tribunal at Nuremberg in 1949 to seven years of imprisonment. He was released in February 1951.

By 1955, Flick was back in business at his old Friedrich Flick Kommanditgesellschaft, controlling 110 companies with a registered capitalization of more than $22 million and with an annual business turnover exceeding $2 billion—making him the second-richest man in Europe. The richest was Baron Gustav Krupp von Bohlen und Halbach.

KRUPP: from 1933 onward, the Krupp family contributed more than 10 million marks annually to Hitler and the Nazi party, and additional sums to the "Heinrich Himmler Circle of Friends"—the twenty-one leading German industrialists to whom Himmler turned to finance "special tasks of the SS." Krupp's predominant role in the German economy was officially recognized with the enactment of a special law in 1943—Lex Krupp—which incorporated the family's 175 German companies and their 60 foreign subsidiaries into a single tax entity, thus avoiding death duties. By then, Krupp's war industries were employing 250,000 persons—100,000 of them slave laborers in the factories at Auschwitz, Markstadt, and five other concentration camps, making Krupp the largest single employer of slave labor. An estimated 70,000–80,000 of these died as a result of "cruel methods of torture and coercion." The Krupp Werke was even privileged by the SS administration to maintain its own "penal camps" at Dechenschule and Neerfeldschule. "Like all other Krupp camps for slave-labor, these excelled in cruelty [even] the established concentration camps, fearsome though these undoubtedly were."[128]

At the end of the war, the Allied High Commission decided Baron Gustav Krupp was too ill to be tried. His son Alfried, who was next in the hierarchy of the Krupp enterprises, was sentenced by the American tribunal at Nuremberg in 1949 to twelve years imprisonment, and all of his property was ordered confiscated. The twelve years shrank to less than two, and Alfried Krupp was released in January 1951—that year of great mercy, and political expediency, when all the convicted industrialists and the marshals of Nazi Germany were set free. And the American high commissioner, John McCloy (himself, in private life, a banker and investment lawyer) rescinded the property confiscation order on the grounds that it was "repugnant to American concepts of justice."[129] Krupp's hundred thousand slave laborers might have taken a sardonic view of that, but of course most of them were in no position to express an opinion. Historically, there is some argument to support Mr. McCloy—slavery was once an American institution, and the confiscation of property never was.

Though the high commissioner would not permit the *confiscation* of Krupp's property, he did allow the commission's experts to continue planning the dissolution of the Krupp trust in accordance with the Potsdam Declaration.

Meeting in Potsdam at war's end, the heads of the American, British, and Soviet governments had decided to break the historic link between aggressive German industry, hungry for profit, and aggressive German politicians, hungry for power. This was to be done by diminishing the influence of the twenty-one largest German industrial and banking families (the same twenty-one who had formed the Heinrich Himmler Circle of Friends). The Potsdam Declaration pledged: "At the earliest practicable date, the German economy shall be decentralized for the purpose of eliminating the present excessive concentration of economic power."

The Soviet Union carried out the Potsdam Declaration

in the simplest possible manner. They just dismantled the German industrial structure in their zone of occupation, carried it off to Russia as war reparations, and nationalized what was left.

For the Americans and the British, it was not so simple. Given their desire to placate the leaders of West Germany, it became too difficult to manage. So it wasn't done.

For example:

The Allied High Commission ordered the Krupp family to sell its coal and steel holdings. But the commission's order specified that these holdings—stolen or not—need be sold only at "full listed value." This proved impossible, particularly since the other German industrialists had made "a gentleman's agreement in the Ruhr not to buy Krupp's coal and steel shares."[130] By 1956, the Krupp family had sold only two coal mines, and some of its raw-material holdings. The commission's liquidation order was abandoned.

Or take the case of Friedrich Flick, who was also ordered to divest himself of his coal holdings. He sold them for $19 million . . . to his two sons, who together with him own the Flick family empire.

Not one of the twenty-one giant economic combines within the western zones of occupation was broken up, or compelled to disgorge any significant portion of its loot. Before, they dominated the German economy; now —illicitly enriched—they dominate Europe.

Schluss.

The convicted war criminals who were amnestied out of the Allied prisons in 1951–52 came home like returning heroes to a prosperous Germany eager to welcome them, and cocky enough to do it openly and in style. This was itself as good a measure as any of the distance the Germans had come in the short years since their defeat. But earlier—at the end of 1945 and in '46 and '47, when the hunted hounds came running home, baying for shelter —the beaten Germans could demonstrate their kameradschaft only in clandestine ways, in secret escape routes that would take the running men further, far enough so

as not to endanger those who helped them . . . out of
Germany.

The first of the Nazi escape routes was organized in
the winter of 1944–45 by an SS bullyboy, Major Alfred
Naujocks, who set up Aktion Birkenbaum under orders
from SS General Ernst Kaltenbrunner, the last head of
the Reich Main Security Office. Aktion Birkenbaum (Operation Birch Tree) was the large-scale forgery operation
in which false papers were made up for the Nazi officials
high enough on the ladder to be in line for hanging, and
thus in need of a bolt-hole. The forgers were concentration camp inmates who had been skilled engravers and
photographers in happier days. When their work was
gone, Naujocks had them killed.

Once the Alt-Aussee line was functioning, the men
who traveled it armed with their false papers made their
way past the Allied border guards and the wandering war-
crimes investigators, down through Austria to Italy and
thence to Rome. There the Catholic Bishop Hudal—mo-
tives uncertain, either as divorced from reality as an
autistic child, or as vicious as a stoat—gave them legitimate Vatican laissez-passers (as did other Catholic priests,
such as the Capuchin monk Father Benedetto), enabling
the fugitives to make their own ways further.

It worked well enough; it got them out of Germany.
Then came Skorzeny.

SS Lieutenant Colonel Otto Skorzeny was famous as
the commando who snatched the captive Mussolini from
his mountaintop jail. He bluffed his way out of an American interrogation stockade at war's end, and went the
Alt-Aussee route with a sum of money estimated at $5
million and "belonging"—after a fashion—to the SS.
Skorzeny went to ground at a farmhouse that he bought
in Ireland while waiting to see if the hue and cry was
up; it was not. Next, he surfaced in Madrid, running an
import-export business—Irish linens and whiskey, Spanish
lace and sherries and wines. The business, though profitable, was a blind. Skorzeny's real business was extending
and improving the Alt-Aussee escape line.

At first, the line ran—as it had before—to Rome, but

now there was money enough for Skorzeny to send tough SS gunmen along to protect the fugitives and to pay their way from Rome to the smuggling fleets that docked at Bari and on to Spain and Portugal, and then from there to the Catholic countries of South America, where a Vatican laissez-passer was the best passport in the world. But that was a long way round and, although the Rome-Bari and Rome-Genoa axes were never abandoned, Skorzeny fiddled around until he was able to buy a steady supply of valid Spanish passports in bulk lots.

Armed with these, he went back to West Germany to put the operation on a real business basis. By then, the Nazi *alte Kämpfer* were getting themselves organized. Several thousand veterans of the Waffen SS had formed a "self-help" organization called HIAG (Hilfsorganisation auf Gegenseitigkeit der Waffen SS) and within a few months they had a million members. Other, similar organizations were gestating—the Stahlhelm ("Steel Helmet") and the Deutscher Soldatenbund (Federation of German Soldiers).

Skorzeny called the leaders of these nascent groups to a meeting in Munich where a general staff was set up to feed men and money into the escape routes, to press for the release and redemption of all war criminals, and to organize all the antiwar-guilt propaganda. The first cover organization—the Committee for Christian Aid to War Prisoners—was formed immediately. Among its sponsors were Cardinal Josef Frings of Cologne and Bishop Johann Neuhäussler of Munich—both Catholics; the Protestants were represented by Bishop Theophil Wurm of Stuttgart and Bishop Meiser of Munich. Two powerful religious organizations—the Roman Catholic Caritas and the Protestant Evangelische Hilfswerk—were brought in; and a weekly newspaper, *Christ und Welt,* began publishing a campaign to end the "persecution" of the war criminals. Sixty leading industrialists contributed large sums to a mysterious bank account called "Komto Gustav" (rumor says it was so named in honor of Baron Gustav Krupp).

All that was the visible part of the iceberg. Underneath were two escape organizations. Die Spinne, run by a Luftwaffe colonel and SS Colonel Eugen Dollman, operated in Germany and in parts of Europe where wanted men had gone into uncertain hiding. Die Spinne gave them protection where they were, or better cover elsewhere in Europe; or moved them on to Spain, where ODESSA waited.

ODESSA (*Organisation der SS Angehörigen*—"Organization of SS Members") was run by Skorzeny, Naujocks, and SS Colonel Otto Bremer. Skorzeny handled the contracts with the Spanish government, supplied the passports—most of them valid Spanish, Portuguese, and South American documents—arranged for funds, and set the travel plans and cover stories. Naujocks and his men handled the tourists going to South America, and were responsible for their reception and protection there. And from a small hotel which Skorzeny bought in Denia—a small fishing and smuggling port on the Spanish Mediterranean coast—Bremer was responsible for the network in Africa and in the Arab countries. Spain was selected as a secure base because the Franco government still remembered Nazi Germany's military help during the Spanish war; and for the fascists in power in Spain, the SS veterans of the "Condor Legion" and the Luftwaffe pilots who devastated Guernica were heroes of legend.

Not every fugitive traveled this way, or went the whole route with Die Spinne and ODESSA; but those who did were enabled to live new, normal lives in the host countries chosen for them and were protected—like Dr. Josef Mengele of Auschwitz; and those who cut loose—like Adolf Eichmann—often came to regret it.

All told, it is estimated that about seven or eight hundred Nazi criminals were handled by Die Spinne and ODESSA—as bloodstained a bunch of bastards as ever fled the avenging angel.

Thus the Germans fought a year-long, two-front campaign to save their beloved war criminals—ODESSA; Die Spinne; the mass organization of SS veterans, HIAG; the army veterans' organization, the Stahlhelm and Deutscher Soldatenbund; Princess Helene von Isenburg's Stille Hilfe ("Silent Help"); Princess Stephany zu Schaumberg-

Lippe's Helfende Hände ("Helping Hands"); the Christian Aid Society; the cardinals and bishops of the Catholic and Evangelical hierarchies—all, in their own ways, mobilized behind the unremitting efforts of their government to save and rehabilitate the convicted mass murderers, "who," as Chancellor Adenauer put it, "in our opinion have not committed any war crimes at all."[131]

By 1951, as we have seen, this war was won . . . and what remained was a mopping-up operation—the return of the released men to respectability and influence, part of the obliteration of Germany's war guilt.

In May 1951, the Bundestag passed a law requiring the reinstatement of all Nazi civil servants—federal, state, municipal—who had been dismissed from their posts by the Allied denazification courts as punishment for criminal activities. Before the end of the year, 129,471 were back in civil service with salaries paid for the years they had been out in the cold.[132] And 92 percent of the schoolteachers, similarly dismissed, had been reinstated as far back as 1949.[133] The process of rehabilitation went so fast that on October 23, 1952, Chancellor Adenauer was able to tell the Bundestag that 66 percent of the senior Foreign Office personnel (including ambassadors) were former Nazis.[134] Three-fifths of all senior police personnel—federal, state, municipal—had been in the Nazi Ordnungspolizei, or the Sicherheitsdienst, or the Gestapo. More than eight hundred judges and prosecutors of Hitler's infamous Peoples' Courts (where hangings were handed out as casually as traffic fines . . . for example, to indentured servants and slave laborers convicted of "grumbling") were by 1952 once again in their judicial places—among these more than 200 who had themselves been sentenced to terms ranging from fifteen years to life imprisonment for their own crimes. Seventeen of these judges were in West Germany's highest tribunal—the Federal Court at Karlsruhe; twenty-seven were presiding judges of provincial courts. And, in the final irony, two-fifths of the personnel in the Federal Office for the Protection of the Constitution had been in the SS, the SD, or the Gestapo.[135]

From February 1951 on, the returning criminals, now

pleasantly called "late homecomers," came under the provisions of the *Lastenausgleich*—which enabled them to call on a fund mounting to $1¼ billion annually for pensions, grants-in-aid, business and housing loans, restitution for property confiscated by the Allies—whether originally stolen or not.[136]

Although these measures were overwhelmingly popular in West Germany, there were some few voices of conscience raised against them; the world reaction was unfavorable, and there was acute embarrassment in the Allied governments—whose benighted beneficence had made it all possible. It became advisable to take a clever step backward . . . or sideways.

With its international image tarnished by the somewhat hasty and overfull rehabilitation of the Nazi war criminals, the Bonn government moved to refurbish "the new Germany" in the eyes of the world. Bonn turned to Jerusalem and offered—at long last—to negotiate reparations agreements with Israel and restitution agreements with the Jewish Material Claims Conference, both to be considered as surrogates for the slaughtered Jews of Europe.

On September 10, 1952, two protocols were signed. Germany undertook to pay $800 million to Israel, and another $112 million to the Claims Conference.

There was much opposition in Israel in this negotiating with "Hitler's heirs," and wild rioting outside the Israeli Parliament by those who saw, clearly, the inevitable results . . . commercial dealings and diplomatic relations with West Germany, the persuasive propaganda use the Germans would make of it all—"If the Jews accept us, who will not?" But Israel was weighed down by the costs of absorbing a mass immigration that had doubled its population within less than a decade, and by the crushing defense burdens imposed upon it by the hostility of the Arab states. So the Israeli leaders, the "realists," forced the agreement through a heavyhearted parliament.

Curiously enough, or—given the German attitudes—not so curiously, Chancellor Adenauer had no easy time getting the agreements ratified by *his* parliament. But his supporters pointed out that it wasn't too bad—the payments would be made over a period of twelve years; since most of the reparations money had to be used to purchase German goods, farm equipment, ships, turbines, machine tools, it would serve as an additional boost to the German economy; and, of course, German industry would take its profit out of all this before Israel ever saw the goods. And finally, it wouldn't cost Germany anything, anyway, because the money would really come from the United States. As the minister of justice, Dr. Thomas Dehler, put it: "The settlement with Israel is a business for which the Americans will compensate us quite handsomely."[137] And so they did. In consideration of German restitution and reparations payments, the American government at the London Debt Conference in 1952 canceled more than $2 billion of West Germany's debts for postwar American aid —leaving the Germans a neat profit of just about $1 billion on the deal.

Even so, since many Germans just couldn't understand why the Jews should get any money at all, the agreements had a difficult time, being confirmed by the Bundestag by a vote of 238 out of 402. Only 83 of the 143 representatives of Dr. Adenauer's own Christian Democrats voted for it. More than 50 percent of the government coalition parties' representatives opposed it. Only the votes of 125 opposition members of the Social Democratic party carried the day for justice, for decency, and for a cynical and profitable maneuver.

No voice was raised in the Bundestag to remind the legislators that their German fellow citizens had, only a few years before, stolen Jewish property conservatively valued in excess of $12 billion—not counting such enormous profits as were sweated from the killing slave labor of over a million Jews.

Never mind. That was long ago, and another government; and besides, those Jews are dead.

All these things happened, in these few years. And there were Jews, watching, who vomited it all out; and decided again, as they had once before, that what no one else would do—they would do.

In December 1952, Malachi Wald called DIN together again.

There were nine of them who met and talked that winter weekend through. Five were of DIN's command group —Malachi Wald; the "little sister"—Hannah Baum; Judah Klein, the wigmaker; Victor Berger; and Ben-Issachar Feld—Benno the Messenger. These were all who were left alive of the band of brothers. And there was Arnie Berg, whom they knew from that first hunting season at Alt-Aussee, seven years before.

Victor Berger brought an organ-voiced, round little Frenchman named Paul Bescanon; and a dour Danziger called Shimon Langer. Bescanon was a member of the central committee of FIR, the organization of veterans of the French Resistance; and Langer of the secretariat of the VVN, the German organization of concentration camp survivors. These two had met in Paris some months before, at a conference of European historians of the holocaust. When the conference ended, they went for a night on the town to cement their common bond of gluttony. They ended up, as such did, having onion soup at Les Halles; and watched—and recognized—the distinguished gentleman indulging his after-theater appetite at the slate-topped table across the narrow room. They finished their soup, finished their marcs, paid, and went down the rain-swept street to their car, and waited. After a bit, the other man came out, ducked his head, and ran toward the metro station; and as he ran, Paul Bescanon let in the clutch and stepped on the accelerator and the car roared into life and hurtled down, catching the running man, flinging him fifteen feet to leave him hanging, a broken dirty doll, on the railing of the metro station. And they went to Langer's hotel, these two, to drink to the blessed death of SS Captain Fritz Hartjenstein, onetime commandant of the Naziweiler concentration camp.

The third of the new ones Wald brought. A towering, thick-shouldered, bright-haired personification of the

Nordic myth, Zvi Sharon had been born in Prague. He was named Herman Conforty then; and he was the youngest of five huge brothers—the delight of their two tiny dark-haired parents, who were—thus admiring of their brood—continuously amazed at the largesse of a beneficent God. God turned against them in 1944, and delivered them to the Nazis, who killed them in the Theresienstadt camp—all but the youngest, who survived, and was scooped up at war's end by the Bricha agents running the underground railway to Palestine. Herman didn't quite make it to Palestine that time. A British coastal patrol vessel intercepted the leaking crock he was on and took him and three hundred other "illegals" to the Cyprus stockade. And there he sat for nearly two years, learning languages, learning Zionism; until finally his quota number came up and the British gave him an immigrant's visa and allowed him and a few score more into the Promised Land. That was 1947, and Herman Conforty was Zvi Sharon, and spoke Hebrew as well as the Czech and the well-bred German he had learned at home. He was nineteen then, and went straight into Hagana, which took him and trained him for field intelligence. At the end of the Israeli-Arab War, that first one, Zvi Sharon went into Mossad—which might be translated as "the outfit," and which is Israel's overseas intelligence organization.

So there were nine of them, met together in a house in Jerusalem, to plan the rebirth of DIN. It was not simple.

The net that DIN had spread over Europe in the post-war hunting seasons had been torn by the passing years. The men and women who had worked with DIN were scattered; some were lost and some were dead, and some were held, now, by the gentle unshakable grip of decent and quite lives—only recently achieved, and precious; the hot anger cooled and the hard trade of killing unlearned and unthinkable. So the first need was manpower, and then—information, and then—money.

Bescanon and Langer were a beginning solution to the first two problems. The organizations they represented were significant within the worldwide network concerned

with the whole history of the holocaust, or with any aspect
or any consequence of it; with anti-Semitism, past or present; with neo-Nazi movements throughout the world; with
the effort to force the prosecution of war criminals by
persistently identifying them and detailing their crimes to
the persistently unlistening world. And Sharon, too, could
help with this—since a section of the Mossad was also
concerned with tracing the Nazi criminals, particularly
those who had gone into the armed forces or the intelligence or police agencies of the Arab countries. So there
were the first channels of information. And there, also,
within these three organizations—however unofficially—
was a partial answer to the problem of manpower, men
who still lived with the memory of the past evil, and the
acid hate for those who had done it. Men, and some few
women, to be selected carefully—to trace and search; and,
ultimately, to do the killing, or to provide the cover and
the safehouses and to plan the escape routes for those
who would.

For the money that would be needed, they would turn
to those Jews who had both money and memories. There
would never be enough money, because there would never
be very many who had money to spare and were sufficiently hardened by hate to spare it for DIN's purpose,
but there were always some.

Thus those nine people meeting in Jerusalem began
the work of DIN again; and thus also, elsewhere, and
about the same time, there were other small groups beginning again; all of them lashed by the same vision of
times past and times present. For the doors that the uncaring world had now flung wide to let the Nazi criminals
free, to let the criminal German nation back again to
wealth and power and unrepentant arrogance, had loosed
the ghosts of the Jewish dead, keening still for vengeance
and for justice. And if the dead could not rest, how could
these—living—be at peace, who were Jews like those dead,
and had come through the same furnace and had not
been consumed? They could not. They would set their feet
again on the bleak road they had traveled before; going,

this time, not so far, nor yet so fast, as they had gone before. For the passing years had brought them all to other kinds of lives than they had lived before; and they had duties owed, lovingly, to the living as well as to the dead, and to themselves also. So they would live these other lives—husband, wife, lover, scholar and vintner and farmer. And what of themselves remained . . . would go to their dark crusade.

In the weeks that followed, they began the work.

Berger and Feld went with the new men—Bescanon and Langer—to Europe, to organize the new network, to establish channels of cooperation with the existing tracing organizations—those Jewish groups which worked legally, hoping to bring Nazi fugitives to trial, or by exposing them to force them from positions of influence and power. Judah Klein and Malachi Wald went to West Germany and Austria and Italy and Spain, to try to organize— somewhere along the route—a penetration of the Nazi escape organization ODESSA. Arnie Berg went to South America for the same purpose; and then on to the United States to raise money, and to see what he could find out about Daugavas Vanagi, the Latvian immigrants' organization in America that ran the escape route to the States and Canada for the Latvian and Lithuanian fascists whose collaboration with the SS had been among the bloodiest in east Europe.

Three months later, they were all back; the network rebuilt, the money and information coming in.

And then the killings began.

Whenever it was possible, or useful, the deaths DIN brought about were arranged to appear of "natural" causes, or "accidental," or—even—"voluntary." At first this was done in an effort to hide the work of DIN from the hunted men and from the ODESSA organization that protected them and still does. Later, the system was continued in order to give DIN's executioners time to escape, or to keep the escape route open for other uses, or to protect the local helpers.

Thus, SS Lieutenant Hans Groetner (of the Ninth Fort

at Kovno and the Jagala death camp in Estonia) was
found dead in a roadside ditch, clearly the victim of some
hit-and-run driver, probably full of German lager; and
much the same thing happened to Hans Stuckart, once in
charge of the Jewish Affairs Bureau in the Third Reich's
Ministry of Interior; and Hitler's plenipotentiary in Paris,
Otto Abetz—who together with SS Obersturmbannführer
Theo Dannecker sent the French Jews to the gas chambers
—was burned to death when something went wrong with
the steering gear of his speeding car and it went cart-
wheeling along the autobahn. . . . Theo Dannecker himself—perhaps in long despond over his lamented colleague—hanged himself in his home one day. So did SS
Lieutenant Kurt Mussfeld, who had run Crematorium
no. 2 at Auschwitz; and so did Karl-Friedrich Simon—
who had advanced from being an SS lieutenant at Auschwitz in the days of the Third Reich to being a police inspector in the new—and clearly much-improved—Germany. Gauleiter Jacob Sprenger committed suicide; and
so did Georg Puetz of the Gestapo, who chose a curious
method of departure—injecting kerosene into his blood-
stream while awaiting a minor operation in a Bochum
hospital. . . .

And so it went; these, and some thirty more, helped out
of the world they had long befouled. These within the
first decade of DIN's rebirth.

And all that time, the hunt went on for others. For
many, many others; among them, for SS General Heinrich Mueller, "Gestapo" Mueller—swallowed up in 1945,
and reportedly now in the Albanian secret police; for
Martin Bormann, Hitler's deputy, whose "grave" was dug
up and found to contain—fittingly enough—the bones of
two dogs, and who disappeared in South America; for
Hans Bothmann, commander of the Chelmno death camp;
for hundreds of others . . . hundreds.

The finding of one of these, Adolf Eichmann, was to
rock the world. No man was sought more diligently than
the former head of Gestapo Bureau 4 B IV—the Jewish
Affairs Bureau which, ultimately, ran the deportations to

the death camps of the east European Jews. Every Jewish tracing organization in the world was engaged—the "legal" ones that sought him for prosecution and trial, like Simon Wicsenthal's Documentation Center in Austria and the Centre du Documentation Juive in Paris, the VVN, FIR, Special Department 006 of the Israeli police, all the "legal" ones, and those others—like DIN—who sought him for killing.

In 1960, the net closed in, and—acting on information supplied by Wiesenthal and others—it was DIN that found him in Buenos Aires; found him, and could have killed him then, but held its hand . . . not out of mercy, God knows! not out of mercy; but because Eichmann was the first of the really big ones to be within the net; and if he could be taken and held and made to talk—he might lead to others, he might "blow" the whole Nazi escape apparatus in Argentina, perhaps in all South America. But DIN didn't have the resources to snatch Eichmann and to hold him safe enough and long enough for interrogation to break him. And the quick methods that the Gestapo knew were forbidden—not by rule, never having been discussed —but by what DIN was . . . and is.

So the command group decided, and Malachi Wald in Tel Aviv went to Isser Har-el—then chief of Israel's security services—and put an "if" to him. "If we could lead you to Eichmann," said Wald, "could you take him to Israel; and would you then hand him over to us for our purposes? And we would then give him back—whole and unhurt—so that the state might—if the state would —put him on trial? If—?"

Har-el went to David Ben-Gurion, prime minister then, and put it to him; and Ben-Gurion agreed. And thus, as the world knows, the Israeli security services took Eichmann out of Argentina—sending a special El Al airlines plane for the purpose, ostensibly bringing Foreign Minister Abba Eban to a state visit, using the unknowing diplomat as an unwitting—and, subsequently, very angry —cover. The operation was no longer DIN's and Isser Har-el ran it himself, going with the group that hauled Eichmann off the street and into a car and, subsequently, piled him—drugged—on the plane as the "second officer" and apparently drunk.

In May 1960, Adolf Eichmann was brought to Israel; and then the whole thing—from DIN's viewpoint and for DIN's purpose—fell apart. Prime Minister Ben-Gurion broke the news to a cheering parliament in public session, and thus to the whole world. That ended it. With the world watching, Eichmann had speedily to be arraigned for a public trial under due process of law; and he knew it. DIN's wedge, the threat of a slow and savage death—of action against his wife and sons, was gone. And, also, the news that Eichmann was in the hands of the Israelis sent the other fugitive Nazis scurrying to new hiding places, with the bodyguards supplied by ODESSA alerted and watching the back trails. So that much of DIN's work and that of all the other hunters during the careful years was wasted.

Dr. Josef Mengele of Auschwitz disappeared from the Argentine vacation resorts he had been moving about in; and three Israelis working with DIN who picked up his trail were ambushed and killed. Martin Bormann fled from Brazil, leaving behind a planted double to lay a false trail—and, following that, one of the hunters from a European group was killed. The Latvian fascist leader Herbert Cukors found safe haven in Paraguay—whose secret police chief is the Croatian fascist Ante Pavelic. But that story ended not too badly when Cukors was enticed to Montevideo and taken and killed by a group headed by DIN's Shimon Langer.

Arnie Berg flew from South America to Canada and on to Winnipeg, to arrive before Alexander Laak could run further for fear of retribution for the hundred thousand Jews he had ordered killed when he had been commandant of the Jagala death camp in Estonia. Berg took his man into the garage of Laak's suburban home, and told Laak just how he intended to kill him—and his wife, when she got home from the cinema. After fifteen minutes of this, Laak begged for the mercy of being allowed to kill himself "decently." So Berg gave him a rope; and left him hanging there . . . a clear case of suicide.

There were other successes, but they were bought at an increasing cost; and in the two years following the public trial of Adolf Eichmann, DIN and the groups that worked with it suffered more men killed than in all the hunting seasons since 1945.

For a time, after the Eichmann trial, there were some who hoped that the Germans might really use a final opportunity to cleanse their souls. In West Germany, the Bonn government was forced by world opinion to extend the statute of limitations—which would have proscribed new prosecutions for war crimes—from December 1965. Buffeted by the wave of loathing set loose when the Eichmann trial revealed the horrors of the holocaust to a new generation for whom all this had been bloodless statistics—only half-believed—the Germans were forced to open the issue once again. A whole new series of war-crimes trials began.

But all this was only a temporary and expedient hypocrisy.

Less than two years later, in July 1962, a survey of senior officials in the Bonn government's legal departments alone still revealed more than two thousand with an active Nazi past.[138] Nine months after the trial in Frankfurt of twenty-two former Auschwitz officers, half the people interviewed in a West German public opinion poll had never even heard of the trial; and of those who knew about it, 39 percent were opposed to it.[139] At the end of 1963, the Ludwigsburg War Crimes Office in West Germany proudly reported that German courts in the years since the war—and including the post-Eichmann trial resurgence—had tried a total of 12,846 persons for war crimes. Buried deep in the report, and not included in the published summary distributed to the press, were other enlightening statistics: of the 12,846 persons tried, only 5,426 were convicted; of those convicted, only 155 were found guilty of murder; of those found guilty of murder, only 72 were sentenced to more than ten years' imprisonment.[140]

Much more typical were sentences like these:

Werner Schmidt-Hammer: for participating in 313 murders—three years' imprisonment.

Edwin Sakuth: for participating in 426 murders—three years six months' imprisonment; and two years' "loss of honor."

Werner Kreuzmann: for participating in 415 murders —five years' imprisonment; and four years' "loss of honor."

Hans-Willems Harms: for participating in 526 murders —three years' imprisonment.

Alois Huelsduenker: for participating in 300 murders— three years 6 months' imprisonment.

Dr. Walter Schultze: for participating in 380 murders— four years' imprisonment.

Hans Richard Wiechert: for participating in 716 murders—four years 6 months' imprisonment.

Oskar Winkler: for participating in 650 murders—three years 6 months' imprisonment.

Dr. Otto Bradfisch: for participating in 15,000 murders —ten years' imprisonment; and 6 years' "loss of honor."

Gerhard Schneider: for participating in 8100 murders —ten years' imprisonment; and five years' "loss of honor."

Bodo Struck: for participating in 5450 murders—four year's imprisonment; and three years' "loss of honor."

Wilhelm Greiffenberger: for participating in 8100 murders—three years' imprisonment; and three years' "loss of honor."[141]

In April 1967, the West German state's attorney, Dr. Adalbert Rückerl, could only admit that "less than ten per cent of the total number of identified and still living Nazi criminals have been brought to trial."[142] But that was more than enough for the German people. Two years before even this "less than ten per cent" was achieved, a government-sponsored public opinion poll revealed: "The great majority of West Germans want the prosecution of

Nazi crimes to end . . . 67 per cent of men and 78 per cent of women want the trials to stop."[143] And the esteemed West German statesman Willy Brandt—himself a "good" German and never a Nazi—could tell a cheering crowd of 400,000 West Berliners that "Twenty years are enough. We shall not be ashamed for these years."[144]

The Germans are not ashamed; and the world is unconcerned.

That leaves—as it has left for more than twenty years —DIN.

Epilogue

I began this book eight years ago.

I have put it often aside, and could adduce reasons for so doing. There was the yearlong emotional drain of reporting the Eichmann trial. There was my work reporting the Israeli-Arab war of June 1967, and the events thereafter. There were, indeed, all the things—personal and public—that can happen to a man and can serve as excuses for work undone.

But the real reason was none of these. It was simply that I felt—and feel—unequal to the burden laid upon me by those of whose lives I have written: to report, and in some measure to explain; to try, somehow, someway, to move the damned unmoving world.

I could not do any of this. But still . . . but, still . . .

The men and women of DIN grow older; and their bleak crusade—though it continues—wanes; and there are none to come after them. But the memory of the Jewish agony in Europe endures and will go echoing through the ages because justice was not done.

And this separates Jew from non-Jew.

The people of Israel today will not entrust any measure of their survival to the non-Jewish world, and what is contained in this book is part of the reason.

And one thing more.

Men denied justice will, themselves, take however much of it they can and in whatever manner open to them. All men. The Jews not least.

306

REFERENCES

ONE / MALACHI WALD

1. *International Military Tribunal Proceedings* (Nuremberg), Washington, D.C., U.S. Government Printing Office, III, 41.

2. Ibid., case IX, document 2265L.

3. Ibid., IV, 14 (document 411).

4. Ibid., III, 524; Official Gazette No. 94.

5. Picture of the Ninth Fort, *Yad Washem Bulletin*, Jerusalem, no. 4/5, p. 25.

TWO / ILLUSION AND REALITY

6. Instructions to Einsatzgruppen, May 1941, in Gerald Reitlinger, *The Final Solution*, London, 1953, p. 509.

7. Ibid., Appendix.

8. Report of Simon Wiesenthal, *Yad Washem*, Jerusalem.

9. *Germans Against Hitler*, Press and Information Office of the Federal German Government, July 1952.

10. Reitlinger, *Final Solution*, Appendix.

11. Miriam Novick, "The Jewish Resistance," monograph published by Beit Lochemei HaGetaoht (Warsaw Ghetto Fighters House), Kibbutz Lochemei HaGetaoht, Israel.

12. Reitlinger, *Final Solution*.

13. War Crimes Trials, Nuremberg, "The Einsatzgruppen Case," April 1948.

14. *The Standard Jewish Encyclopedia*, New York, 1958.

15. Bernard Mark, "Problems Related to the Study of the Jewish Resistance in the Second World War," monograph published by Yad Washem, Jerusalem.

16. Letter from "Antek" (Yitzhak Zuckerman), commander of the Warsaw Ghetto revolt, to "Bor" (General Komorowski), commander of the Polish Armia Krajowa, Warsaw, November 26, 1943 (photostat in author's possession).

17. *International Military Tribunal Proceedings*, III, 42 (document PS-2360).

18. Ibid., XIII, 133–137 (document PS-3363).

19. *State of Israel* v. *Adolf Eichmann*, document 983, Jerusalem.

20. Ibid., testimony, transcript record session 25 (May 3, 1961), p. G1.

THREE / THE JEWISH RESISTANCE

21. Field Marshal von Reichenau, Order of the Day, October 10, 1941, *International Military Tribunal Proceedings*, IV, 14 (document 411).

22. *Israel* v. *Eichmann,* trial transcript, May 4, 1961, p. U1.

23. War Crimes Tribunal, *Subsequent Proceedings,* "The Doctors' Trial," Brack testimony.

24. Y. Smolar, "Minsker Ghetto," *EMES,* Moscow, 1946.

25. Ibid.

26. Reitlinger, *Final Solution.*

27. Reitlinger, *SS, Alibi of a Nation,* pp. 172–174.

28. Ibid.

29. *Israel* v. *Eichmann,* trial, session 27 (May 4, 1961), p. V2.

30. Ibid., p. Z1.

31. "Study of the Jewish Resistance," document of the Second World Congress for Jewish Studies (Section for the History of the Jewish People), Jerusalem, August 4, 1957.

32. Ibid.

FOUR / FOUR FROM THE FURNACE

33. *International Military Tribunal Proceedings,* document PS–3051.

34. Ibid., IX, 252 (documents PS–3058, PS–1816).

35. Ibid., document PS–3063.

36. William L. Shirer, *The Rise and Fall of the Third Reich,* p. 431.

37. Archives, Beit Lochemei HaGetaoht.

38. *Extermination and Resistance,* I, 105 (Historical Records and Source Material), Beit Lochemei HaGetaoht.

39. Archives, Beit Lochemei HaGetaoht, Archives Jewish Historical Institute, Warsaw, Stroop report, May 16, 1943.

40. *Consolidated Weekly Report,* General-Government, Main Division—Propaganda, for all districts, March 21, 1942.

41. American *Subsequent Proceedings,* document NI–14462.

42. *Trial Report,* British War Crimes Trials, Werner Library, London.

43. Jan Sehn (Presiding Judge—The Chief Commission for the Investigation of Nazi Crimes in Poland), *Summary and Report,* Warsaw, January 1946.

44. Affidavit submitted by Israeli Police Inspector Otto Leif to the Central Office for War Crimes Investigation, Ludwigsburg, West Germany. (Photocopies: *Testimony of Treblinka Survivors,* Archives, Bureau 06, National Police Headquarters, Tel Aviv.

45. Ibid.

46. VVN *Bulletin,* published by Ma'ariv, Tel Aviv, April 27, 1961.

47. *International Military Tribunal Proceedings,* XIII, 718–720, Deutscher Reichsanzeiger und Preussischer Staatsanzeiger No. 260.

48. Ibid., XIV, 719 (document EC–410).

49. Archives, Vereinigungen der Verfolgten des Naziregimes, Frankfurt am Main, affidavit of Max Winkler, September 9. 1947, p. xxx.

50. Sehn, *History of Auschwitz*, Warsaw, 1961.

51. Ibid.; Reitlinger, *Final Solution*, p. 461.

52. Sehn, *History of Auschwitz*.

53. Der Hohere SS und Polizeiführer beim Oberpräsidentin in Schlesien und beim Reischsstatthalter in Sudetenland im Wehrkreis VIII, no. 383/40 G.

54. *Affidavits of the Prosecution*, NI–9150, *The Zyklon B Case, Reports of Trials of the War Criminals*, H.M.G. Stationery Office, London, 1947.

55. Account taken from "Affidavits to the Chief Commission for the Investigation of Nazi Crimes in Poland," *Bulletin*, no. 1, Warsaw, 1946.

56. *Proceedings* of the National Labor Relations Board, Sun Tent Awning Case, Los Angeles, 1937.

57. Quoted by Alex L. Easterman in "None Can Plead Ignorance," *World Jewry*, IV (May 1961), 6-7.

58. U.S. State Department Archives, cable no. 354, 1943, quoted by Secretary of the Treasury Morgenthau in *The Morgenthau Diaries*.

59. Ibid.

60. Ibid.

61. Easterman, "None Can Plead Ignorance."

62. *Morgenthau Diaries*.

63. Ibid.

64. Memorandum by Cavendish W. Cannon, November 12, 1941, published in *Foreign Relations*, II (1941), 875-876.

65. Reitlinger, *Final Solution*, p. 405; *Standard Jewish Encyclopedia*, p. 1763.

66. *Morgenthau Diaries*.

67. Ibid.

68. Ibid.

69. *Final Summary*, Report of the Executive Director, War Refugee Board, Washington, D.C., September 15, 1945.

70. *Life* magazine, December 5, 1960, p. 148.

FIVE / THE ROADS

71. *Historical Records and Source Material*, Vol. I, Beit Lochemei HaGetaoht, 1958; address by Zwi Bar-On, *Proceedings of The First International Convention for the History of the European Resistance Movement*, Liège, September 4-17, 1958; *The Struggle of the Jewish Partisans in Eastern Europe*, Ayanot Publishers, Tel Aviv, 1954; *The Great Soviet Encyclopedia*, XXXII (1955), 161-165.

72. Bernard Mark, "Study of the Jewish Resistance Movement," *Yad Washem Studies*, III (1959), 41-64.

73. *Great Soviet Encyclopedia*, XXXII (1955); *Outline of the History of the Great Patriotic War, 1941–1945*, Academy of Sciences of the USSR, Moscow, 1955.

74. Mark, "Study of the Jewish Resistance Movement"; *Struggle*

of the Jewish Partisans in Eastern Europe, Ayanot Publishers, Tel Aviv, 1954.

75. *International Military Tribunal Proceedings,* I, 105; III, 57; IV, 90.

76. Prince Christopher Radziwill, quoted in *Time* magazine, July 14, 1947.

77. *International Military Tribunal Proceedings,* affidavit of Konrad Morgen, Judge of the SS Court of Honor.

78. Ibid., affidavit of Dr. Wilhelm Jaeger, II, 2-7 (N.D.D. 288).

SIX / DIN—JUDGMENT AND VENGEANCE

79. Foreword to the Report to the General Assembly by the United Nations Special Committee on Palestine, 1947, p. xix.

80. Ibid.

81. Leo W. Schwarz, *The Redeemers,* New York, 1953.

82. An authoritative account of the workings of Bricha may be found in John Kimche, *The Secret Roads,* London.

83. Reitlinger, *Final Solution,* p. 130.

84. SHAEF Intelligence Summary, quoted by Shirer in *Rise and Fall of the Third Reich.*

85. RSHA Amt VI reports, quoted by Bob Edwards, M.P., in *A Study of the Master Spy,* London, 1961.

86. General Walter Bedell Smith, quoted by Chester Wilmot in *The Struggle for Europe,* New York, 1952.

87. Accounts of the "Alpine Redoubt" may be found in Field Marshal Albert Kesselring, *A Soldier's Record,* New York, 1954; SS Major General Walter Schellenberg, *The Schellenberg Memoirs,* London, 1956; Wilhelm Hoettl, *The Secret Front,* New York, 1954.

88. Accounts of Operation Bernhard may be found in Hoettl, *The Secret Front; Report* of Simon Wiesenthal, director, Jewish Documentation Center, Vienna, 1960.

89. Hoettl, *The Secret Front.*

90. Wiesenthal, *Report.*

91. Ibid.

92. RSHA Amt VI reports quoted by Edwards, *Study of the Master Spy.*

EIGHT / THE WORLD OF MALACHI WALD

93. "War and Peace Aims," Special Supplement No. 1 to the *United Nations Review,* New York.

94. *The Memoirs of Cordell Hull,* New York, 1948, II, 1289–1291.

95. Declaration of the Federal Council of Churches of Christ, cited in *Report of the Interim Committee to the American Jewish Conference,* pp. 104–105.

96. Memorandum from Sir Alexander Cadogan, Permanent Under-Secretary for Foreign Affairs, at the International Conference of Military Trials, London, April 23, 1945.

97. Raul Hilberg, *The Destruction of the European Jews,* London, 1961, p. 701.

98. *Report on Palestine; the Report to the General Assembly by the United Nations Special Committee on Palestine,* New York, 1947, preface by Senator Robert Wagner, p. xi.

99. Azzam Pasha, secretary general of the Arab League, speaking on the BBC, May 15, 1948.

100. Statistics of Arab and Israel forces are taken from Nathanial Lorch, *The Edge of the Sword,* London, 1961; and Jon and David Kimche, *Both Sides of the Hill,* London, 1960.

101. Part of the Magenta-Milan operation is described in Manya Mardor, *Strictly Illegal,* London, 1964.

102. Ibid.

103. Directive 1067/6, April 26, 1945, to the Commander-in-Chief, U.S. Forces of Occupation, from the Joint Chiefs of Staff (Report of the U.S. Military Governor, "Denazification," *Statistical Annex,* July 1949, p. 280).

104. Ibid.

105. *Nazi Conspiracy and Aggression, Opinion and Judgment,* Office of U.S. Chief of Counsel for Prosecution of Axis Criminality, U.S. Government Printing Office, Washington, D.C., 1947.

106. Hilberg, *Destruction of the European Jews,* p. 682.

107. Mark, "Study of the Jewish Resistance Movement."

108. Hilberg, *Destruction of the European Jews,* p. 682.

109. Ibid., p. 693.

110. Telford Taylor, *Final Report* to the Secretary of the Army on the Nuremberg War Crimes Trials under Control Council Law no. 10, pp. 50 ff.

111. Quoted by Josiah DuBois, *The Devil's Chemists,* Boston, 1952, p. 95.

112. Telford Taylor, *Final Report.*

113. T. H. Tetens, *The New Germany and the Old Nazis,* New York, 1961, p. 63.

114. Ibid., p. 89.

115. Arthur Seittel (advisor on public relations to the U.S. High Commissioner for Germany, 1949–1952), "Seven Were Hanged," *Commentary,* New York, May 1960.

116. Ibid.

117. Ibid.

118. Ibid.

119. Hilberg, *Destruction of the European Jews,* p. 697.

120. *Status of De-nazification Proceedings, U.S. Zone,* Department of State publication 3356, March 1950.

121. *The Prosecution of War Criminals Since the End of the War,* publication of the Institute of Jewish Affairs, World Jewish Congress, New York, 1961.

122. Ibid.

123. Ibid.

124. Untersuchung sasschub Freiheitlicher Juristen, "Ehemalige National-sozialisten in Pankows Dienstein," West Berlin.

125. Alistair Horne, *Return to Power*, New York, 1956, pp. 265 ff.

126. U.S. Department of Commerce, *Survey of Current Business*, no. 9 (1966), p. 34.

127. Dr. Joseph Tannenbaum, *Race and Reich*, New York, 1956, p. 99.

128. Ibid., pp. 198, 206; *International Military Tribunal Proceedings*, documents NI–11675, 11676, 11679, 5823, 5787, 6811, 15364.

129. Horne, *Return to Power*, p. 102.

130. Dr. Nehemiah Robinson, *Spoliation and Remedial Action*, publication of the Institute of Jewish Affairs, World Jewish Congress, New York, 1962.

131. Press conference in Bonn, reported in the *New York Times*, February 19, 1952.

132. Report of Dr. John D. Montgomery, senior research officer, U.S. Military Government, *Forced to Be Free*, Chicago, 1957, p. 81.

133. Ibid., p. 96.

134. Quoted in the *New York Times*, April 26, 1951.

135. Tetens, *New Germany and Old Nazis*, pp. 166 ff.; Federal Court Judge Wilhelm Ellinghaus, *Süddeutsche Zeitung*, December 13, 1959.

136. Ellinghaus, ibid.

137. Quoted in the *Frankfurter Rundschau*, February 24, 1953.

138. Survey quoted by Rawle Knox, *London Observer* Foreign News Service, July 8, 1962.

139. Public opinion poll conducted by the Divo Institute, reported *INA*, August 17, 1964.

140. Report of the Ludwigsburg Central Office for War Crimes Prosecutions, Federal Ministry of Justice, Bonn, November 1963.

141. Herman Langbein, *Survey of German War Crimes Trials*, Vienna, 1963.

142. Quoted in *Jerusalem Post*, April 19, 1967.

143. Tübingen public opinion poll, quoted by Reuters, March 4, 1965.

144. Quoted in *Newsweek*, May 10, 1965.